ANTIQUES YOU CAN DECORATE WITH

OTHER BOOKS BY GEORGE GROTZ

FROM GUNK TO GLOW

THE FURNITURE DOCTOR

THE NEW ANTIQUES: KNOWING AND BUYING VICTORIAN FURNITURE

INSTANT FURNITURE REFINISHING AND OTHER CRAFTY PRACTICES

Antiques You Can Decorate With

BY GEORGE GROTZ

A PRACTICAL GUIDE TO WHAT THEY ARE, WHERE TO FIND THEM, AND HOW MUCH TO PAY FOR THEM

WITH MORE THAN 400 DRAWINGS BY THE AUTHOR

DOUBLEDAY & COMPANY, INC., GARDEN CITY, N.Y.

LIBRARY OF CONGRESS CATALOG CARD NUMBER 66–20923

PRINTED IN THE UNITED STATES OF AMERICA

For the Peg O' My Heart.

LET THE READER BEWARE

To be seen carrying this book on the streets will put the bearer in clear and present danger from irate attacks, insult, and verbal abuse from apparently refined and gentle strangers who will turn out to be outraged antique dealers. To walk into an antique shop with this book under your arm . . . the mind rejects the horrors that could befall you!

The trouble is that this book tells the truth about the antique business, and the truth is a notorious hurter—especially when it hurts in the pocketbook, where antique dealers hurt the easiest.

The first of the hard truths that this book develops is that MOST PEOPLE ARE PAYING MUCH MORE FOR ANTIQUES THAN THEY WOULD HAVE TO if they understood how the antique business works. (Wholesalers will sell to you at the same price that they sell to dealers. And, believe me, that's where the highway shops get their merchandise—from wholesalers, not from secret arrangements with little old ladies in the country as they would have you believe.)

The second truth—albeit something of a well-worn truth and not exactly news—is that MISREPRESENTATION IS RAMPANT. Especially in furniture, for, as every dealer knows, "that's where the money is." And this book explains how to look for and understand the ways in which misrepresentation is done.

So don't say I didn't warn you. If you propose to carry this book on the streets be prepared to defend yourself. If you propose to carry this book around with you as a price guide to antiques you can decorate with—which it definitely is—you had better cover it with brown paper and leave it in your car where you can sneak out to refer to it.

(As the old Marine sergeant used to say, "I didn't join this outfit to make friends.")

GEORGE GROTZ

PREFACE

Listen, Gentle Reader . . .

. . . Do you think this is just another book about antiques? A book for the little closed group of antique-o-philes who go around writing books for one another to read?

Well, if you do, you are lead-pipe wrong!

Because this book is a secret message from antiquesville to the outside world. And my message is this:

Antiques are not just for the cognoscenti, the "in" group, the "know it alls." Antiques are for everybody. Or at least they can be. You don't have to spend twenty years learning enough about them so that you won't get stuck every time you go into an antique shop that uses a price code. Actually, all you need to know can be put into a book just like this.

Of course, I am assuming that what you are interested in is using antiques in your house as useful conversation pieces and intriguing decorations. If you have in mind becoming a collector of one-armed dolls from Eastern Tasmania or some other esoteric thing, you are on your own. On the other hand, if you limit yourself—as most people do—to a reasonable interest in antiques that will fit into home decoration, well then, believe it or not, this book covers ninety-nine percent of all the antiques anyone in his right mind would ever buy.

It is also about things that you CAN buy, things that are really available in antique shops and that come up at auctions at reasonable prices.

That is because this book wasn't written by cribbing from other older books in libraries or private collections. EVERY SINGLE PIECE in this book was for sale in some antique shop or at some auction during the time this book was being written. (I have Polaroid photographs of almost every piece to prove it.)

I did not start out with the preconceived notion that I should have thirty-five-percent Early American, sixteen-percent Chippendale, twenty-percent Empire Period or this or that percentage of Victorian or lamps or brass or whatever. That's the impractical sort of thing you find in those magazines you buy at the supermarket—pictures of things only millionaires can afford. This book was compiled by going out into the marketplace and seeing what was actually there. I went to where the antiques come from—not to the big cities where antiques have already passed through several pairs of hands (each pair making a profit) but to the places where antiques first enter the market. These are the rural areas of the New England states, New York, New Jersey, Pennsylvania, Ohio, Virginia, North Carolina, and Georgia—in descending order of importance.

Now, at this point some mean-looking little old fellow is undoubtedly going to get up in the back row and shout: "Ah, you don't know what you're talking about! I live in Arkansas and we have the finest antiques in the country!"

Well, maybe so, grandpa, and I don't want to hurt your feelings, but in the first place such states as yours are migration states and their antiques (with only minor characteristic variations that don't affect their value) are the same as those found in the Eastern states.

In the second place, I happen to know for a solid-gold cinch that seventy-five percent of the antiques sold in your state—and other unlikely states for original antiques—were hauled there from the East. And I don't mean by covered wagon, either, but in some antique dealer's station wagon or moving van. In the case of Texas—as unlikely a place as I can think of—I'd even raise the ante to ninety percent. Why, nowadays they are hauling the stuff from New Bedford to Dallas by trailer truck. I've seen the truck—with a crew of four. Even the oxbows (supposedly from Granddaddy's covered wagon) that people in Texas are always hanging on their walls don't come from Texas. Being a sensible Easterner, when his oxen died Granddaddy threw the oxbow at some Indians or burned it for firewood, and then switched to horses. Those bows come from Connecticut and Pennsylvania, where all the oxen were bred in those days. Even more nowadays come from Canada.

Well, that's my answer to the mean old troublemaker in the back row. It may not be a very good answer, but it's the only one I've got, so it will have to do. "Never explain, never complain," as the old lady said as she kissed her cow.

GEORGE GROTZ

January 15, 1966
San Miguel de Allende, Gto.

TABLE OF CONTENTS

Part Two

Part One

WHAT ANTIQUES ARE

Or, reason vs. the "arbitrary and capricious" 1930 law, in which our fearless author challenges the massed might of Federal bureaucracy. (If this be treason, damn the torpedoes and full speed ahead!)

Every once in a while somebody asks me, "Well, what is an antique? How do you know when you've got one?" That seems like a simple-enough question, and so when I start hemming and hawing they begin to think my mother writes these books for me.

But I still have to begin to answer the question by saying, "Well, it all depends on how you look at it." It isn't a question you can settle by looking the word up in a dictionary, because the Federal government has passed a law to tell us what antiques are, a law that stuns the mind, offends the sensibilities, and is enough to turn a Roosevelt Democrat into a Vermont Republican overnight.

Actually, this law that so ridiculously defines an antique is part of the tariff schedules that govern the duties on things imported from foreign countries. And the sense of the section dealing with antiques is logical: they should be let in free because their arrival hurts no particular native industry. Well, that's all fine, but then the law goes on to define antiques as things made before specific dates—dates that are utterly ridiculous today. For instance, according to the law, Martha Washington's rugs aren't antiques!

Here is the pertinent section of the law—in all its arbitrary and capricious glory. (The lovely term "arbitrary and capricious" is one that the Supreme Court has used in the past in rejecting similar laws when test cases were brought before it.)

Rugs and carpets made prior to the year 1701; violins, violas, violoncellos, and double basses of all sizes, made prior to the year 1801; ethnographic objects made in traditional aboriginal styles and made at least 50 years prior to their date of entry; and other antiques made prior to the year 1830,* except rugs and carpets, violins, violas, violoncellos, and double basses, and ethnographic objects made in traditional aboriginal styles; all the foregoing articles, including such articles which have been repaired or renovated without changing their original form or character.

Obviously, the correct definition of an antique—as any ten-year-old child should be able to figure out—is that it is almost anything that reminds us of the past, of our forefathers, and of the roots of our current culture.

But before developing that theme, let's look first at the effect that this law has on men who have grown up under the concept of government "for the people." Like all bad laws—Prohibition is the great example—it makes criminals of honest men and undermines the moral values of all concerned with it. No man with any guts at all is going to honor what he knows is an unjust and burdensome law, and law-enforcement officers with the intelligence to understand the situation are going to be corrupted because they feel like idiots when they enforce it.

To show you what I mean, let us pull the covers off what happens at a port of entry to the United States when you

* Changed since this book went to press to 1866, which makes the law thirty-six years less arbitrary.

bring antiques in. I've gone through this in returning from Canada and Mexico, and I've been told in confidence by men I believe that the same thing happens even more blatantly in the case of antiques being imported from Europe and the Far East.

I speak specifically of the importation of antiques from Canada, because this is where the vast majority of imports on the American market come from, imports such as those in this book, which are within the purchasing power of people of average means, ranging from $5 to $500 or $600 for major pieces of furniture.

The daily volume of this importation, incidentally, is, during the summer months, an average of one trailer-truck load and fifteen pickup trucks. I know it's hard to believe, but I've been there and I've seen it.

What happens with all this stuff is this. Having been up to Defoy (directions for finding it are given elsewhere in this book) or some other furniture mine in Quebec or the Maritimes, you return to your most convenient port of entry.

A customs officer will signal you to pull up to one side and will walk casually around your truck or peer a few moments into the windows of your Volkswagen; and then he'll invite you into his office. He goes behind his counter while you stand out in the room on the guilty side. (And if you have any sense, boy, are you guilty!) He asks you to tell him what you have in your load (he doesn't tell you, you tell him) and asks to see your receipts or bills of sale. If you are new at the game, he will explain the situation to you.

To begin with, you are told about the ruling that any antiques you have can enter the country duty-free. But on items manufactured after 1830 you will have to pay an import tax of ten to fifteen percent, depending on such various classifications as furniture, china, silver, fabric. The tax will be figured on what you paid for the item as determined by your receipt or bill of sale. (Think that sentence over for a minute with your larcenous mind, and we'll get back to it in a minute.)

Now, your first objective is to pay no duty (import tax, that is) on several of the pieces that you feel, guess, or even know were made before 1830, and you can't load a truck with antique furniture in Canada without having a couple of these. You point these pieces out to the inspector, and do you know what he tells you? He tells you he can't judge the age of your pieces and that the burden of proof of age is up to you. The only way to prove age is to have the antiques shipped by bonded carrier to Boston, where the customs officer has an appraiser. If the pieces are judged antique, you can either go there to pick them up or have them re-shipped to your home or place of business. In most cases this will cost you as much as you paid for the piece! Often more, since the purpose of going to Canada in the first place is that you can get things cheap.

As far as the inspector is concerned everything on your truck is subject to tax, and to get it in tax-free you would have to go to a great deal of trouble and expense. On top of this, you know darned well that the 1830 ruling is wrong in the first place. You can see the sense in accepting an arbitrary hundred-year-old basis, but you are going to have to be awfully well brain-washed before you will admit that your cast-iron device for peeling three apples and an onion all at once, which was patented in 1888, isn't an antique. Not to mention a 1910 hanging lampshade of colored glass, a French hussar's helmet from World War I, and on and on.

The common practice of every red-blooded believer in Jeffersonian democracy and Simón Bolívar is to fight back against governmental tyranny by adhering, as a true revolutionary, to one's own standard of values in this situation. In other words, to cheat.

(In my own case, this is also something of a religious matter, as I was early taught that the angels in heaven sing every time you cheat a chain grocery store, the telephone company, or the New Haven Railroad.)

What it comes down to is that almost anyone in Canada—and especially in Quebec, where the Canadian government's attitude toward the French-speaking population is deeply resented*—will gladly write you out a receipt for $5 for an 1850 chest of drawers for which you have in actuality paid him $35 or $50. That would be for a piece in the rough. For a fine refinished corner cupboard for which you paid him $125, you might as well have him put down $25 or $35 so as not to press your luck.

Furthermore, it is easy enough in Canada to buy blank receipt books. You can even make a collection of them, each in a different style of typography. These, some Separatist will be happy to fill in for you on the principle that if you get back at one government you get back at them all.

I once presented such a form to an inspector (legitimately in this case) which was covered with French words so atrociously scrawled that neither the inspector nor I could translate a word. Desperate to get the business over, I pretended to be able to make out the hieroglyphics. "Well, this must mean the chair," I said, "and that the wine press, and that the so on and so forth." His only interest was in getting his forms filled out and filed, and he went along with me. The only actual check he made was to see that I had approximately as many pieces in and on top of my bus as I

* *Vive les Séparatistes!*

had listings on my various receipts. Since he did it by looking through the window, it was a rough check, indeed.

But enough of revolutionary talk. I am in no way trying to incite you antique lovers out there to overthrow the government of the United States of America in all its glory by force of arms. I'm inciting nothing. I'm just reporting on a little righteous Civil Disobedience that points to a crying need for reform in one of our laws.

It would be too much to hope for that a new law be enacted that would admit the antiquity of items manufactured over fifty years before the date of purchase, but this would certainly be more closely related to the accepted definition of antiques. Roughly, the accepted definition is this: manufactured things—whether by hand or by machine—that are old enough in each case to invoke in us a sense of our past, a feeling of times gone by.

There are many ways of stating this principle. Anything that is interesting *because* it is old is an antique. Of course, it is assumed that the "thing" was in some way wrought by man and is being made by him no longer or not in the same way. An object is not made antique merely by the passage of time but by changes over a period of time in the way man lives.

At various times in history, time has almost stood still for centuries, and things that man has made and used have become antique very slowly. It is when civilization is making progress and man is finding new ways to live and fight and love that antiques come into being. Antiques are the artifacts from whatever way he used to live and fight and love, before the newest way was invented to cope with the problem of staying alive on this earth.

On postcards of sixty years ago that picture the San Francisco fire of April 18, 1906, we see women standing on a hillside in utterly impractical clothes watching a city disappear in wild flames. The colors and the detail range between the improbable and the impossible. Nobody makes cards like that anymore. Such an approach to reporting would be a disaster today. But cards like this were the *Life* magazine of our grandfather's day, a small window on the simpler world our grandparents lived in.

Helmets, guns, uniforms, and other relics of the First World War are established "collectors' items." I talked yesterday to a teenager who wasn't even born until World War II was over. (I am growing old, my tea is getting cold!) To his generation, an M-1 rifle is an interesting sort of primitive weapon. The point is that, in our era of rapid technological advancement, antiques are coming into existence faster than you can blink your eyes. I read last week that some university had decided not to junk, but to preserve for posterity, an "antique" electronic computer!

And so, when dealers complain to me that you "just can't find antiques anymore," I feel sorry for them, because they just don't understand the situation. They aren't keeping up with the old times. Of course, you can't find Sheraton tables and primitive pine, but the whole world of Victorians is opening up, and hundreds of dealers are doing wonderfully well because they have accepted the march of time and turned to the furniture, lamps, and tools of the times of Abraham Lincoln and General Custer and Teddy Roosevelt and Woodrow Wilson and Jimmy Walker and the whole last exciting hundred years of American life.

An antique is not something made before a certain date but something out of the past that reminds us of a way of life that was different from our own. This is a book about current antiques, not the ones you could have bought fifty years ago. It is about the antiques, among others, that are flooding out of the last hundred years into the shops of today. Just as the ones you could have bought fifty years ago are now mostly in museums or collections of the rich, the current antiques will find their way too into museums and collections a hundred years from now. The process goes on and on.

An antique electronic computer, indeed! Wow!

Which reminds me. Antiques don't have to have beauty or grace or even charm. The essence of an antique is that it tells us something of the roots of our culture and goes to the sources of who we are. A painting of the Hudson River School is an antique. But so is a Model T Ford.

A hundred years from now, the fuddy-duddy dealers will still be complaining that they can't find any of the good stuff anymore. You know, the stuff with real character—like Early Plywood!

WHERE ANTIQUES COME FROM

Or, on the trail of the vanishing pine: where the pickers go to find the stuff in the rough.

I guess there isn't any point stalling around. I know why you opened this book to this chapter. You want to know about the place in Canada. After you've found out, you'll slip the book back on the counter, casually sidle over to another counter next to the door, make believe you have just remembered an appointment, and slip out the door free. Well, that's the way it goes. Some days you make a sale and some days you don't.

So what you want to know is the name of the secret place in Canada where the "good stuff" can be bought for practically nothing, the place you have to marry into an antique dealer's family to find out about. That is if you're lucky and the father-in-law you've picked happens to know about it. It is my guess that up to the publication of this book not one dealer in twenty does know about it. Most dealers buy from pickers, and pickers don't tell dealers *anything*. They make Macy's and Gimbels look like a couple of blabber mouths.

Well, here it is: the name of the place is Defoy. It is in the Province of Quebec about three-fifths of the way from Montreal going toward Quebec, only a little south, a quarter of a mile east of superhighway 9. It is across the highway from Daveluyville—which is also developing into a really good antique dump, by the way. Get someone to direct you to the barn of M. Rheault.

Anyway, Defoy is on a graded (dirt) road, and there isn't any town—just sheds and sheds and sheds loaded with the stuff. The whole thing is the business of the brothers Leo and René Beaudin, and it is the central distribution point for the rape of Quebec—and the Gaspé Peninsula as far as antiques are concerned.

I have never been there when there weren't seven to ten trucks, including a couple of trailer trucks, lined up waiting to be loaded, with license plates from all over the United States. On weekends it's bedlam, because that's when the pickers are bringing the stuff fresh from barns and farmhouses within a four-hundred-mile radius. (Why the stuff comes from this area, I'll discuss later in this chapter.)

To get the best prices, you have to wait your turn in line and buy from the wholesale shed—or the great pile that the pickers are unloading into faster than the work crew can put it away. To get into this line, you have to come with at least an empty Volkswagen bus with a rack for overflow on top. You'll be able to jam that bus full and cover the top with *pine* for $75.

Over in the retail shed—about forty by one hundred feet—you can find prices like these: dough boxes (without tops) for $3, with ends made of planks over two inches thick; really ancient-looking pine cupboards with only the remnants of the original paint on them for $20 to $35 (which sell for $125 to $250 refinished in a "suburban" shop); solid pine, round-top traveling trunks for $3; Victorian clocks for $1, earlier ones from $5 to $10; oxbows for $6; simple pine drop-leaf tables from $3 to $9, depending on how much paint is on them or whether they need minor (hinge) repairs. On and on it goes like that, for rows and rows, the finer pieces going for higher prices but still way down there.

The only exceptions are some typically Early French pieces, which command a high price in Canada. (They consider that they are selling the "junk" to the United States dealers!) An armoire with "diamond point" carving on the door panels will go for as high as $300 in the rough. Pieces like this are never completely refinished—just scraped down to the pine, with traces of the old paint showing.

There are two exceptions in the articles that might as well have come from the United States: chairs of the arrow-back and rabbit-ear variety, which are by comparison ridiculously high at around $14, and Victorian pine chests of drawers, the common "cottage furniture" made as late as the early 1900s. These are $20 and $22 in the rough, the same you would have to pay in New England. The word has gotten around—even to Defoy—and the standardization in price is remarkable. It is the same in New England, around Providence (the biggest wholesale center in the United States—see the following chapter) and even on high-priced Cape Cod.

There is another sort of wholesale center in Quebec, which is only fifteen miles east of Montreal (Defoy is 140 miles northeast), and this is Richelieu on Highway 1. Here, the prices are almost twice as high, but still cheap by United States standards.

Now that I've spilled the beans about Defoy, let's get back to the overall picture of where the antiques come from and why.

To begin with, the idea that most antique dealers like to convey is that they buy their merchandise from very secret sources. You are led to believe they are little old ladies in New Hampshire farmhouses whom the dealer has been cultivating for years.

Well, that doesn't happen to be true at all. Dealers actually get their merchandise off the backs of trucks, driven by men called pickers. These are the middlemen of the antique business, and there are thousands of them. They make regular rounds to their customers in cities and suburbs and resort areas throughout the country.

Dealers do buy at local auctions, but usually their customers are there too, bidding so high that there isn't any profit left for a dealer. Dealers also buy when an estate is being liquidated, but there isn't enough of this going on to amount to ten percent of the average dealer's stock. He needs stock, and he has to turn it over a couple of times a year to stay in business. To do this, he has to stay in his shop waiting for customers, and that is why the useful service of the pickers has come into being. Maybe that isn't the way it used to be—say, fifty years ago—but that is the way it is now.

The question is, where do the pickers find the stuff? They find it in areas and pockets of declining population and economic depression. The passing of the small farm is one factor that causes household items to come on the market. This was still happening fifty years ago in Connecticut, but by now most of the farms are occupied by refugees from New York City. The next source was southern Vermont, New Hampshire, and Maine. There are still some sources left in the northern parts of these states, but not many people lived there, and there wasn't too much to begin with.

As I have said, the farm things are coming from Canada, especially Quebec and the Maritime Provinces, which accounts for the function of Defoy and the five to ten truckloads that leave there daily.

There are two other places where farm antiques can still be found—western New York State and western Pennsylvania. There are pockets where mills have closed in small towns or where the valleys are too small to accommodate milk-cow herds of economically feasible size. (That, incidentally, is why dairying has gone out of style in New Hampshire but not in Vermont—Vermont has larger valleys—and why New Hampshire is "better pickings" than Vermont.)

Cities and other highly populated places can also become depressed, as has happened in the last twenty years to the mill towns of New England, particularly in southeastern Massachusetts. This area, once highly populated and wealthy, includes New Bedford, at one time one of the richest cities in the country. Also struck by the movement of industrial mills to the South were southern New Hampshire, a lot of Rhode Island, and western Massachusetts.

The biggest solid area of depression is the southeastern corner of Massachusetts, including New Bedford. As a result, a wholesaling area for antiques from the houses of the well-to-do and the wealthy, the once stately homes of mill owners and the whaling captains of New Bedford, has sprung up just east of Providence on Route 44 and on Route 114A, which crosses Route 44 and goes east into Seekonk, Massachusetts, and along 114 toward New Bedford.

Here the situation is a little different from the situation in Defoy. You have not just one wholesaler (with a little

retail on the side) but around thirty dealers who have retail shops. They sell at prices so low as to amount to wholesale prices in comparison to the prices prevalent in city, suburban, and resort shops. You can buy almost anything for about half the price you would pay in the summer at Cape Cod (a resort area), which is only seventy miles away. If you are an established dealer or even if you aren't a dealer but are prepared to buy a station wagon full, you will receive an additional discount, probably around ten percent.

This area has become pretty widely known among dealers over the last fifteen years, partly because a number of these shops advertise in *Hobbies* and, more recently, in *The Antique Trader*. (Especially well known are two dealers in Rhode Island—Bob Harpin in West Warwick and Peter Potts in West Kingston, Rhode Island.) Pickers from all over New England have been bringing merchandise into this area to compensate for what is already coming out of it. They don't get as much money here for their things as they would by going into New York City and northern New Jersey, but they can get rid of a truckload in a hurry and head back home the same night. This saves them the expense of spending a couple of days selling a piece here and a piece there farther south. Of course, pickers who have refinished their things tend to go to Connecticut, New York, or New Jersey or save them to sell during the summer in the resort areas along the coast of New England, where thousands of summer shops flourish. A lot of the pieces are Victorian, but if a piece is pine, it is scraped down and stained and becomes ersatz Early American. (See the chapter "Prevalent Fakes.") But there are also many "really good things" from the big old houses in southeastern Massachusetts that are being torn down. Country or farm objects are being brought in by the New England pickers and by the truckload from Canada.

Money is made by moving antiques from one place to another. Dealers from the South and Midwest come to this area by the hundreds to load up and return home to tell their stories about secret little old ladies living on farms in New Hampshire. One dealer here, who has no shop but just a big white barn, buys as much Empire furniture as he can and sends a truckload a week to regular customers in the South. Empire is the popular period in the South for historic reasons, while you can't find a stick of it in Boston.

Victorian goes mostly to the Midwest, because that is *their* period. (Victorian is sent to the dump in Boston, and it is only beginning to pick up—because of the craze for Golden Oak—in the New York City area.) It also moves as far west as Seattle, San Francisco, and, especially, Dallas, where it goes for prices that make a New Englander's eyes pop. One operator takes six trailer truckloads to Texas every year, mostly from this area, but also from Canada.

On a smaller scale than in the New Bedford-Providence country, but with a tendency to have better stock—that is, less Victorian—similar groups of retail dealers who also sell at wholesale exist in western New York State and Pennsylvania.

So these are the places from which the antiques are coming and will come for the next couple of decades. (See the following chapter for the names and locations of the shops in the areas and a survey of where the shops are all over the country.) But what will happen as these sources gradually dry up? My crystal ball tells me nothing. Obviously, anybody who can read the future doesn't advertise it; he goes to a racetrack or down to Wall Street and gets rich.

But there are educated guesses, based on straws in the wind. Clearly, Victoriana is the next wave of antiques. (See the discussion of these waves in the preceding chapter.) During the Victorian era, which coincided with the industrial revolution, the United States and England exported staggering amounts of their production to relatively underdeveloped countries overseas—to South America, Spain, the Mediterranean. As these countries develop, all that Victorian furniture becomes junk to them. It is already being bought up in Spain and shipped back.

That is one possibility for the antique business to consider. Another thought is that, as foreign travel increases and the world shrinks, we may broaden our interest in antiques to include those of the whole world.

As to future depressed areas . . . sorry, folks, the crystal ball is clouding over. That's all for tonight. Someone turn on the lights, and don't forget to leave your contributions on the table by the door as you leave. And I don't want to hear any coins clinking, either!

WHERE TO BUY THEM

A guide to the wholesale areas of the Northeast, where the dealers go for stock, and you can too.

It seems you can buy antiques almost anywhere these days, and at least half a dozen directories of shops all over the country are being published. The ads in *Hobbies* and *The Antique Trader* make a pretty good directory in themselves, because the advertisers are not only *in* business but are *doing* business. The directories are all good and useful, but the trouble with them is that they include anyone with a couple of lamps in his garage who hangs out a shingle with the word "Antiques" on it.

On the other hand, *Hobbies* and *The Antique Trader* are the publications that dealers use for buying and selling among one another. You know they really have things and don't have wild ideas about prices—which the amateurs and dabblers in the business often do. Because people are loath to part with even the oldest copies of these publications, here's the information you will need to get your own subscriptions:

Hobbies
1006 South Michigan Avenue
Chicago, Illinois
(Published once a month, one-year subscription for $4.)

The Antique Trader
Box 327
Kewanee, Illinois
(Published twice a month, one-year subscription for $3.)

The pages of these two magazines are crammed with advertisements for articles that are for sale at the right prices. In fact, it is in these two "open markets" for dealers that values are established. (But you don't have to be a dealer to buy from any of the advertisers.)

The rest of the areas and shops I'm going to mention are based on my personal experience, and if there are any significant omissions I'll try to make up for them the next time I write a book. But I don't think I've missed any of the really important marketplaces in my travels, which have taken me all over the country. I do skim lightly over the less important parts of the country.

The best general area is the northeastern section of the United States, because more people have lived in it and moved out of it over the years. So I'll start out with the two best places there, cover each of the northeastern states individually, and then skip around the rest of the country where concentrations of dealers can be found in key cities.

Southeastern Pennsylvania

Beyond the shadow of a doubt, the heartland of American antiques in this decade is southeastern Pennsylvania. This is where the really old things are coming from today in any quantity, as they used to come from Massachusetts and Connecticut, and later from Vermont, New Hampshire, and Maine. The prices are naturally a lot lower here than after the stuff has been distributed around the country and among the thousands of shops along the coast and in other resort areas of New England.

Most of the pieces are coming out of the rolling hills of the Pennsylvania countryside, where the old stone houses still have the look of Revolutionary days about them and where, in the small towns, history is engraved on little

plaques all around you. The area reaches from Philadelphia to Lancaster and Harrisburg, and then back to Reading, Allentown, and Trenton. There isn't anything in those cities —not even many shops. Where the antiques show up is in shops along the old highways. Starting from Harrisburg and going east, Route 422 is the main artery of this antiqueland. The stuff flows from the whole area into the Harrisburg region. There is an association of some fifty dealers there—any one of whom will give you a map showing the locations of the others. From the Harrisburg region the stuff flows down into Bucks County, north of Philadelphia. You will find the good pieces in almost any of the roads through this surprisingly rustic countryside. But the throbbing center is the tiny town of Lahaska, on Route 202, five miles below New Hope, Pennsylvania, right on the Jersey border.

Lahaska is the wholesale-retail center to which buyers come from all over the East Coast, Midwest, and far West, and it is impossible to say now how many shops have located there. I counted twenty-two, and at the rate they are opening the number might be doubled by the time this book is out. Here is where you find the traditional gold—old cupboards, completely repaired and scraped down to the raw wood—usually pine—for $125. One shop will give you a choice of eight of them. You find all kinds of antique ironware at the lowest prices in the country, because you are so near the places where it is being forged—in both senses of the word.

One place that is even better, some seventy miles west of Lahaska, is a single enterprise, Merritt's Antiques, a couple of miles north of Douglassville on Route 422. Douglassville is between Reading and Pottstown on Route 422.

Merritt's is the biggest wholesale center in the country, and retail buyers are not turned away. Three or four large trucks dump their loads here every week. I have seen twenty grandfather clocks piled up in the yard like coffins waiting for a place to put them under cover. You can buy any kind of antique there, and dealers in their station wagons arrive not only from the East Coast but from as far as California and Texas.

Merritt's advertisements in *Hobbies* and *The Antique Trader* say, "Not only do we have what we advertise, but an unbelievable selection of goods." And you had better believe that it is unbelievable. It is awe-inspiring. And the prices are the best in the country.

Sheds beyond sheds are loaded with china in all tastes, glass, chests and cabinets, clocks, chairs and tables, stacked to the roof. In one corner I saw almost forty tilt-top tables, which is more than you could find in all the shops from

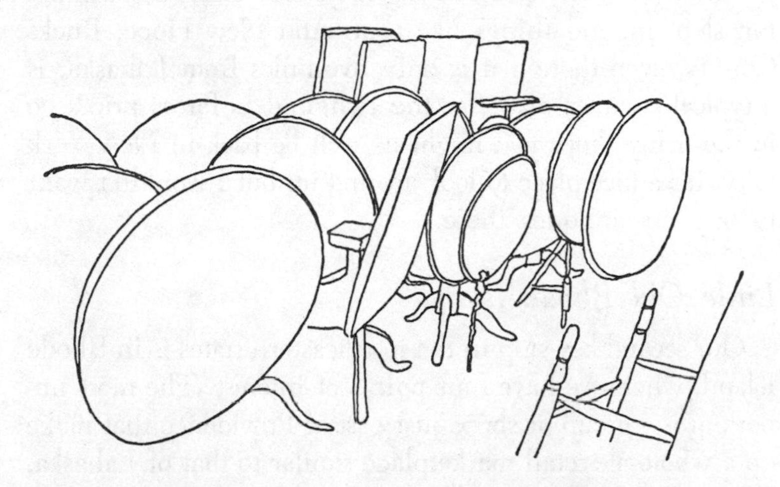

Providence to Boston and in Cape Cod and the rest of Massachusetts. There are a hundred grandfather clocks—good ones—and maybe two hundred wall clocks; three-drawer pine chests, completely scraped down, for $22 and $25; lift-top commodes for $27. We are on an ascending market, and by the time this book gets to print, they will cost more, but they will still be the same degree cheaper than anywhere else. (Incidentally, I saw pieces that had just come in from New Hampshire—I wish I knew where!—and so Merritt's sources of supply are not limited to Pennsylvania. But this is typical of the shipping around the country that goes on.)

The spring antiques show held in the armory in Harrisburg is turning out to be one of the best in the East. More dealers are bringing more stuff and more buyers are buying it. In 1965 so much business was done the first day—because the pieces were there and the prices were right—that many dealers sold out and spent the night driving back to their shops to load up for the next day.

There are many shops in Philadelphia, but, like Boston and the middle fifties of New York City, the price range is for the really rich—$12,000 highboys that George Washington slept in, and things like that. And New Hope, Bucks County, even though it is only five miles from Lahaska, is a typical summer place for the rich, and as far as prices go in the many shops you might as well be back in New York City. It's a nice place to look around in, but I wouldn't want to buy my antiques there.

Little Old Rhode Island

Our second key stop in the northeastern states is in Rhode Island, where we have four points of interest. The most important is a group of shops just east of Providence that make up a wholesale-retail marketplace similar to that of Lahaska. The difference is that the merchandise tends strongly to Victoriana. Dealers from the Midwest, Texas, and the far West come here to load up. The shops are on Route 44 going east out of Providence, on Route 114, which crosses Route 44 a few miles outside of Providence, and around the nearby town of Seekonk. There is no point in giving you more specific directions, because if you stop at any one of these shops you will be given a map showing the locations of all the others in the area.

A few miles farther northeast from Providence, along Route 44, you come to our second point of interest in Rhode Island. This is Leonard's, the most impressive antique shop I have ever seen. Supermarket would be a better word than shop. Mr. Leonard has eleven employees selling, repairing, and refinishing just about every kind of American antique furniture from every period up to Early Victorian. It takes five rooms of an old stone house to display samples of his standard stock. Behind the house are the cabinetmaking and refinishing shops and three enormous sheds packed to the ceiling with stock that Mr. Leonard scours the country for, buying up whole estates before they ever get to the auctioneer's block. Leonard's sells an average of a bed a day, every day of the year—authentic cannonball and pineapple post beds. There are rows of slant-top desks—all the really old ones—stacked three tiers high. Thirty or forty tilt-top tables, birdcages, and snake legs are piled at random in a corner. It's enough to make your mouth water for a moving van and a good moonless night.

You won't find any cheap pieces or bargains here, but because of the volume of business done you can be sure the prices are as close to a fair market value as any place in the country. Leonard's ships to almost every state and all over the world. A great many of his sales are to interior decorators, but the collector is always welcome.

For our next stop we go back through Providence and west of it to the fabulous compound of Trader Bob Harpin at 20 Centre Street in West Warwick. From barns back of his beautiful Colonial house, Bob and his wife, Cookie, have been doing a mail-order business through their full-page ad in *Hobbies* for almost twenty years. The difference between this place and Leonard's is that Trader Bob got on the Victorian band wagon long ago and has been riding it high ever since. He has lots of earlier things, but the emphasis is on Victorian furniture and lamps. The prices are good, and this is one of the places where prices are established. Virtually everything is sold "in the rough" or "as is," and you get to do your own repairing and refinishing when necessary.

Finally, there is a flock of dealers in southern Rhode Island around Kingston and Peace Dale who carry a general line of Early American at a lower price range than any other place in New England. I don't know why, and I suppose that when they read this they'll all rush out and raise their prices, so you had better hurry. One of the best places to start is with Cleb Davis, proprietor of Dove and Distaff in Peace Dale, or with Peter Potts in West Kingston, or with James E. Scudder in Carolina. They will give you an association map showing where the other dealers are.

Southeastern Pennsylvania and Rhode Island are the two choicest areas for antiques in the country, along with Defoy, Quebec. The other states of the Northeast and the key antiques cities in the rest of the country follow, not in the order of importance.

New Jersey

There are a lot of "suburban" shops in the New Jersey towns near New York City and down the resort coast for about forty miles south. They all have a fine selection of the really good things, because this is part of the Gold Coast of the United States and the people have the money. This is fine with me, but if you are a bargain hunter—and what real antiques fiend isn't?—the area to comb in New Jersey is the hill country just west of the concentration of population around New York City. The artery is Route 202, running southwest from New York City toward Bucks County, Pennsylvania, and very close to the fabulous Lahaska.

Some of the good old pieces are still coming out of the extreme southern part of New Jersey and filtering into shops on Route 9 between Atlantic City and Cape May, the "old road," parallel to the Garden State Parkway.

Connecticut

This used to be the best state in the Union for antiques, because it was settled so early and so thickly populated. But, being next to New York City and containing that part of the Gold Coast that runs from White Plains to New Haven, it was the first state to be picked over and in the last fifty years it has been downright gleaned. Of course, there are plenty of shops along the southern coast of Connecticut, but the merchandise is mostly imported. The rest comes from the liquidation of local estates. Prices are sky high, with the exception of the famous old shop of the Liverant family (including Zeek, the Seeker) in Colchester, about halfway between New London and Hartford. There are several other good shops, with good selections and reasonable prices, around Colchester, and it is well worth a visit.

There are also some fine shops around West Hartford featuring really old, more or less primitive furniture. But not cheap—because Hartford is a rich city.

Massachusetts

In Massachusetts you have the same situation we found in New Jersey. There are plenty of shops in the rich towns around Boston and the resort areas along the coast, especially on Cape Cod. But all the antiques are imported and sold at the highest price level. The only exception I have found is a covey of shops in and around Harwich, off the beaten track about halfway out on Cape Cod.

One interesting place on the Cape is The Old Yankee Peddler, which carries the finest line of pine reproductions —unfinished—that I have ever seen, and at the lowest prices. It is on Route 28, the southern route out on the Cape, near South Yarmouth.

The southeastern bulge of Massachusetts that includes Taunton and the old whaling cities of Fall River and New Bedford is the area from which a great deal of Victorian is coming on the market. But it all moves quickly into the shops in East Providence and Seekonk, Rhode Island.

Whatever antiques are left in the western part of Massachusetts seep into the shops along Route 5, which runs north and south between Holyoke and Bernardston. Incidentally, in Leyden, west of Bernardston, you start looking for Hugh Sloane, who can sell you all kinds of pieces of old houses in case you are restoring one. Lots of the paneling, boarding, and mantels that went into the restoration of Old Deerfield came from the stacks in his barn.

Vermont

For some reason Vermont sounds to most people like a great place to find antiques. But the trouble is that too few people have lived in Vermont, and there was never any great quantity of antiques in the first place. The antiques that really are there in those beautiful old towns and houses are owned by people who have no intention of selling them, because they think of them as their furniture.

However, if you insist on looking for yourself, the greatest concentration of shops is on Route 7, running up and down the western side of the state. They are mostly between Rutland and Bennington.

New Hampshire

By contrast to Vermont, southern New Hampshire offers pretty good hunting, but the shops are not clustered. The best way to find them is to buy one of the guides that are on the market. The best one I have found is *Buxton's Guide to New England Antique Shops,* published by John S. Herold, Inc., Greenwich, Connecticut, price $2.95. It has lots of maps and pictures, and it lists the bigger shops that are really in business throughout New England. It also contains information on the major shows and antique fairs and a bibliography of books on antiques which, strangely enough, lists no books by that well-known antiques writer, George Grotz. But that's the way the cookie crumbles, and I still think it is a great guide.

You will run into some fine shops, with local things from the hills, along Route 4 in New Hampshire. This highway runs through some of the most beautiful country in the world between Portsmouth and Concord.

Maine

The coast of Maine is practically infested with antique shops. But, as on the coast of Massachusetts and Cape Cod, the vast majority are summer shops catering to tourists and to people who can afford to have summer homes in a resort area. This is especially so south of Portland. The prices begin to come down when you get up to the Boothbay-Camden-Rockland area, especially after the season is over and the summer people have gone home.

On the whole, Maine does not offer much, because, as with Vermont, it never did have much of a population. Whatever antiques are around are being bid up by the rich summer people—and the summer crowd in Maine is about the richest in any of the resort areas of New England.

New York State (outside New York City)

To begin with, you can forget about the northern section of New York State, because antiques simply don't come out of mountains. As for the rest of the state, you will find the usual number of shops in each city and its suburbs. The only outstanding area is the west-central section around Ithaca and south of the Finger Lakes, but the shops are widely scattered. There are fine shops in and around Cooperstown, where you will also find the very interesting American Farm Museum.

New York City

Victorian furnishings are the fad in New York City. They are "the newest thing," and New Yorkers wouldn't live in the terrible place if they weren't hung up on being sophisticated. But the rents are high, and dealers have to sell things on which they can make a high profit. The prices that New Yorkers pay for the commonest type of oak furniture (circa 1915) are enough to stun a person from any other part of the country. A round-top oak table, for instance, can bring $135. New Yorkers seem to be able to afford the high cost of being sophisticated; that you could never stick one of us country bumpkins like that is a secret I think should be kept from them. After all, they are helping to support a couple of hundred pickers around New England who are bringing the stuff into the New York shops (including me, a couple of times a year). The early Victorian you find is priced closer to reality, but it is still higher than any other place in the country. If you want to see fabulous collections of Victoriana, however, these are the shops to look at, as follows.

For the wildest variety of really far-out decorative pieces —from lamps, whatnots, furniture, bentwood rockers, and shaving mugs to bubble-gum machines—the place to start is the Circa 1890 shop just off Second Avenue on east Seventy-eighth Street. Then see the cluster of shops a block below on east Seventy-seventh Street. You can cruise Second Avenue all the way from Ninetieth Street down to Sixth Street in the east side of Greenwich Village—"the East Village," as New Yorkers call it. On the way down the avenue you will pass at least twenty shops. A few more are scattered around in the East Village, especially on Eighth Street.

The highest concentration of shops is all the way over on the western edge of Greenwich Village on Hudson Street, which runs north and south and is really the downtown extension of Ninth Avenue. Most of the shops are on Hudson Street between Tenth and Eleventh streets, but there are also a number around the corner on Bleecker Street; two or three of these are the best in the city.

The Rest of the Country

Strewn across the rest of the United States of America are some fifteen thousand antique shops, and to cover the whole scene would take another book. I could tell you that in Dallas the best streets are Fairmount and McKinney; but then there are the cities of Austin and Fort Worth—and around five hundred shops in Texas all told. The touring and evaluating of these would take a book in itself. But the problem has really been solved for us all with a listing by city and state of about eleven thousand antique shops; it is the *National Travel Guide to Antique Shops,* published by Antique Enterprises, Inc., 333 South Beech Street, Casper, Wyoming. The price is $4 postpaid.

"Yes, but which are the *best* cities or areas to go to if, for instance, we were going to take a vacation trip?" Well, the answer is that the antique business—and the interstate distribution of antiques—has developed in such a way in the last twenty years that it just doesn't work that way anymore. Asking that question is like asking what city or state I should visit to find the best A&Ps. The only difference among shops is that, like supermarkets, they carry stock that tends to cater to the taste of the customers in their respective areas. I have mentioned this kind of variation, and I have stressed the special nature of the antique-bearing areas of eastern Pennsylvania and parts of New England.

About all I can offer is a few generalities. The states outside the Northeast where antiques are most popular are Ohio, Florida, Texas, and, on the West Coast, California (especially San Francisco) and Washington (especially Seattle). Antique shops are thickest around centers of wealth, which in turn leads to their becoming centers of culture and sophistication.

So get the two guides and the two magazines I have mentioned, and happy hunting! They are the *National Travel Guide to Antique Shops; Buxton's Guide to New England Antique Shops; Hobbies* and *The Antique Trader.*

HOW TO BUY THEM

A fundamental technique for taking unfair advantage of antique dealers.

The thing about buying antiques is that you first have to start thinking about antique dealers as if they were people and therefore subject to the ordinary laws of human psychology. I know this might be difficult for you at times, but try! Most dealers I know consider themselves to be a little cracked—or else why would they be in a miserable, thankless business they wouldn't get out of for all the tea in China?

I have been doing a lot of research on the problem in the last few years, and I have come up with a theory about deal-

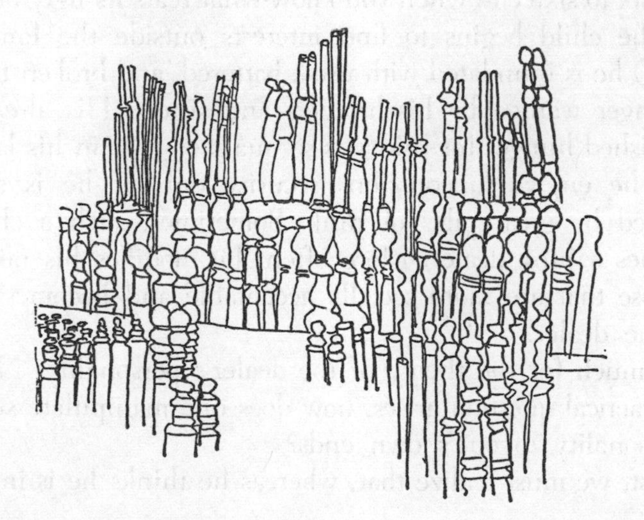

ers which, if fully understood, makes it possible not only to understand the working of their minds but also to manipulate them to your own ends.

To do this I have naturally had to read widely in psychology and conduct many in-depth interviews, mostly with my subjects under the influence of a cup of peyote tea.

The Grotz Theory of the Antique Dealer Psychosis is this:

The antique dealer invariably starts out as the youngest child in a family of from three to fourteen children. This means that two things happen to him in his formative years. First, in the years from zero to six, the bigger kids in the family are always taking marbles away from him. (I use the term "marbles" as a symbol of all his toys.) The result is that there is established in the tender psyche of the child an insatiable hunger to have stuff of his or her own. Now, if things were to stop there, all we would have when the child grows up to adulthood would be the fairly harmless personality of a "collector."

But a second thing happens to the child. In the years from six to sixteen (when you-know-what rears its ugly head and the child begins to find interests outside the family group) he is inundated with used, battered, and broken toys no longer wanted by his brothers and sisters. His already established hunger for things is so qualified that in his later years he enjoys subconscious security only if he is surrounded by great piles of junk. Sometimes, such a child becomes a junk dealer. More often, he modifies his needs to those that are more socially acceptable and becomes an antique dealer.

So much for the theory of the dealer's personality. Now the practical question arises, how does one manipulate such a personality to one's own ends?

First, we must realize that, whereas he thinks he is interested in buying and selling for a profit in order to make a living, actually his whole inner drive is directed at creating a situation of security by surrounding himself with ever-new pieces of junk—for which we read antiques. He is constantly driven to relive the experience of his years from six to sixteen.

Therefore, the way to arouse a dealer's interest and weaken his intention of profiting from his dealings with you is to dangle before his beady eyes the promise of the junk (read antiques) that his poor, greedy little psyche lusts for. So you must bring with you some interesting junk that you are willing to sell for what you paid for it, or even slightly less if the situation calls for a sacrifice. And—I can't emphasize this point too strongly—you also *must offer him the promise of more and different junk to come on future visits.*

You can carry your bait in the back of your car or station wagon, but I find it much more effective to pile it helter-skelter in a rack on top. This way, when you drive up, the dealer can see it through his window. You don't even have to open the ploy, because the dealer will invariably ask you first about your load, especially if you have something crazy on top of your car, like a gum-ball machine.

That is the cue for the all-important second part of your gambit. You tell him it is for sale, and you tell him you are helping your mother clean out the attic, or that you and your spouse have just inherited an old house in the country and you are trying to empty the barn your grandmother has been cramming with old things for years, or that your brother drives a truck for the Salvation Army and is always dropping off things that are too old for the workshop to restore. Almost any story will do.

What all this does is to awaken in the poor creature a desire to have you like him and want to come back to his shop. It doesn't matter whether he buys anything from you then and there or not. It is probably even better if he doesn't, because this keeps his poor sick appetite unsatisfied. And if you find something in his shop that you want to buy from him, he is going to give it to you at the best price he can to encourage your friendship and early return with other worn-out toys.

On a less artistic level, there is another way to manipulate a dealer into giving you his "best price." (There is always a lower price than the one marked on an item, because dealers sell to each other at a small "courtesy discount.") It is this: Never walk into a shop and announce that you are just looking around in case you see something interesting. Or that you are looking for a present for your Secret Pal. Or that you collect something, or even that you are looking for a particular antique. What you are doing, you say, is looking over the contents of all the shops in the area, because you have just bought a house that is much, much bigger than your old one, and you want to decorate it from top to bottom with antiques.

If you want to lay it on really thick, you can also have a sister who is also buying a much, much bigger house a couple of months from now. This all endows you with the rosy aura of a quantity and repeat customer. It is not a method of depth-psychology for antique dealers, but it is common psychology, and it works.

Now, I am aware that you will think I do not have a strictly honest mind. But let me remind you that we all must make a go of this life the best way we can. And I too had certain problems in my childhood.

Be that as it may, this short but meaty chapter should be worth the price of this book to you.

PREVALENT FAKES

Or, there's hardly anything you can believe in anymore.

There is going to have to be a certain amount of overlapping between this chapter and the next one (on frauds), because when you sell a fake, you have committed a fraud, and you are intending a fraud when you make a fake.

The basic distinction is that a fake is something that is done physically with something, and a fraud is a misrepresentation. A dealer buys a Victorian dry-sink, for example, scrapes the false graining off it, stains it light walnut, and sells it for Early American. He has made a fake and misrepresented it at the same time. And, into which chapter should the practice go? I don't know, but it is in this one right now, though I lean to thinking it should be in the next one. Such is the curse of being part organizing German and part self-questioning Irish. As my dear old mother would say, it's just another cross I have to bear, though why I should drag you into the mess I don't know.

In no particular order, then, let us proceed with the most prevalent fakes you should watch out for. Not that you shouldn't buy fakes if you like them, but you shouldn't pay for them as if they were genuine.

All fakes divide themselves into two groups, because there are fundamentally only two ways of making things. In the first group, the raw material, which is wood, exists in a solid state and you shape it by cutting away from it. Shaped pieces can be assembled into articles of furniture, mostly, and into sleighs, spinning wheels, cranberry scoops, kitchen ware, and other implements.

The second group comprises things in which a liquid or malleable material is given shape in a mold or form, which is ordinarily used over and over. In this group we have the things made out of glass, pewter, iron, silver, china. Copper and tinware is shaped on forms. Even things thrown on a wheel for shaping and baked are usually kept uniform by shaped scrapers held against the spinning clay or other material.

Articles more or less mass-produced by means of molds or forms are by far the fakes most difficult to detect—in most cases almost impossible—because all you have to do is find an original mold and you are in business. This kind of fakery can be done on a small scale or an incredibly large one.

The funniest large-scale operation I ever heard of was the Japanese factory reproducing English china of many styles and grades. This they were exporting to the United States, and to get through customs, each piece had to have "Made in Japan" stamped on the bottom. Well, this was such a large operation that the group of plants involved naturally controlled the politics of the town. One day, they had the name of the town changed to Usa, and for many years they shipped china into this country with the legend "MADE IN USA."

On a smaller scale, I once sold a dealer four deeply pocked and rather unattractive pewter plates that I had found in a cellar. I couldn't understand what he wanted them for until I met him at an antique show where we both had booths and I saw that he was selling antique pewter spoons both cheap and fast. He put only a couple out on the table at a time, but he had a Campbell's soup carton full of them out in his station wagon. And after we had gotten friendly, he admitted that he had found an old mold.

Take cast-iron toys and banks. Any foundry can reproduce them for you. All you need is one example of the original product. Thousands of exact reproductions were made and used as premiums by a book company back in the twenties. The company had its name on the bottom of them, but this could easily be ground off, the piece repainted, and the new paint artificially aged. With the price of these toys and banks zooming the way they are—mechanical banks start around $60 for the commonest, mostly sell in the hundreds, and go up to the thousands—well, you can call me a cynical old man if you want to, but as my Uncle George always said, when you can make something for a nickel and sell it for a dollar, as soon as that gets around there are going to be a lot of fellows getting into that business.

People are even faking glass, in which there is enough profit to make it worth while. A few years ago a museum that unfortunately is best known for its fakes bought a collection of Sandwich glass at a "bargain price." When its authenticity was questioned, and the matter even got into the hands of lawyers, it turned out that if the original molds are used, there isn't any way of telling. You can't tell by the composition of the glass, because the old formula is known. Even so, in the old days the formula varied from one lot to another—at least enough to confuse the issue.

Oil paintings are very easily copied by competent artists. They buy old paintings that were ruined by water or not good in the first place. They remove the remnants of the paint and start out with a genuine old canvas on an old stretcher. Cracks are made by applying a varnish over the paint before it is dry and then baking it. Such fakes can be detected, but only at considerable expense, and the paintings usually aren't *that* expensive. They often are ancestor portraits that sell for a round $500 and are guaranteed to bear a remarkable resemblance to the purchaser.

Old wooden signs are also suspect—even when the lettering is raised, supposedly from the action of the elements on the surface of the wood surrounding the painted areas. The technique is to paint the letters on new wood in liquid wax and then use lye to eat into the wood around them.

The most widespread of painting fakes are those done on glass for the doors of old clocks. Nice little old ladies all over the country have taken this up as a money-making hobby, some of them even advertising in small magazines.

Hitchcock chairs—or at least the decoration on them—are also suspect. Redecorating, of course, is obvious. But I knew one dealer who used to touch his up just gently and sign them on the back of the seat, as Hitchcock used to do. He admitted to me that he had signed at least four hundred chairs in his time. He always waited until he had found six matching ones, and then sold them in a set—for a premium price.

Which brings us rather neatly, it seems to me, to the subject of things made out of wood—especially furniture. Here the faker has many tricks, but there are many ways to find him out.

His two basic problems are to make new wood (or recently reworked old wood) look old and so to change or modify a piece as to make it look a lot older than it is.

Now, making the surface of wood look old is not hard at all. All this talk about the original patina that comes from wear and about time being impossible to reproduce is hogwash. Any competent wood finisher can do it and do it fast.

The edges are rounded with sandpaper and some depressions are sanded out where they might logically exist because of wear—the tops of front rungs in chairs, for instance. The piece is distressed by beating it with chains and mallets and maybe gouging out a few places. The whole is resanded and a dark walnut stain rubbed on hard with burlap or other rough material. The finish is applied, and this too is distressed in turn, though more gently than the bare wood was. Then another thin finish is applied to make it look as if someone had tried to restore a legitimately distressed underfinish. It all takes skill, but that doesn't take long to learn. More detailed instructions are given in a book I once wrote called *The Furniture Doctor*. And I'm afraid I have to admit that I didn't learn what I tell there from hearsay.

If the faker started out with a brand-new reproduction, or was trying to make a fifty-year-old piece of Victorian pine look three times as old, that is the process he would use. The question is, how do you detect it?

If the faker knew what he was doing, it would be impossible to tell by looking at the finish itself or even by feeling it. But he might not have bothered to age the underside of the top of a chair or table or whatnot. Even more important, he might not have been able to get really wide boards, such as were used before true mass production of furniture began after the Civil War. After that time, when a wide piece was needed for a table or bureau top or a chair seat, the wood was planked up. When this has been done, the lines between the separate pieces, while they can be very well obscured, can never be fully concealed.

Old wide boards have two characteristics that guarantee that that is what you have. One is that over the years they invariably warp to some extent. This doesn't happen with box pieces very often, but with table leaves it always does.

The other thing about wide boards is that they shrink over the years. A table with a round top supported by a column measures less across the grain than it will the length of it. If it is perfectly round it is a fake. In the case of

drop-leaf tables, the top of a really old one will have split lengthwise down the middle or will have sprung two of the hinges. Both faults can easily be repaired, but if there is no evidence of repair, there is something the matter in Denmark.

New hinges, also, would be suspicious; the old ones rarely broke—they just pulled out the screws.

The best signs of reproduction or of artificial aging in chest pieces are in the construction. In a really old chest of drawers—Early American, whether a primitive piecc or a choice example of the city cabinetmaker—signs of hand planing on the sides and, especially, the bottoms of drawers is a key indication of real age. If the bottoms of the drawers are quite thick and were beveled to fit the slots in the sides, it is the real thing. Also look for the runners of the drawers to be worn down or to have worn grooves in the pieces that support the drawers.

Also on drawers, the manner in which the sides were dovetailed to the front is probably the quickest clue to age. When some faker has stripped and aged a pine chest made in the Victorian era, the frequency and regularity of the dovetailing shows that it is machine-cut, and this is a dead giveaway. There will be eight to a dozen dovetails. In the older, handmade pieces, the dovetails were cut out with hand tools and there will be only from three to five of them. They will not match exactly and may not all be the same distance apart, though the old fellows did their best.

Speaking of drawers, the neatest trick of all is to apply a false front. This is done with the older case pieces where the front of the drawer had a rounded lip extending all the way around so as to conceal the crack between the drawer and the case. If the faker has found a really old piece, where the lip is mostly broken off, he planes a quarter of an inch off the whole front of the drawer and glues a new piece of the same kind of wood back on. Then he carves the edge. Any crack between this false front and the original front is not only almost invisible, but is easily concealed entirely with stain. The same thing can be done to the front of a drawer that never had a lip to begin with. This might be a cruder old piece or one that is not very old at all.

There are two tip-offs. The most obvious is the presence of two sets of holes in the back of the drawer front for attaching the drawer-pulls, and only one set in the forward part. The other is that the grain on the front of the drawer will not correspond to the grain on the back. A lot of people —including museums—have overlooked this one.

So far we have been looking at fakery from the aspect of the techniques used by the fakers. Now let us look at it from the aspect of the commonest fakes to look out for.

To begin with, nobody goes to the trouble of faking pieces of which there are a good many around. You can feel perfectly safe about Victorian furniture—for a while, anyway. Also, nobody is going to become involved in fakery unless there is a reasonable profit for the effort. This means that you don't have to start to watch out until you have pieces retailing for $50 and up. And the higher up you get, the more suspicious you should be.

This leaves us mainly with Early American—mostly pine,

but also cherry, maple, and any of the other hardwoods occasionally used. Because there is a great demand for primitive-pine case pieces and a very small supply, fakery is most rampant in that category. Everybody wants three- and four-drawer chests of drawers, dry-sinks, and cupboards. These, the faker supplies in three ways.

The first way is by turning to the vast supply of low-priced "cottage furniture" that was made all during the Victorian era and was being sold by Sears, Roebuck (to indicate the volume involved) right up to the First World War. This gives us about sixty years of production. In the beginning it was painted mustard, with simple striping or stenciled decorations. Later it was given false graining and the tear-drop knobs of Victorian. I would estimate, from what I have seen in my travels, that eighty percent of what is sold today as Early American pine dry-sinks and chests of drawers is faked from cottage pieces.

The first way to identify them is by the fact that their sides are paneled as opposed to being solid wood. The other tip-off is the dovetailing discussed a few pages back. You look at the drawers of chests and, in the case of dry-sinks, at the corners of the boxes on top.

A second great source of fake pine chests is the Empire furniture made just before the Civil War and still valued very low in New England, though selling for pretty good prices in the South at this time. Empire is made of very solid pine coated with mahogany veneer. For the last fifty years, New England dealers have been stripping off the veneer by letting the pieces soak in the lake until it peels off. They square them up while the glue in the joints dries out, round the edges, finish them with a dark brown stain, and there you are. They can be detected by the massiveness of the pine used. The framing of the chests will be almost three inches square. And if you visualize them with the veneer back on, you can see the heavy, square, boxy lines of Empire.

Another telltale characteristic of Empire is that it had overhanging top drawers, and it is a lot of trouble for the faker to cut these off and lower them—though this is done sometimes. Even if there are two drawers on the top level and they don't overhang, they are still a giveaway, because early primitive pine just didn't have divided drawers.

When it comes to the cupboard pieces, the faker has nothing he can modify, and he has to resort to building the whole thing from scratch. But the simple construction of these pieces makes it easy for even an amateur carpenter to knock one together in a day. The subtlety comes in the fact that the faker uses old boards of random width that have been taken out of the attics of old houses. Only ten years ago I was offered thirty cents a square foot for the boards in my attic. There are dealers and builders all over New England who have barnfuls of old boards taken from houses that had to be torn down for one reason or another. The current price is about fifty cents a square foot, but people who build their own antique cupboards collect their own boards or pay only half of that. And they use the old nails out of their boards.

To detect one of these fake cupboards, whose edges have been worn and to which the stain has been applied, is one of the hardest things for the layman to do. The only clues are the instances in which the faker has skimped in his craft. Where the boards have been cut to length, there often are curved lines indicating that a circular saw has been used, as opposed to the straight lines left when a hand saw was used to "cut off." Inside, you might find traces of old paint on one board and not on the one next to it. Or you might find a faded strip where the board was at one time nailed to a beam. The biggest giveaway is empty nail holes in places where there was never any reason for nails in the construction of the cupboard. These can be detected even if they have been filled with plastic wood and painted over.

Another common trick of the faker is to cut things down to popular sizes. For instance, church benches simply weren't built to seat two or three people. But four feet is the desired length for a bench these days, and the faker cuts a regular eight-foot bench in half. This required him to make two new end arms, but that's easy.

In the same fashion, all the cute little apothecary chests—usually with four levels of three square drawers each—are cut out of much bigger chests and set on four-legged frames.

When you see a cute little Early American pine three-drawer chest that is only as high as a Victorian commode—well, that's what it is. Some faker has taken the doors off and built in two drawers like the one already there. I knew a cabinetmaker in Connecticut once who had a contract to bring these in by the truckload to a famous New York City department store.

Another piece that is often faked—but not as often as case pieces—is the cobbler's bench. Like the cupboards, cobbler's benches are made up of old boards and old nails—and the ways of detection are the same.

To wrap this up, I want to get back to the possibility of fakes made out of cherry, maple, and mahogany. These are rare because of the difficulty of finding wide-enough boards. Nobody ever planked his attic floor with random-width cherry. And it is too easy to detect planked-up wood in a table leaf or the side of a highboy. Here, of course, we are getting into pieces that sell at far beyond the common market price and therefore beyond the range of this book.

And now for the frauds.

THE COMMONEST FRAUDS

Misrepresentation and other tricky practices to watch out for.

Fraud is a funny thing, because to commit it you have to know you are doing it. You can't stick up a gas station and not know it. But you can misrepresent something without knowing it, especially when it comes to antiques, which come pretty close to being infinitely varied in number and type and style. Anybody who says, "I know my antiques," is just sticking his neck out, even if he limits himself to a field as small as buttons or toy fire engines. One of the fascinating things about the antique business is that you never stop learning.

Some people think they don't have anything more to learn, and it is awful to have to listen to them. These characters come in two styles. One is the kind who really does know a lot and has been in the business for years. Even when you disagree with her (it's *always* a woman) you can't argue because there is always a fifty-fifty chance that she'll pull out a book or an old magazine article and crow loudly. This also means she will "have it on you" from then on. And if there is anything I can't stand it's a know-it-all lady dealer having it on me.

The other kind is just plain ignorant, and—happily—is most often found in thrift shops. I say happily because she will underprice things just as often as she will overprice.

But as far as arguing about the overpriced things is concerned, just forget it. She will keep them marked up to ridiculous prices until doomsday. If she thinks an Eastlake mirror is Sheraton, that's that. It is Sheraton because the lady who donated it said so. And Mrs. so-and-so knows her own furniture. (This is an actual case and it has been bothering me for years, because the piece was the only Eastlake mirror I have seen that was made of solid cherry, and I thought I could steal it for five dollars. This is an example of why you can't know everything. I spent two years researching for a book about Victorian furniture once, and I would have *sworn* that there was no such thing as an Eastlake mirror made of cherry. But there it was, staring me in the face!)

But she was nowhere nearly as bad as the little old lady I ran into one night in a little shop outside Orleans on Cape Cod. The shop was a Cape Cod with a front porch, if you can visualize that, and the porch and two downstairs rooms were packed with stuff. The place was on the main highway, with plenty of parking space, and I figured she must do a terrific business. A location like that would rent for $1500 for the season, at least. (Yes, Virginia, you *can* make big money in antiques. You have to if you are going to pay rents like that, at least for good locations in resort areas.)

I left my wife in the car, because I just wanted to case the joint. Besides, she said there wasn't any point in her looking at another shop because there would just be something else she'd want and I wouldn't let her have.

The first thing I saw under the light on the porch was a Victorian Jacobean chair so rickety that I thought I might be able to get it for $5. It had no cane. When she came to the door, I asked her how much it was, and she said $65. She said, "It's very old, you know." Well, I knew. They date around 1875. So I just shook my head and followed her inside.

The first thing I happened to look at was an oak library table with legs shaped like urns, circa 1910. I told her I was in the business, and asked her how much she would "have to get for" the table. (That's the sort of phrase that dealers identify one another by.) She said she'd have to get $125 for that and added, "It's Sheraton, you know."

I began to feel like Alice through the looking-glass and looked back at the door to see if it was really a mirror that I had stepped through. The next piece was a Victorian (or later) carpenter's tool chest that she told me was a sailor's sea chest. She wanted $125 for that too. Suppressing a hysterical giggle as well as I could, I asked her how business was this year. Predictably enough, she told me it was terrible. This was only her second year, she said, and she was thinking of selling out, but nobody would give her enough for her stock. I left the poor woman in her fantasy world and drove sadly home.

The point of all this is that you have to be careful about jumping to conclusions when you think a piece of furniture is being misrepresented. There are all degrees of ignorance, and I don't think there is an experienced dealer in the country who doesn't have a story about the time he picked up something for twenty-five cents and sold it to another dealer for $5—only to find out a couple of weeks later that it was worth $500. Oil paintings are the worst in this line. Many's the dealer who has sold an "ancestor" portrait for $200 or $300 only to find that it was done by Gilbert Stuart or someone almost as good. The only place to go when you are in doubt about a painting is to a museum. For American things, the Boston Museum of Fine Arts is the best.

Assuming you have fallen into the clutches of a tricky-dicky dealer, what are the items and practices to watch out for? Far and away the greatest area for misrepresentation is so-called Early American Primitive Pine. As I have pointed out in the previous chapter, this is because there's hardly any left, the demand is enormous, and there is the vast supply of Victorian pine, most of it covered with false graining, that lends itself readily to aging. Many pieces have been changed or built from scratch.

Other things aren't changed but are misrepresented. The newest of these are the Victorian ice chests, which were probably being made up to the First World War. They look like a short coffin and stand on short, heavy, turned feet. All the dealer does is pull out the tin and call them Early American blanket chests. Sometimes they aren't even scraped down and stained, and you are sold some original milk paint to dress up the swindle. They are really coming onto the market now—and detection is pathetically simple. In the first place, no real Early American was ever made of such heavy pieces of pine. Chests were given turnip feet, all right, but never of such bulk and weight. Secondly, you will be able to find nail holes inside the chest that can only be accounted for by its having been lined with sheet metal, usually galvanized sheet iron.

Very similar are the large Victorian tool chests that carpenters locked for the night and left on the job. They usually have inset metal handles on the end, which are obviously of Victorian design. They are being sold as sea chests, of which there are still plenty around, but nowhere nearly enough to fill the demand. The fraud is ludicrous, because if a man wanted a box to carry on and off a ship and down a cobbled street, he would build it, or have it built, as light as possible. Real sea chests were made of three-quarter-inch board and didn't have any legs, though a lot of them were set on frames or had legs attached after the owner was through with going to sea.

Another growing class of misrepresentation is the selling of mass-produced reproductions as the real thing. They are sold to the dealer unfinished, and he just slaps a coat of stain on them. (Do you see what I mean about some things being fakery and fraud at the same time? This is both, but I finally decided it was *more* fraud, or misrepresentation, than fakery, so I put it into this chapter. If you want it in the chapter on fakes, clip it out and paste it in back there.)

The commonest of these reproductions are ladder-back chairs and captain's chairs with the heavy rolled back. But small bedside tables, harvest tables, and even drop-leaf tables and slant-top desks are being made in rapidly increasing quantities. They are all in pine because the hard woods cost so much. And the world is rapidly being flooded with carved duck and goose decoys.

Of course, you can detect all these reproductions because they are just too good. There is no evidence of their having fallen apart and been glued back together again. Some other hints are given in the preceding chapter.

Now, here's one I really don't know how to classify. A lot

of dealers in Victorian have started calling Eastlake furniture Jacobean. I think the confusion (if that is what it is) comes about because there *was* a fad for reproductions of Jacobean chairs (but chairs only) at the same time that Eastlake was going strong—about 1870 to 1890. But Eastlake is Eastlake and Jacobean is Jacobean, and never the twain shall meet. At any rate, this misrepresentation has even appeared, unwittingly, of course, in the pages of that Johnny-come-lately authority on antiques, *Woman's Day*.

One summer recently I ran into a beautiful instance of fraud on my own Cape Cod. It didn't happen in the shop of "an old established dealer," for established dealers are almost always honest; they have to be, to maintain their clientele. This incident took place in one of the thousand or so resort shops that infest the shores of New England every summer.

The woman who ran the shop had a lift-top commode of pine with squarish lines, which would put it in the second half of the Cottage Furniture period (1845–1890+), which puts it at approximately 1875. But on the back of it she had pasted a piece of an old newspaper, which carefully displayed the date 1796; this, she pointed out, definitely established the age of the piece.

The funniest part of the farce was that another commode stood right next to it that had the curved lines suggestive of Empire and was earlier than the first piece—perhaps 1850. In the bottom of this, my wife found several small pieces of what was obviously the same newspaper—only these hadn't been pasted on anything yet.

Then you have to watch out for the cozy little couple who invite you into their parlor to see their special things that aren't for sale—not much they aren't—and it's called "selling from the parlor." But if you really like something, darned if they aren't hard up this month and could let you have it for a song because they do want to be your friends and so few people appreciate the really good things. This line may or may not be accompanied by enough sherry to get a longshoreman dead drunk. Yes, beware the sherry at all costs, or be sure to leave your checkbook home when you stop by to see this friendly pair.

And I hardly need to remind a smart old dog like you to look out for the recently painted piece that is going for half, or less, of what it would ordinarily be worth. This is a sure sign that somebody has scraped it down and found the legs to be worm-eaten and pulpy. Standard practice with the tricky-dickies.

Oh yes, I forgot to mention the lamps. The first one you have to watch out for is the student lamp, which has been widely reproduced for years. The reproduction is as good as the old ones, but don't swallow some bill of goods about how Barry Goldwater's great-great-grandfather used it crossing on the *Mayflower*. The right price to pay will be found in the second part of this book.

The other lamp that people have been fooling around with is the enormously popular *Gone With the Wind* Lamp, so called because such a lamp was featured in the movie of the same name. Lamps of this type weren't made until shortly after the Civil War—but why should a little detail like that bother us?

Anyway, the problem is with the globes, which are of glass and rather precariously supported. There are a lot more bases around than globes, so on a lot and for this reason, plain globes of current manufacture have been painted to match the design on the base. In the original globes, the design was *in* the glass, and these gentle forgeries are easily detectable.

Globes with designs *in* the glass—all-purpose designs of a sort—are also being manufactured now, but the designers are so fearful of offending that the designs don't match those on *any* bases, and they are not too hard to detect.

As far as cast iron goes, you can trust anything but the toy banks (see preceding chapter), the trivets, and Franklin stoves. Trivets are widely reproduced, but the reproductions always are decorative "improvements" on the originals. As for the stoves, the reproductions sell for as much as the originals do.

CODED PRICES

It's a troublesome problem, and everything depends on the integrity of the dealer.

Coded prices remind me of the time I went into New York to see my lawyer about my income tax. I wasn't in trouble or anything, but I'd been traveling around a lot finding out things for my faithful readers, and I figured I might be entitled to some king-sized deductions. Well, Marty and I have been friends for a long time, and so my feelings weren't hurt when he told me he was above doing income taxes these days but that he had a very talented accountant with an office on the same floor. I let the word "talented" go by, and we went down the hall to this fellow's place of business. Pretty soon I was spreading my records out on his desk and explaining the situation to him.

He kept nodding his head, and when I was all done, he said, "Yes, Mr. Grotz, that all seems to be perfectly clear. Now, just how much income tax can you afford to pay?"

Marty, who was listening to all this, finally convinced me that the guy was another amateur humorist, so I let him go ahead and prepare my form. Now I'm just waiting for seven years to be up. Or doesn't the statute of limitations apply to income taxes?

I always remember the experience when I go into a shop and see a tag on something I want that reads "FLp-M22." It's as if the dealer were saying to me, "Well, Mr. Grotz, how much can you afford to pay?" Or "How much can I stick you for?"

I ask the dealer how much he wants for his little treasure, and he comes over and looks at the tag. Then he stares up at the ceiling, supposedly figuring out what the code translates into in dollars and cents. But I happen to know that the code tells him how much he paid for the piece, and he is trying to figure out how much more than that he can get out of me.

And so, like almost everybody else I know, I think coded pricing is an evil and nefarious practice designed to catch as many suckers as possible.

But I have gotten friendly with some dealers who use code, and I have to admit that they have their side of the story too. They have given me two different reasons why a dealer will use code.

The first reason applies to the dealer who is getting a lot of primary stuff. That is, he isn't buying from pickers but directly from "the little old ladies." He is buying the contents of houses, which are usually sold to settle an estate. And if he hasn't been in the business over a thousand years, he will often get things that he isn't sure of the value of. Now, such a dealer will naturally have other dealers coming into his shop a lot to see what's new. So he puts the stuff he is unsure of on the table or floor with a coded price tag on it. When a dealer shows interest, he starts fishing to find out what he thinks it is worth. He'll say, "Well, what will you give me for it?" Or he'll name a price just to get the dealer's reaction. Or he'll tell him some enormous price he paid for it to see what the dealer says. After four or five such sessions, he'll have a pretty good idea of the item's value.

Well, how can you object to that? After all, the man is in the antique business to make a living, and to do that he has to get the best price the market will bear for everything that passes through his shop. A dealer like this gets in a lot of pieces that he can't make anything on or has to throw away, and he usually has such good buys that you can't refuse to have anything to do with him because he uses coded prices. In fact, dealers like him are in or close to the prime areas where the antiques come from (see the chapter "Where to Buy Them").

But there is another kind of dealer who uses coded prices and should be avoided, unless you know your values pretty well. This dealer sells from a lah-de-dah shop or a house in a fancy suburb, because he caters to interior decorators. He sells fifteen to forty percent less than he does to the general public. He gives an interior decorator a bill at the retail price, which the decorator gives to his customer. But after the customer pays the bill to the dealer, the dealer kicks back fifteen to forty percent of the amount to the interior decorator. The price has been decided on between the dealer and the decorator—at the highest figure the decorator thinks his customer will bear. All of which is fine if you have plenty of money and you think interior decorators are cute, which they usually are.

I've been talking in generalities here, and the trouble with generalities is that there are exceptions. In this case the exception is the fabulous Leonard's, a few miles northeast of Providence on Route 44.

This is the largest antique shop in the country and, strangely enough, probably the least publicized. Mr. Leonard never ran an ad in the trade or public press until 1964, although he has been in business since 1931. He had been a printer before that, but in those days there were a lot more printers than there were jobs. He was "over thirty," and the great depression was at its depth. He started from scratch, and yet today Lester Leonard's "shop" is the Macy's

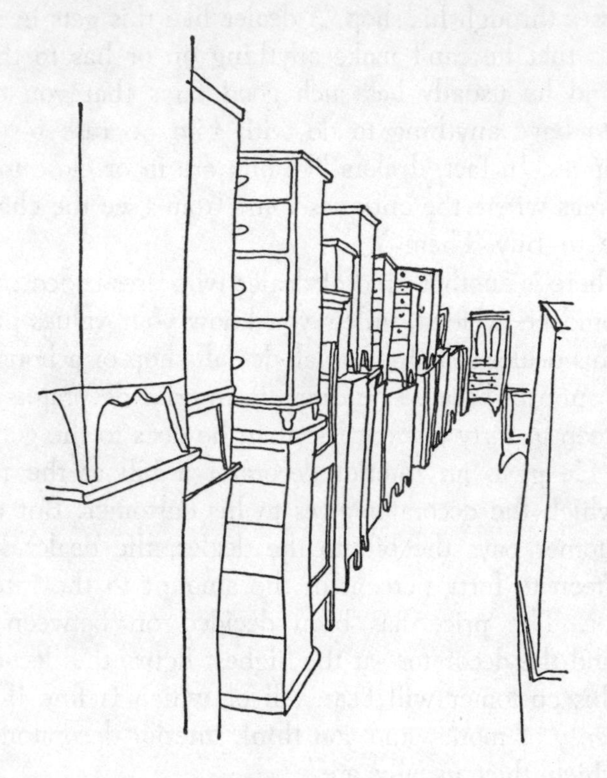

and Gimbels of the antique business—a department store of "antiques you can decorate with."

A gentle, humorous man, who looks over his glasses with a deceptive air of simplicity, Mr. Leonard employs eleven men in his refinishing shop alone, and last year filled orders for buyers in thirty-five states, all over Europe, and places like Saudi Arabia. Fine beds—cannonball, pineapple, and tester—are his specialty, and he sells an average of slightly more than one a day for every day in the year. To keep his three giant sheds full of the material for this business, he travels thousands of miles a week—four days on the road—buying estates big and small and sends his trucks to pick up the things. "Just estates," he says, because it takes too much time to buy at auctions.

When he is away, the "store" is tended by his wife and his assistant, Bob Jenkins, who is a treasure house of information.

Getting back to the use of code, it is Bob who points out that to run an operation of this size, you have to have the interior decorator trade. It is because of this volume that Leonard's can keep its prices reasonable and standard—in fact, to an important extent Leonard's sets the standard for the whole trade. When you come in "off the street"—whether you are a dealer or collector—you are given a reasonable price. You can't build a business like Leonard's with hanky-panky, trying to find suckers. Only straight dealing can do it, or the word would soon get around.

And since the word on Leonard's—as everyone in the trade knows—is "absolute integrity," there is an argument for using coded prices in this case. However, Leonard's is a far cry from some "Olde Gyppee Shoppee" by the seashore! That's where coded prices mean "Beware."

INVESTING IN ANTIQUES

As with the stock market, it's best to be just lucky, but with antiques it's hard *to lose.*

How much interest are you getting on your furniture this year? That's right, I didn't say your government bonds, I said your furniture. Was it five or ten or twenty percent. Or maybe you don't even understand the situation. (The rich get richer and the poor get poorer. Hallelujah, I'm a bum!)

Look, let me tell you a couple of stories. I've got a hundred like them, but two will do:

First story: A few years ago a young couple I knew asked me over to their house to look at a bedroom set they wanted to sell. He had moved down from the city and was raising rabbits, but something had gone wrong in the hutches that year, and he needed some extra money to pay his alfalfa bill, or something. So they figured they would sacrifice this fancy set they had paid $600 for only three years before. They told me they would let me have it for only $400. I winced internally and told them I only bought antiques but that I could give them the names of some places that dealt in used furniture.

As a rule of thumb, the most these fellows can pay for something is one third (if they like you) of what they can sell the stuff for. After all, they have their expenses and they have to make a profit to feed hungry mouths at home.

So the highest offer my friends got was $50. They advertised the set in the newspaper at $200—and they didn't get a single inquiry. They still have their bedroom set. They sold their car instead and bought one thousand turkey eggs—but that's another story entirely.

Second story: In 1938 a friend of mine named Howard took his wife Gladys for a Sunday afternoon drive out of New York City. Just across the Jersey line, on Route 9-W, they saw an auction going on outside a big square white building that had been a church but was now an antique shop. They stopped, or there wouldn't be any story. Well, with over two hundred people there and three dealers to make sure that nothing went too cheap, they bought a Sheraton desk for $110. In 1954 a *dealer* offered them $350 for it. In 1964 another dealer offered them $450, and they sold it in Florida in 1965 to a private collector for $650. I've seen it, and I think they should have gotten a $100 more than that.

That's the end of my stories, and I am sure that even if you had the meanest intelligence, you wouldn't have to have the moral spelled out for you.

But why does this happen? Simply because, out of each century, only a certain number of artifacts survive the junkyards, and that number, once the artifacts have been made, can never increase. Meanwhile, the population expands and the number of people who want those artifacts does increase. The people who want the stuff make up the richest segment of our society, and they don't want reproductions, they want the real thing.

In other words, the value of antiques isn't decided in some smoke-filled room but on an open market, in the same way the value of the industry of our country is determined on Wall Street. But antiques are far more secure than stocks, for each era or generation of them is in absolute limited supply. Even if their value dips along with everything else in a depression, after the depression is over they snap right back and go even higher. Lying around for ten years just increases their value, whereas a steel mill that is closed down for ten years (not to mention the taxes going on) would be worth a lot less. Old-fashioned is fine for antiques, but nobody wants an old-fashioned steel mill.

Now, that is the fundamental picture: all antiques rise in value as a result of inflation and the expanding population—like stocks, real estate, and even gold. But also there is a variation in the speed with which different styles and groups of antiques rise in value. There isn't anything classed as an antique that doesn't rise at least as fast as a government bond. But there also are antiques that at some time in their history will rise at an incredible speed. This usually happens just a few years after they have come onto the market as recognized antiques, of popular appeal.

(Let's deal with "popular appeal" right now and get it

out of the way. Very few people want things connected with death, sickness, or bodily functions of a private nature. For instance, you may have an old tombstone that is very interesting, but Jim Wharton had one around his shop, Stuff for Sale, in Westbrook, Connecticut, for five years and couldn't get a dollar for it. For all I know, he still has it. Nor will anybody buy "potty chairs," which are of the vintage of Boston rockers and Hitchcock chairs. They were regular bedroom furniture in the days before indoor toilets, and nice to have in the winter. People are amused by them, but they just don't want them in their houses. While Boston rockers are up to around $50 to $60 at the time I write, potty chairs still go for $5 to $10—and then only to cabinet-makers who rebuild them into plain chairs or "Boston rockers." There are other articles, but you'll recognize them when you see them, and besides, I like my books to sell in family bookstores and not under the counter.)

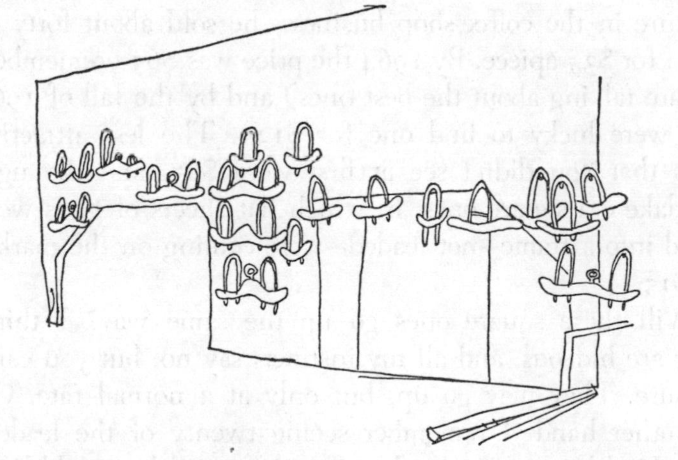

Now let's get back to the time in the history of an antique when its value rises the fastest. Do you remember those leaded glass lampshades that used to hang over your grandmother's round oak table in her sitting room (right behind the parlor, which was used for funerals and weddings only) or in her dining room, if she was a little bit ritzier than my grandmother? (We ate in her enormous kitchen, whose floor she scrubbed on her hands and knees every Saturday morning.)

All right, so you remember. Well, these first began to show up in the interior decorating pages of the women's magazines around 1957–58, and in a shop that carried Victorian you could sometimes pick out a nice one that looked like an inverted flower made out of beautiful stained glass for $10 or $15—even in New York City, where things are high. New antiques catch on first in New York (the avant-garde and all that), and to find one outside the city at that time, you would have had to go to a real junkshop. Well, in 1959 my friend Roy, of Roy's Antiques (what else?), at 249 East Seventy-seventh Street in Manhattan, began selling them at $20. In 1960—the year of his ill-fated adventure in the coffee-shop business—he sold about forty of them for $35 apiece. By 1964 the price was $65 (remember, we are talking about the best ones) and by the fall of 1965 you were lucky to find one for $125. The less attractive ones that you didn't see at first were $65, and the ugly Eastlake era square ones, in which flat sheets of glass were fitted into a frame—not leaded—were coming on the market at $15.

Will these square ones go up the same way? I think they are hideous, and all my instincts say no, but you can't be sure. They may go up, but only at a normal rate. On the other hand, I remember seeing twenty of the leaded-glass kind hanging in Roy's coffee shop, and he would have sold me the lot at $30 apiece. For $600 I would today have $2500 worth of merchandise. And if I had hunted them out in junkshops two years before that . . . wow!

Once the early spurt is over, the price either remains the same for a few years or drops a little—but not much, not more than ten percent. Then the item joins the great mass of antiques that rise in value at a gradual five to ten percent a year, a rate faster than can be attributed to inflation alone. The difference is accounted for by the fact that you have something that is in absolutely limited supply. They might not all be on the market yet, but the trade knows just about how many are left in attics and old houses and how fast they will be coming on the market.

Now, your obvious question is, what item is going to spurt in value next? Well, it's like these fellows who give you advice on the stock market and horse races. If I knew what the future held, I wouldn't be writing books. I'd be out in the marketplace getting rich. (But in the second part of this book I haven't been able to resist making some guesses about specific pieces.)

There are some generalities we can count on, however. One is that home furnishings will always be the soundest investment—as opposed to things that people collect, such as buttons, dolls, campaign ribbons, glassware. For one thing, the market on such things cannot be broken by mass forgery. Oh, anything can be forged, but when it comes to furniture and any of the larger things made of wood, it can't be done on a mass scale, as it can be with metal things such as silver, pewter, and ironware, and glass and china. (See the chapter "Prevalent Fakes.")

For another thing, there is the economics of faking something. Take the round, leaded-stained-glass hanging shades we were talking about a minute ago. There simply isn't the mass market that would make it reasonable to mass-produce them, and to reproduce them one at a time would cost a fantastic amount.

Now, I wouldn't be a bit surprised if it was becoming

feasible to fake early prints, such as Currier and Ives. And I mean making the higher priced ones exactly like the originals. If the interest in decorated tinware keeps up, that could be a trouble spot one of these days. In fact, if someone doesn't start mass-faking candle molds pretty fast, I am going to be deeply disappointed in the American con-man. The classic twelve-hole size is up to $24—even higher in suburbia shops—and it shouldn't be hard at all to tool up a one-man factory in a garage to make them. They have only about fifty cents' worth of tin and solder in them, and you could sell them to dealers for $12 and still make a killing. Hmm.

Probably the most important generality of all is that the best area for investment is in late Victoriana—which is to say, after the Civil War. This includes home furnishings in Eastlake, Mission, Golden Oak, and Art Nouveau.*

For speculation you might buy things from the Roaring 20s—so-called modernistic stuff . . . beds made out of clear plastic, even things to do with the depression, such as statues of F.D.R. steering the ship of state with a clock mounted in his stomach, a refrigerator with the coils mounted on top, parts of automobiles and airplanes, Early Plywood furniture. But from here you are on your own; my crystal ball has a dust storm in it today.

But late Victoriana is the big thing, because you can find it. It has started to appear in antique shops—though it hasn't completed the process of moving out of the junkshops *yet.* In New York City there are a couple of dozen shops that carry nothing but late Victorian. They are in Greenwich Village, over in the East Village, around the St. Mark's

* For more detailed information about these styles than is given in this book, see *The New Antiques: Knowing and Buying Victorian Furniture* by George Grotz, Doubleday & Company, Inc., Garden City, New York, 1964.

Place area, on lower First and Second avenues, and the rest on Second Avenue in the fashionable Upper East Side and on Seventy-seventh and Seventy-eighth streets just off the avenue. In Dallas and Chicago, Victoriana is catching on. The main prime source, of course, is the Providence-New Bedford-Fall River area. (See the chapter "Where Antiques Come From.")

Just so that you don't think I'm the only one turned on to Victoriana, I'd like to close this chapter with a quote from my friend Amy Vanderbilt, who knows a lot more about interior decoration than I do. Her etiquette is a lot better than mine too, but I guess you knew that, what with her having that big book out on it.* Not that I'm jealous or anything. After all, I don't need much etiquette. I haven't been to a tea party in years. But anyway, what she wrote was this:

"When I was quite young, my mother told me, 'Never throw out anything Victorian.' I must say that I didn't believe her at the time, and I discarded over the years a number of things—*Tiffany glass,* for example—that she treasured and I did not. She had quite a collection of dark green pressed glass, too, that I abominated. I still don't like it, but I wish I had kept it as an investment.

* *Amy Vanderbilt's New Complete Book of Etiquette,* Doubleday & Company, Inc., Garden City, New York, 1963.

"Before I was born, my grandfather, who had sense about these things, packed several barrels of old glass and china for me when I should appear. Many of these things lend a beautiful background to my own Victorian brownstone in New York today. Antiques—even the most recent ones—are like money in the bank."

SECRETS OF REFINISHING

The instant refinisher rides again, or the shortest course in furniture refinishing ever offered.

Well, here we are back at the old stand, and I will admit that I had to give the matter a lot of thought before I decided to call this chapter "Secrets of Refinishing." After all, it might seem to some people that a fellow who has written three books on refinishing wouldn't have any secrets left. In fact, I think I just heard a voice in the back row muttering, "That blabbermouth never kept a secret in his life!"

I guess I'll have to admit that in the first book I told everything that my Uncle George taught me back in Vermont,* and in the second one what I learned running my own shop in Connecticut,** and in the third one the sneaky tricks I learned that year I worked in New York City for

* *From Gunk to Glow,* available from the author at $1 postpaid. Send check, cash, or money order to George Grotz, East Poultney, Vermont.

** *The Furniture Doctor,* Doubleday & Company, Inc., Garden City, New York, 1962, $4.95.

the AAAA Find 'em, Fool 'em and Forget 'em Door-to-Door Refinishing Agency.*

But on the other hand, an unfortunately large number of people don't own those books—not to mention the number who never even heard of them, or me, or my racket—oops, profession. So I don't think it is really cheating to repeat in this book a few of the most important things that anyone who is new at the game should know.

This raises the question of whether it's against the law to commit plagiarism on yourself. And if I sued myself, how much could I collect? And what if I lost? Wouldn't that mean that I had won? The whole thing is too complicated for me—I'll just have to leave it up to my lawyers.

So, now that we are all sufficiently confused for the day, let's get down to business.

The first thing to do is to identify your problem. As I see it, there are the following possibilities:

1. The piece has its original finish, but it is filthy dirty.

2. It has the original finish, but that finish is scratched, scuffed, worn, or just falling off (dirty too, but that is now an unimportant problem).

3. Someone has put several coats of varnish or shellac over the original finish, and it is all lumpy and dirty and generally cruddy.

4. Someone has put one or more coats of paint over the original finish.

5. The original finish itself was a coat of milk paint (usually red or blue), which means the thing is a primitive country piece. Milk paint was used from the early Colonial days up to, generally speaking, the Civil War (though I

* *Instant Furniture Refinishing,* Doubleday & Company, Inc., Garden City, New York, 1966, $1.95.

wouldn't be shocked to hear that there is still some old character in the depths of Vermont *still* using milk paint).

6. The original finish was paint of the kind used by Victorian furniture manufacturers. They applied false graining and other decoration to their pine pieces: chests of drawers and commodes, including the popular lift-top commodes, of which you can buy unfinished reproductions.

7. The piece has no finish at all: either because, by the time you got hold of it, someone had stripped it or because it is an unfinished reproduction.

All right. Now, for each of these possibilities there is an *easiest* way, and for some there are ways that are just right. Here are your prescriptions:

1. *Dirty original finish.* Never use soap and water. You can use a damp rag to wipe off anything that dissolves in water, such as candy or spilt coffee. Do this first. Then remove the general overlay of grime with mineral spirits, which is usually sold as "paint thinner" or turpentine. Apply very freely, and rub the surface with a rag. Mineral spirits will clean your piece better than soap, because it will dissolve all the old oil and wax. (Soap gets the oil but not the wax.) Also it will not cause a clear finish to blush or haze as soapy water is very likely to do. Once the piece is clean, wipe it dry and apply an oil-base furniture polish. This will dress up an old finish better than a wax.

The same process also applies to dirty painted pieces when you want to preserve the decorations, which more and more people are doing with decorated Victorian pieces these days instead of stripping them and trying to pretend they are Early American pine. (See the chapters on frauds and fakes.)

2. *Ruined original finish.* Don't scrape it, don't sand it, don't use paint remover. Those are the hard ways. Instead, first clean the piece with paint thinner as explained above.

Then you can try one of the niftiest tricks in the whole trade. This is called reamalgamation. In other words, you rebrush the finish right on the surface with a solvent for it. There are two solvents, and you have to try both on some inconspicuous part of the piece to see which works better. They are lacquer thinner and denatured alcohol (shellac thinner).

Just pour some of the right thinner in a bowl, dip your brush in it, and start brushing it on the surface as if you were applying a coat of shellac or varnish. Amazingly it works. When the finish has redried, rub it down very lightly with fine steel wool, and then apply wax or polish.

3. *Several coats of clear finish* (or a single coat that is too far gone to reamalgamate). It doesn't matter whether your finishes are shellac or varnish or both. Don't scrape, don't sand, don't use paint remover. Instead, buy a quart each of lacquer thinner and denatured alcohol. Mixed 50-50, the two solvents now become a remover for the clear finishes—with a big built-in advantage over any paint remover. Combine them in a can or large instant-coffee jar, and pour the mixture on the surface. Swish it around until the finish is gooey, and then wipe it off with anything handy.

Now, the advantage of this process is that it leaves remnants of the original finish in the pores of the wood, and this is the equivalent of a sealer-coat or primer or first coat—whatever you want to call it. Also it doesn't take the stain out of the wood, and it doesn't raise the grain. So you are already way ahead of where you would be if you had scraped or sanded the piece. And you are your sealer-coat ahead of where you would have been if you had used paint remover, which seeps into the pores and sometimes even takes out the stain.

After you have removed the finish with lacquer thinner

and denatured alcohol, the surface is ready for a final coat of finish in an hour. Or, for a lovely, dull antique effect, you can simply wax the piece, and the job is done.

Incidentally, if after removing the finish this way you *want* to take out the stain to make the piece lighter, rub it down with fine steel wool and lots of Clorox or any other liquid laundry bleach. Wear rubber gloves, of course. This process will also remove your sealer-coat from the pores of the wood, and you will have to let the piece dry for at least twenty-four hours before applying a new finish.

4. *Paint over the original finish* (one or more layers, it makes no difference). I think the best secret of refinishing that I know is to stay away from anything that is painted. But sometimes, when a thing is painted, the price is irresistible. I would certainly never scrape paint off chairs or washstands even if I got them for nothing. The only time it is worth removing paint is when the result will be a cherry or maple drop-leaf table, for instance, or a *really* early piece of pine.

Here, the best thing for the amateur to do is to stick with paint remover. Sure, you can use lye or sodium hydroxide or trisodium phosphate or caustic soda, but all these things are either tricky or a lot of trouble to use, and it takes a lot of time to set up the operation. They are all right for someone who is in the business, but if you are doing only one or two pieces at a time, paint remover is the thing. And I wouldn't recommend one over the other, because you more or less get what you pay for.

What I would recommend for tough jobs is a little patience. After you have applied a good coat of remover to one of the flat surfaces of your piece, immediately slap on to it a sheet of waxed paper. This prevents the paint remover from drying and keeps the volatile stuff in it working on the paint. Let the paint soak overnight. The next day you can scrape off the coats and clean off the remnants with lacquer thinner and steel wool. This process makes your paint remover go a lot farther and saves a lot of work.

5. *Original milk paint.* Milk paint may be all that is on your piece; or, after removing many layers of regular paint, you come to this final coat that even paint remover doesn't work on.

The secret is ammonia. Work outside because of the fumes, and in the shade to slow down evaporation. The stuff works very fast. After it has soaked into the paint only a minute or two, you are ready to scrub the milk paint off with a brush or steel wool. Rinse the piece with buckets of water or the stream from a garden hose. It is going to take a couple of days in the sun for the wood to dry out enough for you to start putting on a few finish.

Ammonia will often turn wood a rich brown, which is really a fine color and brings out the grain as well as any stain could; when the brown happens, a lot of people leave it in. But if you don't want it, Clorox or other bleaches will take it out in a few seconds. After rinsing the paint and ammonia off with water, just wipe the wood dry and apply the bleach immediately—full strength, of course. No additional water rinse is needed.

6. *Victorian paint.* This stuff sometimes seems to have been made out of fine cement, and no liquid at all will touch it. Of course, you can scrape it off if you have a couple of weeks to spend on a small chest of drawers, for instance. But the only practical solution is a belt sander. (No oscillating or vibrating sander was ever worth three cents!) With a belt sander you can get the average piece down to raw wood—and the corners cleaned out with a scraper—in a couple of hours. Sanders begin at about $60 from Sears, Roebuck or Montgomery Ward and are well

worth it, but you can also rent them at places that rent tools.

7. *No finish at all.* Strictly speaking, this isn't a matter of refinishing but of applying a finish. I'm tacking it on to round out the picture. If you use a sander or a scraper, or if you have bought an unfinished reproduction, you are going to be faced with the situation.

To begin with, practically all raw wood needs some degree of stain in it to bring out the characteristic grain or figure of the wood. Good stains are mighty hard to buy in this country. Don't ask me why, but all the big companies who make stain put pigment in it—instead of selling clear, transparent dyes such as are used by all furniture factories and professional refinishers. But you can get transparent dyes from a mail-order house specializing in woodworker's supplies. One house is Albert Constantine and Son, Inc., 2050 Eastchester Road, Bronx, New York. Tell Mr. Constantine I sent you, and tell him he should put my books in his catalogue so I can make more money. (Enclose 25¢ for his great catalogue.)

A fellow who sells only one stain—a sealer stain but a great shade of antique brown—is Francis Hagerty, Cohasset Colonials, Cohasset, Massachusetts. He mostly sells fine unfinished reproductions of Early American in kit form, but he will sell you the stain separately. (Another 25¢ for a catalogue.)

Maybe the best of all are the small finishing kits (including stains) that you can get from the Sturbridge Yankee Workshop, Sturbridge, Massachusetts. That's where the reconstructed New England Village is—the most interesting place I've ever seen. It was started by a couple of antique collectors (brothers) who went berserk. They collected so many barnfuls of the stuff that they had to collect a whole village full of old houses and stores to show it in.

After you have gotten the wood the color you want it, you have to seal the stain with shellac or a can of clear spray. Then rub the surface with fine steel wool and wax it. Some people use two coats of shellac (both thinned to 50-50 with *fresh* denatured alcohol). For tabletops, the second coat can be varnish. When this is dry, it also gets a light rubbing with fine steel wool and is waxed.

In the case of a sealer stain such as Hagerty's or the stain from the Sturbridge Yankee Workshop, you need no finish. When it is dry, rub it down with the steel wool and wax. That is the easiest way.

I make it all sound easy, don't I? Well, as the fellow who cleans up after the elephants in the circus says, "That's show business!"

Part Two

CURRENT ANTIQUES AND THEIR PRICES

How this selection was made and the prices established.

In the following pages there are well over four hundred items represented and described, and you may very well ask, Why stop there? It is a good question. The answer lies in the use for which this book is intended. It is not supposed to be a dictionary of antiques but a practical guide to the decorative antiques—the ones you use in decorating your home as opposed to things you collect—that are *actually available* in antique shops around the country.

At first it looked like an overwhelming task to choose the examples, because there are thousands of items for sale in antique shops. But as I toured the sheds and shops with my trusty Polaroid camera—the drawings are all made from photographs of items actually for sale—some helpful facts began to emerge.

The first is that there is an awful lot of junk in antique shops that nobody would want in his house. Second, only about a third of the items in shops are things you could use in interior decoration. The rest are things you collect or oddments you leave lying around because they are interesting to talk about.

This cut the number of items down to a couple of thousand possibilities, and I was still *fairly* overwhelmed. Relief came quickly, however, when I reminded myself that this was a guide to values and not a dictionary. Sure, there are some eighteen different kinds of Hitchcock chairs. But we only have to show one kind and talk about it a little to give you a reasonably accurate idea of how much they are all worth—which indeed depends far more on condition than on variations in style. In the case of Windsor chairs, there are at least two whole books about them. But if we establish the fact that one piece with arms is going for $125 and one without is around $85, we don't have to show all the variations to enable you to figure out that one with a "desk arm" is going to cost a little more or that one with worn-off legs will cost a little less.

Incidentally, unless otherwise noted, all prices are for pieces in good condition and with good original finish or nicely refinished. The condition of pieces "in the rough" varies so much that all you can say is that a piece in the rough is worth the price given here less the cost of refinishing.

After visiting and photographing things in about forty shops in the northeastern states, I stopped seeing anything new—anything that I hadn't already photographed. Over and over again, shops would have the same basic stocks, with minor variations. And so, after making sure that I hadn't missed any area in the Northeast, I toured the rest of the country to find significant local variations. But I found only concentrations of interest in various periods—Empire in the South and Late Victorian (Eastlake) in the Midwest. There was nothing available in the rest of the country that wasn't for sale in the Northeast. For this there turned out to be two reasons. The first is that the vast majority of the antiques sold outside the Northeast are imported from the Northeast. Yes, even in San Francisco—remember, it burned down in

1906! In Texas a good ninety percent of the things for sale are imported from the Northeast.

The second reason why just about everything is available in the Northeast is that whatever wasn't made there originally is brought in from the rest of the country.

One factor in the pricing done in the following pages is that prices vary in different parts of the country. If a dealer in Dallas imports—or buys from an importer—a round oak table that comes from Fall River, Massachusetts, the customer is going to have to pay for the transportation and the time and trouble somebody went to. The same with Empire furniture, which is regularly sent into the south from Rhode Island. And when you buy something in a shop in New York City, where the rent is $400 a month, the customer is going to have to pay that rent—and also the rent that the dealer has to pay for his own apartment in New York City. You must remember, then, that the prices I have given are the basic low ones of the marketplaces for antiques in the Northeast. The marketplaces (discussed in the first section of this book) are southeastern Pennsylvania, especially Bucks County, and Rhode Island. If this makes all the dealers in Boston, New York City, Philadelphia, Dallas, and San Francisco hate me, I can't help it. These are the prices at which things can be bought on the open market if you go there to get them. If you are going to have somebody else bring them to you, naturally you are going to have to pay the difference. Business is business, and *c'est la guerre*. I will not be intimidated. I will not deign to argue. The rest is silence. Which, coming from me, is a break.

Beds

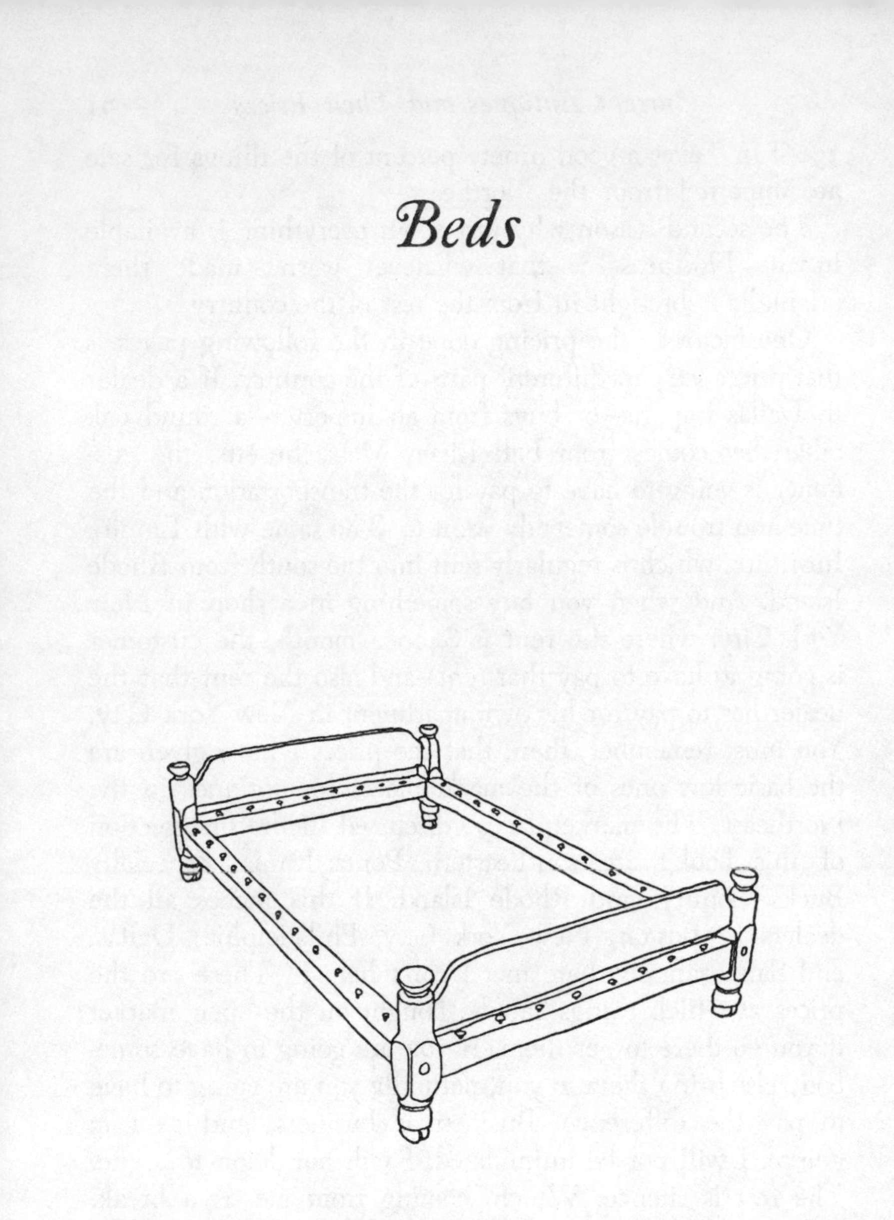

1 This is actually a trundle bed and it is more curious than useful. However, it shows the way these early beds were constructed. The pegs on the top of the frame were used for stretching a net of rope to support the mattress of straw or feathers. Sometimes holes were drilled in the frame for the ropes. These beds are all quite early. This one is about 1750 and valued at around $125.

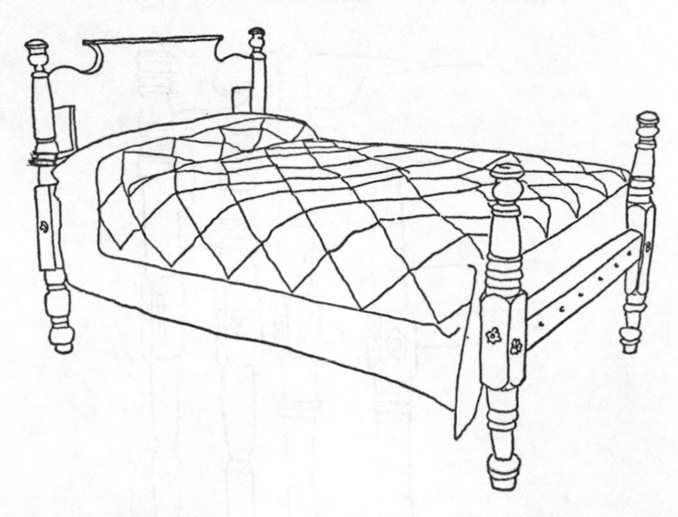

2 Here is a classic made up with a patchwork quilt in all its pre-Revolutionary glory. The woods were usually maple for the posts and stretchers. Cherry, mahogany, poplar, or even pine was used in the headboards. The stretchers were two feet above the floor, and when you mount a mattress and spring on the frame, you are riding pretty high. Rigged to take a standard three-quarter spring and mattress, a beauty like this goes for $350 to $400.

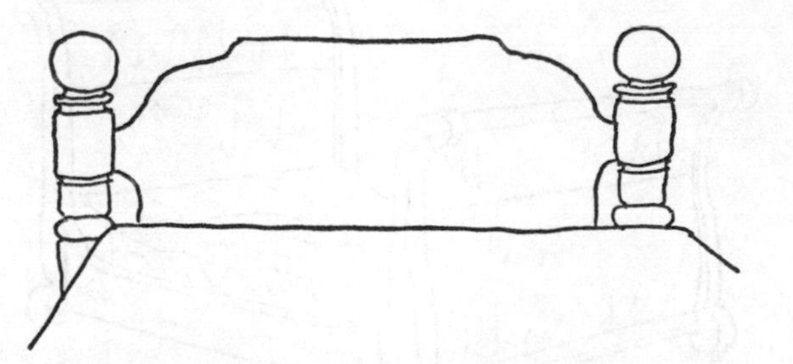

3 The cannonball version of these beds came in the early 1800s. They were popular for decades, so there are a lot around selling in good condition and fitted for mattresses at around $225, depending on the woods used in the headboards and footboards.

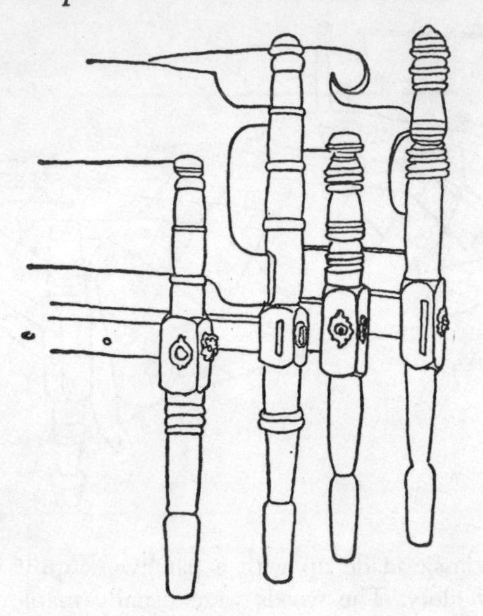

4 Here are a couple of the many variations of the bed shown in illustration no. 2. A column carved with a pineapple design was also popular but is now rare enough to be worth an extra $75 on the price of the bed. The side stretchers fit into slots on the posts, where they were bolted firm, with decorative little medallions hanging on small nails to cover the heads of the bolts.

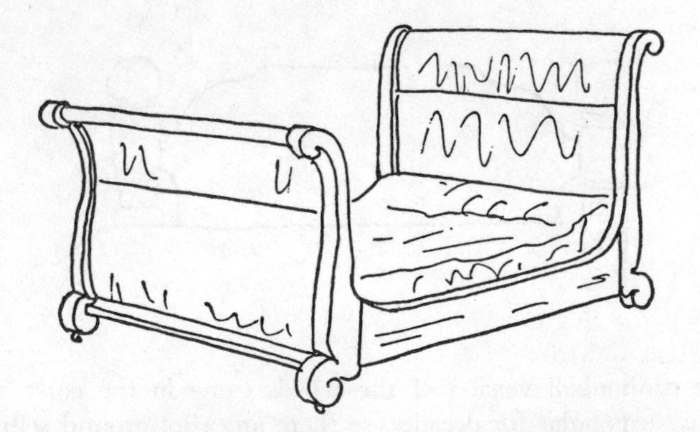

5 These "sleigh" beds are the American version of Empire, and so date from the 1830s up to the Civil War. Like all Empire they are more popular in the South than anywhere else. They were made of blocks of well-dried soft pine and then covered with very fine Honduras mahogany veneers with the figures carefully matched. You just don't see mahogany like that anymore. In fact, the even-grained stuff that furniture manufacturers sell today isn't really mahogany at all, but just miscellaneous woods from big trees in Africa and the Philippines. Someday Empire may catch on across the country, but at present its appeal is low, and these beds really are undervalued at $85 to $125, depending on how massive they are and the condition of the veneering.

6 After the Civil War came the Early Victorian or Renaissance style with imposing beds like this one, which would go right through the ceiling of a modern house. In this early version the wood is walnut with panels of highly figured walnut veneer, and sometimes even rosewood in the trim. If you have a house that can hold one, the usual price is only about $125.

By the turn of the century, imitations of this bed were being made of pine and painted with imitation wood graining. These were a more reasonable size and are currently coming into vogue. With good original paint they are worth around $85. Often there was a matching chest and dresser with teardrop pulls. This brings us up to around 1900, and such a three-piece set, when you can find one, is a great bargain at around $200.

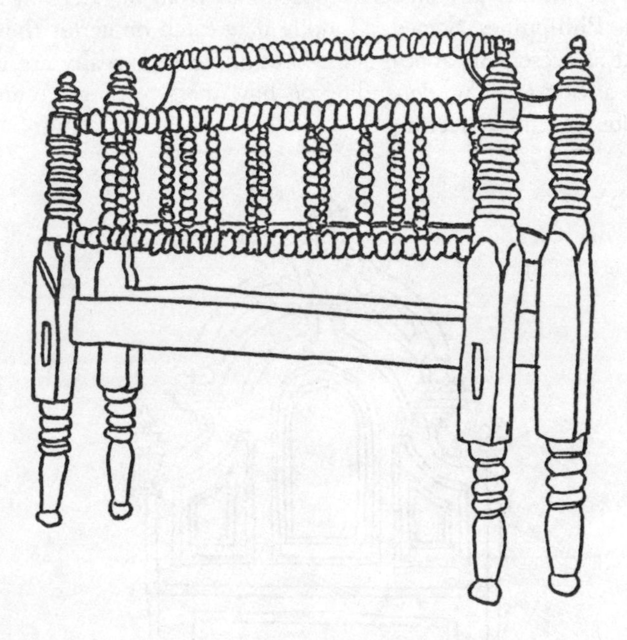

7 Here is an Early American edition of the spool bed that was to become ubiquitous (I always wanted to use that word!) in Victorian times. This one, with maple posts and turnings and pine headboard, dates from the 1700s and is worth around $400. (It was made, of course, by one craftsman on a hand lathe.)

8 The mass-produced spool beds of the Victorian era, which were made all through the 1800s, are still comparatively high in price because people like them and it is so much work to refinish them. (The best way is to take them apart and put the pieces in a lathe to scrape and sand the old finish off.) They run from $130 to $165, depending on the beauty of the wood revealed by refinishing—mostly maple, of course, for the turnings.

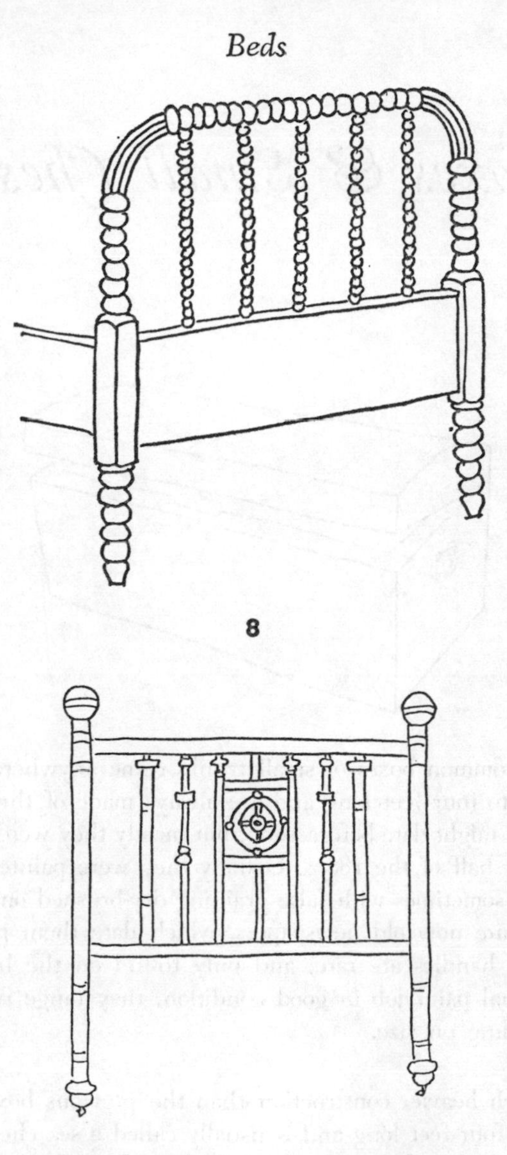

8

9 I remember carting brass beds to the dump after an auction back in Killingworth only ten years ago. But with the growing fad for Victorian, especially in New York City, they are now very popular with interior decorators for what they call "fun" guest rooms. Well. Anyway, fitted up for a modern spring and mattress these will now run you up to $85 for a sturdy, bold, and very brassy one.

Boxes & Small Chests

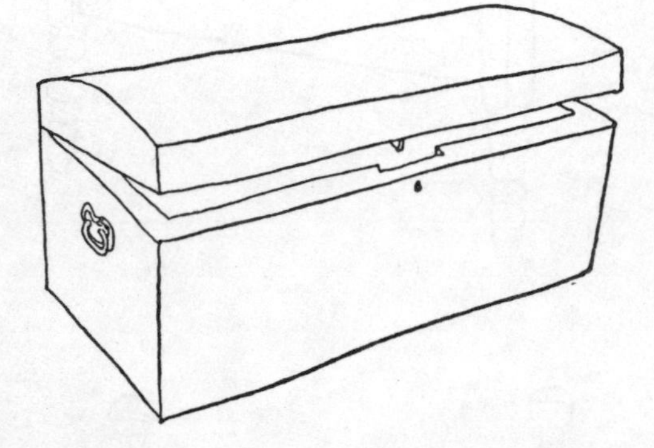

10 These common boxes or small trunks come anywhere from two and a half to four feet long and are always made of thin pieces of pine. A few might date before 1800, but mostly they were made during the first half of the 1800s. Usually they were painted with red milk paint, sometimes with false graining dry-brushed on, and lined with what are now old newspapers, which date them pretty accurately. The handles are rare, and only found on the bigger ones. With original paint job in good condition, they range from $12 to $25 depending on size.

11 Of much heavier construction than the previous box, this style runs about four feet long and is usually called a sea chest, and undoubtedly some of them were used by sailors, especially during the heyday of the whaling industry (mid-1800s). But they were also used by everybody else as a foot-locker in which to store clothes and personal belongings. Always made of pine, with the hand-craftsmanship obvious, they sell for $25 up to $40 for one with the original paint in good condition. Barbarians, of course, refinish these.

Lately any Victorian (post-Civil War) carpenter's tool chest that even vaguely resembles these boxes is being sold as a sea chest for about the same prices. These boxes are much cruder, without the molding or top that extends over the sides. Also the corners are not dovetailed and the boards are not single wide ones as in the old chests.

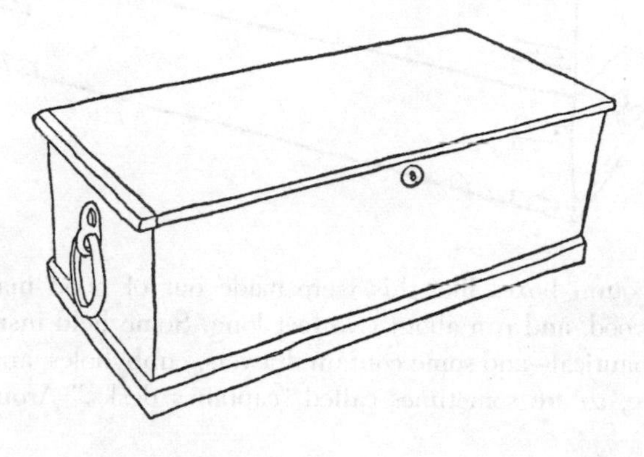

11

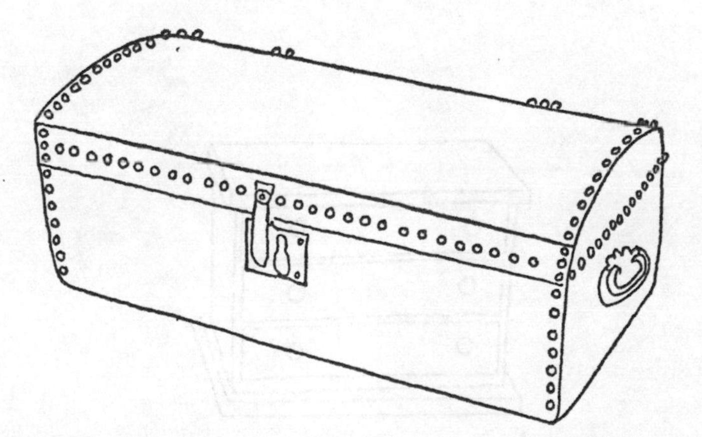

12 A later Victorian version of the box in illustration no. 10, covered with leather and studded with brass tacks. Usually about two feet long. If the leather is in bad shape, it is stripped down to the pine, as this one was. About $20.

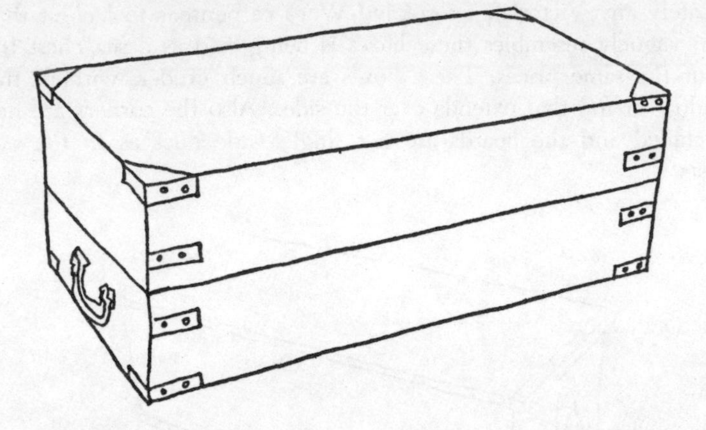

13 Brass-bound boxes like this were made out of good mahogany, even rosewood, and run about two feet long. Some held instruments —usually nautical—and some contain drawers, cubbyholes, and a writing surface, so are sometimes called "captain's desks." Around $35.

14 An early pine jewel (?) box only about ten inches long. Undoubtedly originally painted, this one has been nicely refinished without any sanding or scraping to remove the signs of wear. Early 1800s, possibly earlier. Priced at $18.

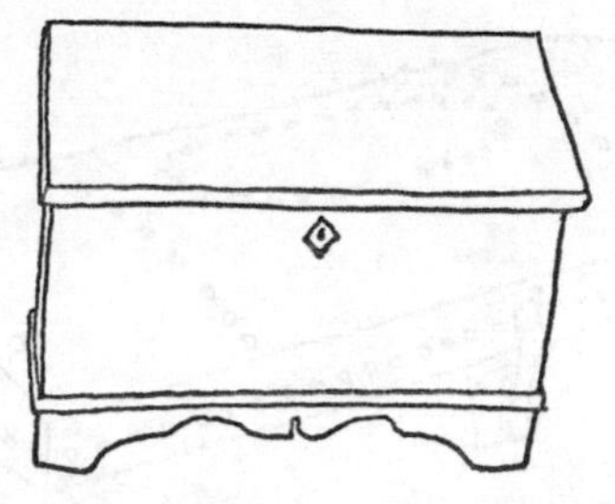

15 Another ten-inch-long chest, from Pennsylvania, with original faded yellow paint on pine and inlaid keyhole. Dating back to Revolutionary days, this box was quite reasonably priced in a show at $22.

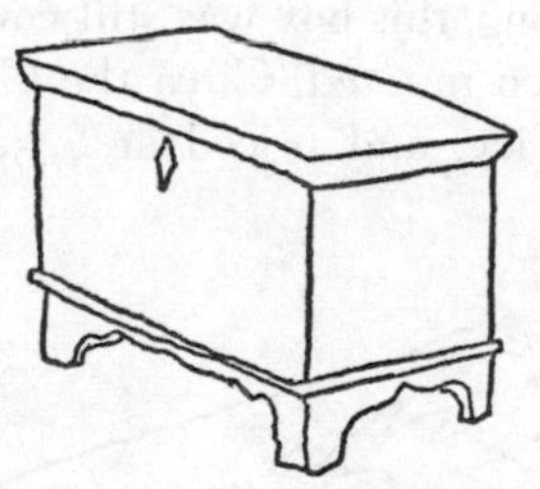

16 Similar to illustration no. 15, but sixteen inches long, this box was only $18, which proves something, though I'm not sure what.

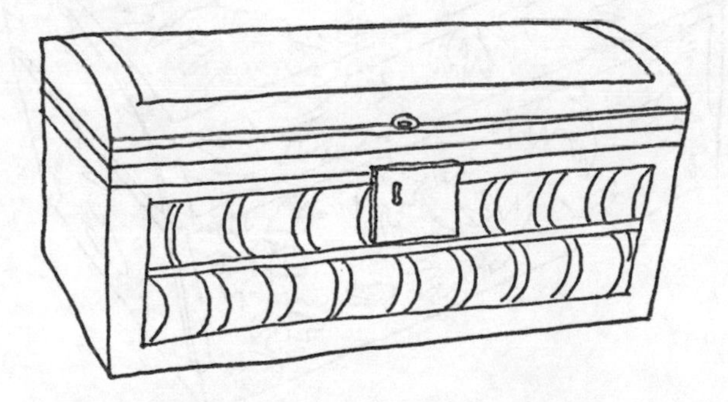

17 The excellent condition of the painting on this early box about twenty-six inches long, plus the fine old hand-hammered iron lock, date it as probably pre-Revolutionary, and the price is right at $42.50. Pine, of course. Dark-red milk paint, with design in black.

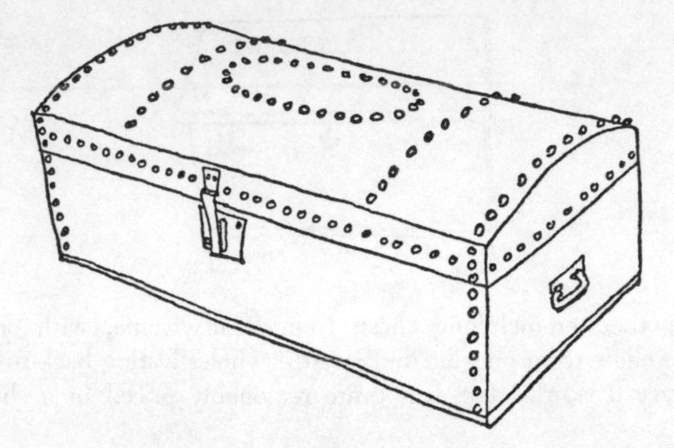

18 About three feet long, this box was still covered with the original leather, which had been restored. Circa the Civil War, according to newspapers pasted inside, and priced at $45.

19 Going back to the early 1800s, this pine box was covered with a brocade and was very finely made. Only about eighteen inches long, and priced at $18.

20 The dolls were stuffed cloth from about 1910 and priced at $12.50 each. The two-foot-long pine chest had been refinished and lined with wallpaper—$22.

Chairs

21   **22**

21 In fine condition, this Windsor had been refinished, revealing maple turnings, plank pine seat, and ash and hickory in the back. A classic of Early American craftsmanship, these chairs hang together even if all the glue has given out, and just rattle when you shake them. Reglued, they are wonderfully sturdy even when over a hundred and fifty years old. An armchair in such fine shape as this one brings over $150. The side chairs, $85 to $100.

22 This square-backed version of the Windsor side chair came into style around 1800 (the round backs were pre-1800) and is called the "birdcage" or "chicken coop" style. But the price runs the same as the round-backs: $85 to $100.

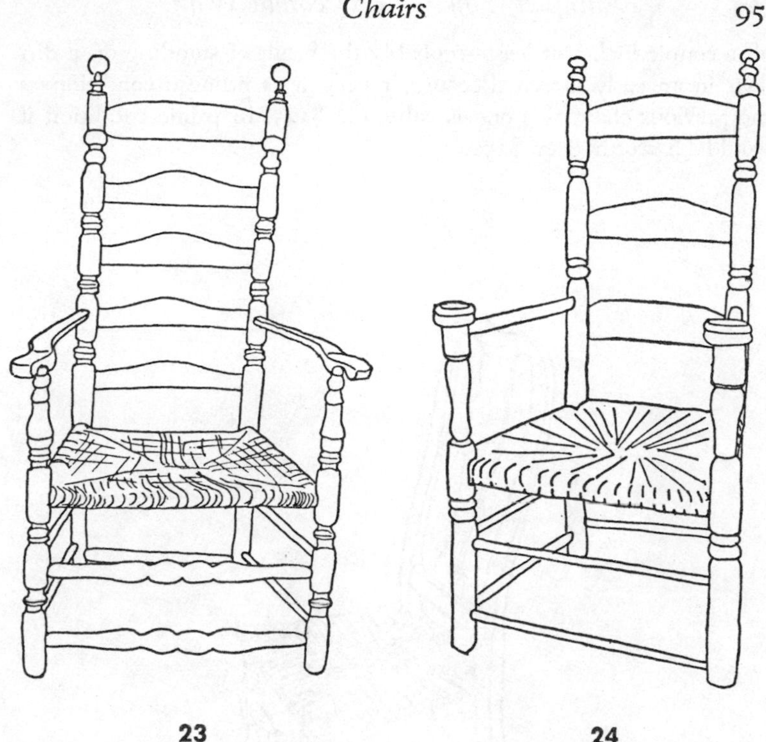

23 24

23 A fine example of the very early ladder-backs, this chair dates from the early 1700s, and of course only a very hard wood like maple would have stood up under all the use it has had. The front rungs are worn flat. A new rush seat has been put in—maybe the third or fourth one. Priced at $165.

24 This variation of the previous chair is called a post-arm and is believed to be even older, though when you get back around 1700 the age of things made by country cabinetmakers becomes very hard to date closely. A country cabinetmaker (also carpenter) and his son might make a chair according to exactly the same design over a span of sixty years. Note that the bottoms of the legs of this chair are worn off a couple inches at least—probably the result of standing on a dirt floor in an early tavern. Because it isn't in as prime a condition as the previous chair, this one is valued at $125. In prime condition it would be worth over $250.

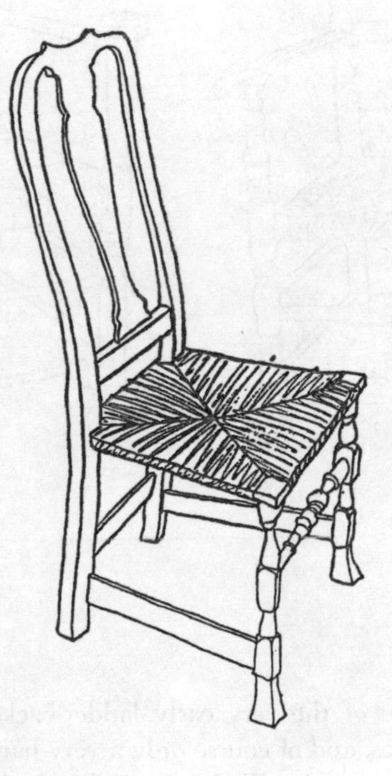

25 A country Queen Anne chair with eccentric legs. These copies of the styles popular in Boston, Philadelphia, and New York were always subject to the creative whims of the country carpenter-cabinetmakers who made them up on order for the local gentry. Perhaps as early as 1740, this chair can come in any wood that was handy, and is valued at around $125.

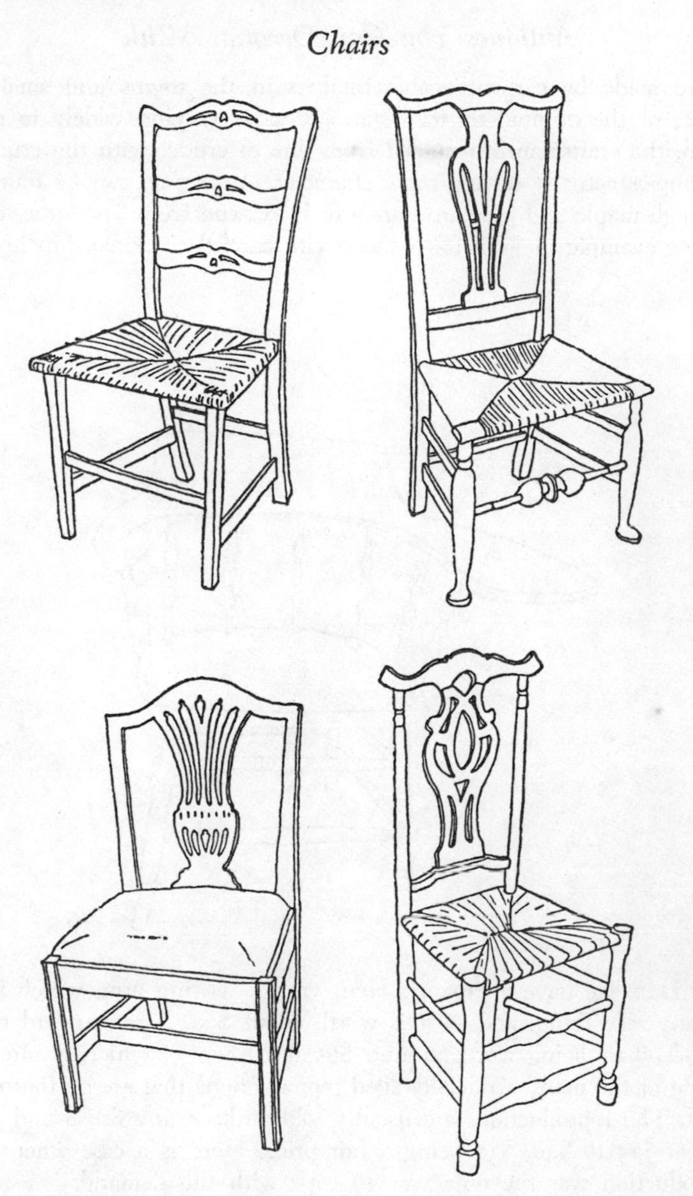

26, 27, 28, 29 Three widely varied examples of country Chippendale with no. 27 featuring Queen Anne (Dutch) feet and a turning on the front stretcher. These chairs all date from the second half of the eighteenth century and, like the preceding country Queen Anne, were made by carpenter-cabinetmakers in the towns and smaller cities of the original thirteen states. Besides varying widely in design, the craftsmanship ranged from fine to crude, with the cruder examples actually having more character. Any wood can be found, though maple and pine are standard. Prices run from $75 for a very crude example to $150 for a chair with careful workmanship in it.

30 Here we have a captain's chair with a writing arm, which is a pretty rare thing, and so it is worth about $90. The standard captain's chair being worth around $65 if authentic, which is rare in light of the many artificially aged reproductions that are on the market. The reproductions are usually sold without any finish and run from $25 to $40, $30 being a fair price. Here is a case where reproduction was the only way to cope with the demand.

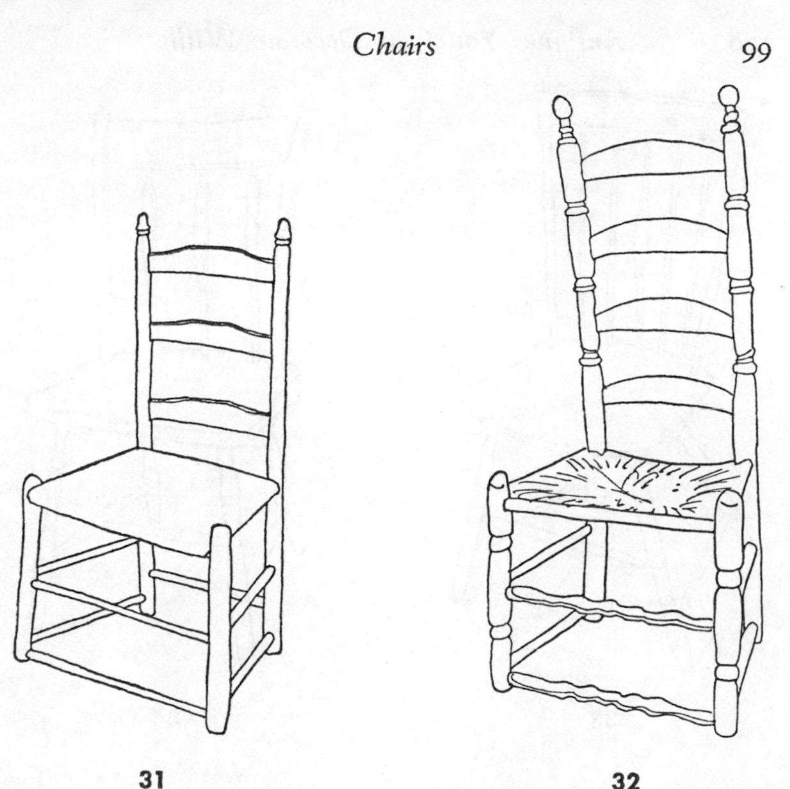

31 32

31 This is an early 1800s version of the ladder-back chairs in illustrations no. 23 and no. 24. That is a long time ago, and you will notice the extensive rotting and wearing off of the bottoms of the legs, which is common in these chairs. Maple posts and stretchers, with hickory or ash slats in the back. Widely reproduced—and beautifully and cheaply by Jeff Elliot down in North Carolina. But there isn't much trouble telling the difference between a reproduction and the real thing when you are talking about a chair that is over a hundred years old. The signs of wear and use are perfectly obvious. With a new seat, these are worth $35 to $45, and going up fast.

32 Another old ladder-back, but without arms, and well worn in the feet and front stretchers, that should go for around $75.

33 Here we have a late Sheraton-style Windsor, similar to the bird-cage style shown in illustration no. 22, but coming a little later—say around 1820 to 1830—as indicated by the bamboo turnings, slat back, and shaped center spoke which points toward the "arrow-backs" to come. Worth about $75. Same woods as other Windsors described previously.

34 Now we come to the arrow-back, and 1820 to 1850 is a good guess for age. Around $55 would be a reasonable price considering the bamboo turnings on the legs. (See next chair.)

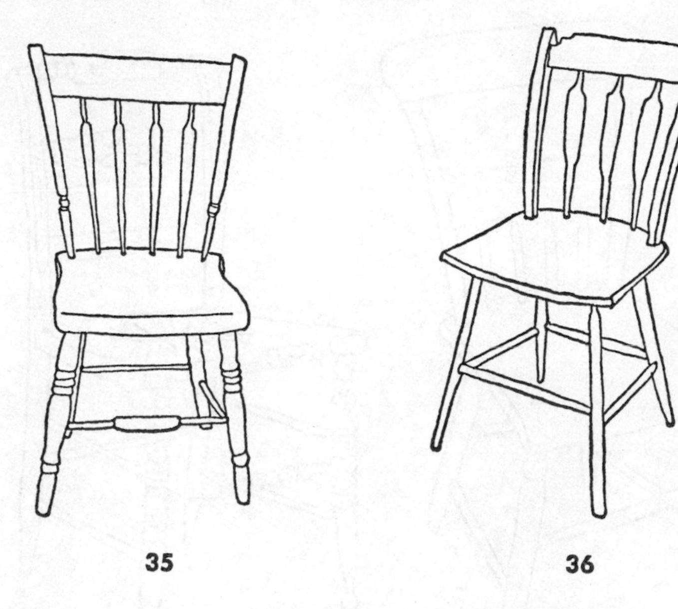

35 36

35 Here is an arrow-back dating a little later than the previous one. See the Sheraton-style leg turnings that are indicative of the Hitchcock to come. Around $55. Although this chair is as early as any Hitchcock, if not earlier, the price is less simply because the Hitchcock has a cachet about it. Prices are determined by public demand.

36 This straight-legged arrow-back is another version of the popular Sheraton-inspired common man's chair, worth around $45. Incidentally, with plain spindles in the back, this would be called a "rabbit-ear" and be worth about $10 less.

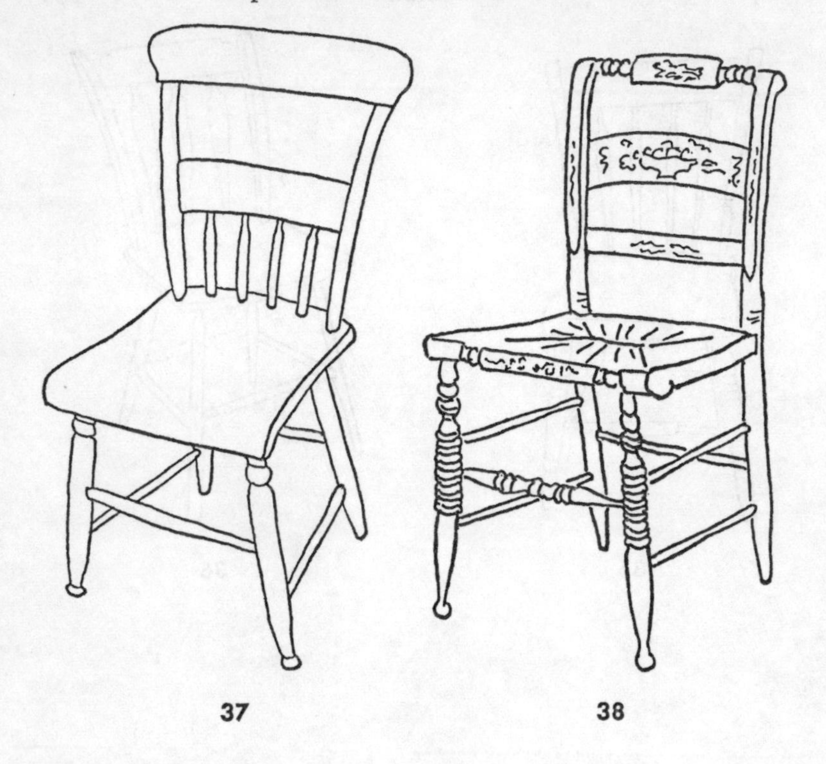

37 38

37 Now we are up to 1850 and past it with this simple country or "kitchen" chair. Pine plank seat and maple posts and stretchers. Contemporary of the Hitchcock and part of the beginning of mass production in the United States. There were a lot of these "just chairs" made from 1840 all the way up to 1900. Worth nowadays around $20 to $30 refinished.

38 One of the real classic designs, the princess herself of all the Sheraton "fancy" chairs that sold like hot cakes all over the States from 1830 to 1890—the fabulously popular Hitchcock chair. Prices of these chairs have soared in recent years. Almost all the chairs on the market have been redecorated—sometimes slyly—and reseated. If the redecoration has been done authentically, such a chair is worth a good $85. A chair with the original decoration only about half worn off would be worth about the same. With the original decoration in "good" condition you are in the $125 class. With the decoration in "fine" condition, you are going to be bidding against museums. And if you find one virtually unused in some attic you would be talking about a couple of thousand dollars.

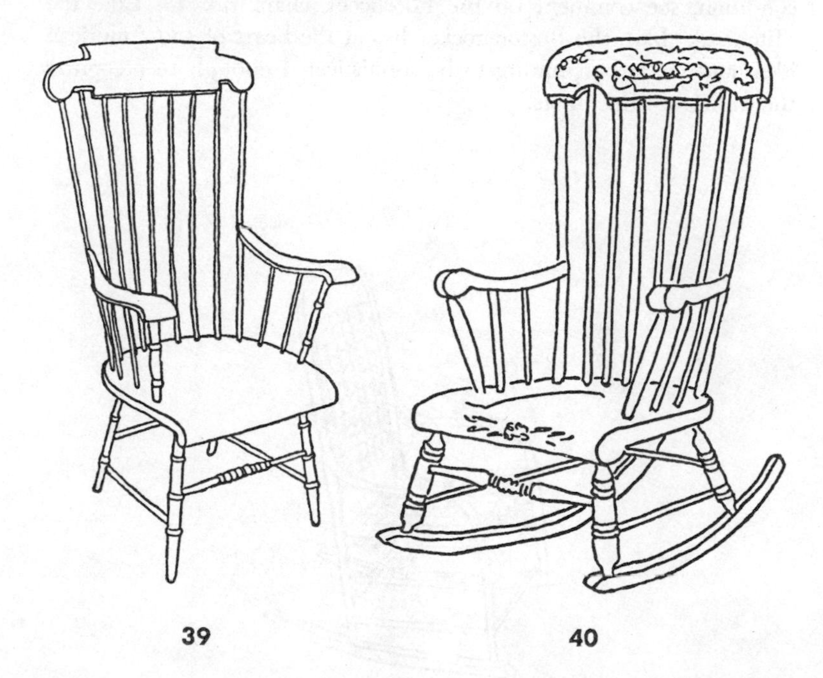

39 40

39 This is the so-called Salem chair. With rockers it became the Boston rocker. Part of the fancy-chair movement of the mid-1800s, contemporary of the Hitchcock chairs, and the first sign of the mass-production factories that would shape the America of today. Like Hitchcocks, these are almost always redecorated, because they were comfortable and used. Pine seats, maple turnings, hickory spokes. Redecorated or with enough original decoration so you are able to make it out—around $85.

40 There she goes, Miss America herself—the incomparable Boston rocker! A contemporary of the Hitchcock chair—1830 to 1880—designed for comfort and a perfect example of functionalism in design. Plank pine seats, maple turnings, hickory spindles, the same bronze powder decoration as the Hitchcocks, the same derivation from the Sheraton style of the American Revolution and as hundred-percent American as you can get. Redecorated or with half the original decoration still there, $100. Should you find one in mint condition, see comment on the Hitchcock chair, no. 38! Like the Hitchcock chair, the Boston rocker lies at the heart of the American idea, and we are beginning to be sophisticated enough to recognize the value of such roots.

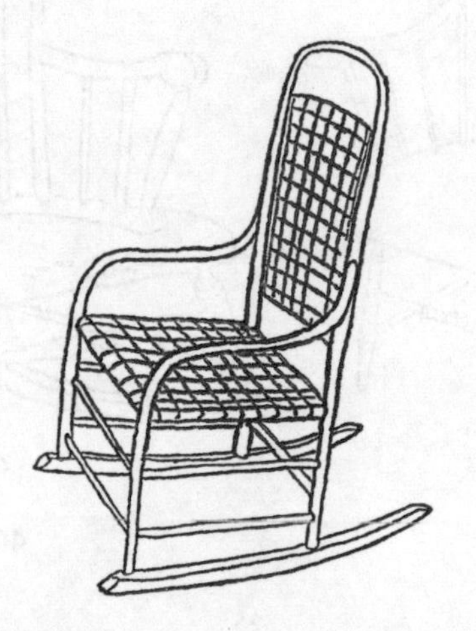

41 In spite of what certain instant experts on those New York magazines are trying to tell us, this is not a Shaker rocker. Simple and charming it may be, but Shaker it ain't. Actually, many of these chairs–with and without rockers–were made by a small factory in upper New York State. Seats and backs were originally of woven splint, bent pieces of hickory, the rest maple. They are believed by many people in the area to have been made sometime "back before 1850," therefore in the "fancy chair" era, contemporary to Hitchcock chairs. These chairs are hard to price fairly. At the time I saw this one the going rate was $45 to $65, but it may double in a couple of years because of this Shaker cachet it has picked up.

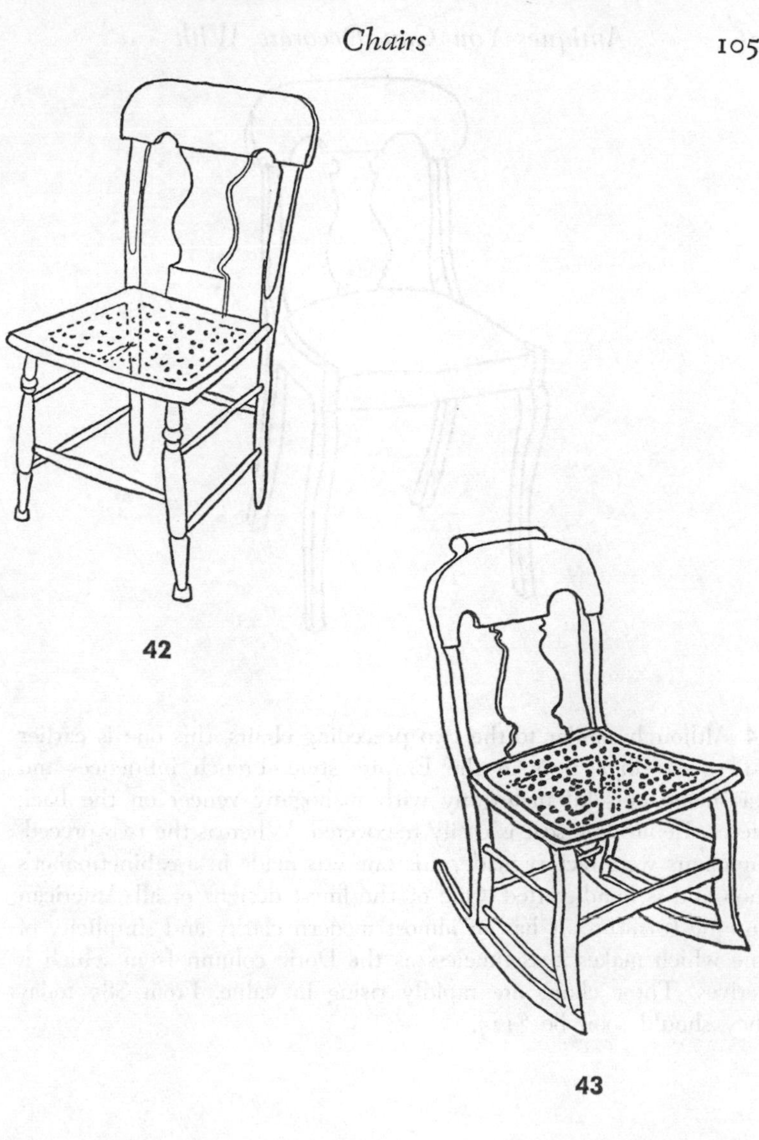

42, 43 Here we have two fiddle-back chairs. Chairs of this type are often made entirely of maple with fine bird's-eye figure in the back. They were originally stained to resemble mahogany, but they look a lot better refinished light. Refinished and recaned, they are worth around $45. They date from around 1850–60.

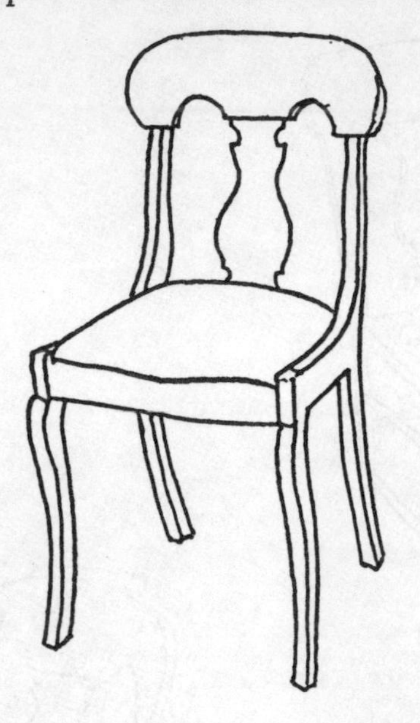

44 Although similar to the two preceding chairs, this one is earlier —1810 to 1840. It is in the Empire style—French influence—and was made of solid mahogany with mahogany veneer on the back pieces. Removable seat is easily re-covered. Whereas the two preceding chairs were factory-made, this one was made in a cabinetmaker's shop and is hand-crafted. One of the finest designs of all American antique furniture, it has an almost modern clarity and simplicity of line which makes it as timeless as the Doric column from which it derives. These chairs are rapidly rising in value. From $85 today they should soon be $125.

45

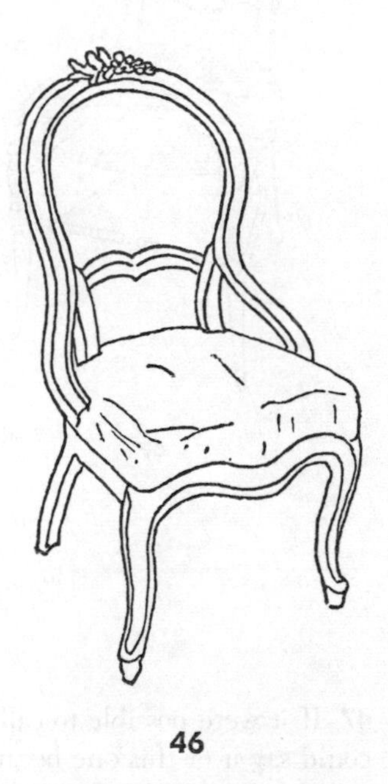

46

45 Like the preceding Empire chair, this Early Victorian or Louis XV chair has classic lines derivative of the French influence on American furniture during the first half of the 1800s. Also made of solid mahogany and hand-crafted. With the old varnish removed, the wood is rich-looking and still pretty dark. Reupholstered—and re-uphostering is always necessary—such a chair sells for $165. It is well worth it, solely as an investment.

46 A Louis XV chair, this is of the same construction as the preceding one. The deep "finger-molding" is all hand-carved, as are the roses and other decorations often found on the backs of this style. This chair is worth about $120.

47 If it were possible to call any Victorian "fancy chair" typical, you could say it of this one because it is typically untypical. Fancy chairs were a great craze during the second half of the 1800s, when the country was expanding rapidly. They were shipped out of New England by the hundreds of thousands to the hotels, the riverboats, and even the humblest farmer's cottage, where they were a touch of longed-for refinement from the East that had been left behind. All kinds of woods were used, but maple predominates, for strength. A chair like this should sell, refinished or repainted and decorated, for $45.

48 A humble rocker with cane seat and back from the late 1800s. Mass-produced, as were all the following chairs in this section except the last two. The expense of recaning pushes the price of this one up to $35.

49

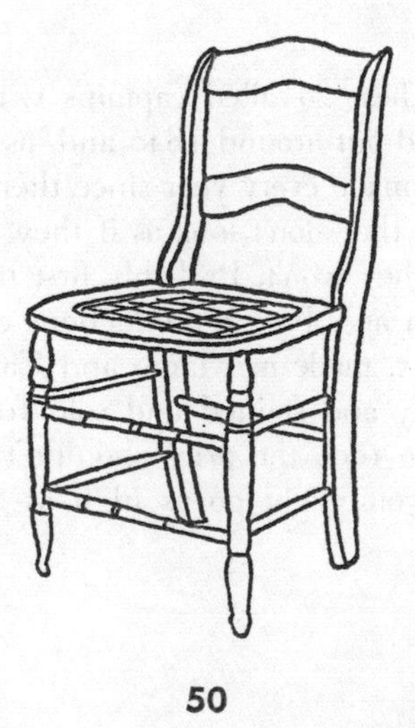

50

49 A post-1900 Victorian chair in the very sturdy Eastlake style. The wood used was oak, with burl walnut veneers sometimes being pasted on for decoration. More popular in the Midwest than any place else, this style of chair is worth $30 to $35 there, though you can still pick them up for $5 or $6 east of Providence.

50 An unpretentious, light but sturdy chair of the 1880s. Usually all maple except for mahogany slats. Sometimes the back posts were also mahogany. Recaned, around $25 to $30.

51 These so-called captains with their bulky pine backs and seats started out around 1840 and, as one authority says, they've probably been made every year since then. They especially appeal to men because they don't look as if they will break if you lean back in them, and they won't. Probably first used in taverns. The price depends a lot on age. Fine reproductions can be bought unfinished for as low as $15, made in Maine and Canada. These are regularly aged artificially and stained and sold for $40. For one actually going back before 1900 the price shouldn't be more than $65. For a really old one you might go as high as $125.

52, 53, 54 Three variations of the preceding captain's chair that can date from 1880 to 1910, these probably should be called office chairs or hotel chairs. For that matter it would be better to call the captain's chairs tavern chairs, but nobody does. These pieces of Victoriana were made mostly of oak with hickory for the bent pieces. Caned or otherwise seated, they sell for around $30.

55 **55A**

55 A simple Victorian kitchen chair—so-called—usually entirely of oak, including the seat, from 1890 to 1920. Sells for around $12.

55A I don't know why it is, but as a rocker this chair has a lot more charm than it does as a straight chair. In this version it is another Miss America, Victorian division. Actually Golden Oak division, around 1900 to 1917. You can still pick these up for $10 or $15 around Providence, Rhode Island, and southeastern Massachusetts; for even less in a junkshop. Not refinished, of course. I'm almost afraid to tell you what they get for them in New York City around Greenwich Village after they have cleaned off the old finish and then just rubbed some linseed oil onto them, but I suppose I have to—$65 to $80! Well, you know what hicks those New Yorkers are

—you can sell them almost anything. They are only asking $35 for the straight version. Incidentally the chairs are, of course, all oak with a design pressed into the back. Since nobody else has named them yet, I call them "pressed oak" chairs.

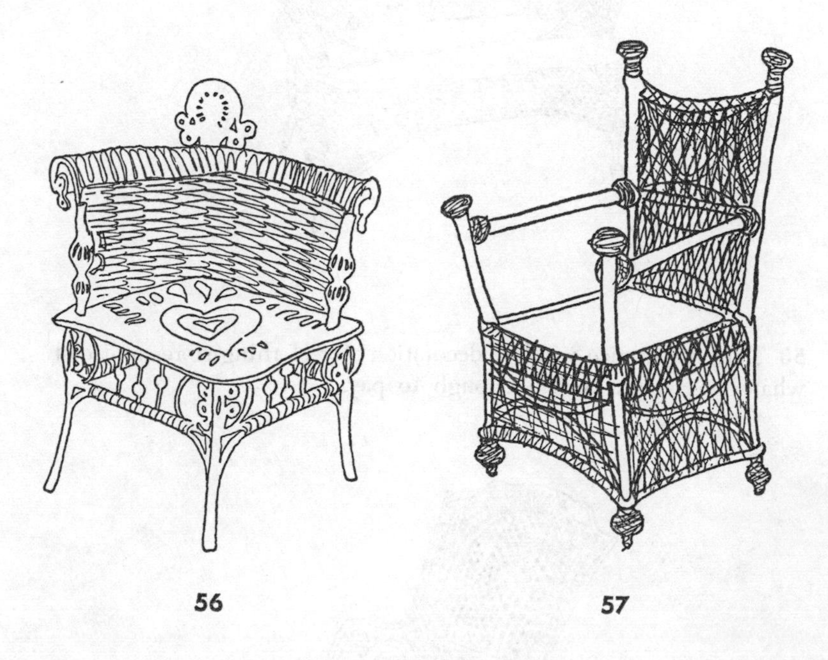

56 **57**

56 These old things, 1910 to 1920, are also sold in New York City, often painted white, but you really have to use them for decorations rather than to sit in. The reed they are made of doesn't have many more years of life left in it. Free anyplace else, around $45 in New York City.

57 Another ugly little beauty without many years of life left in it. Around $30.

58 They make nice window decorations for clothing stores and cost whatever you are foolish enough to pay.

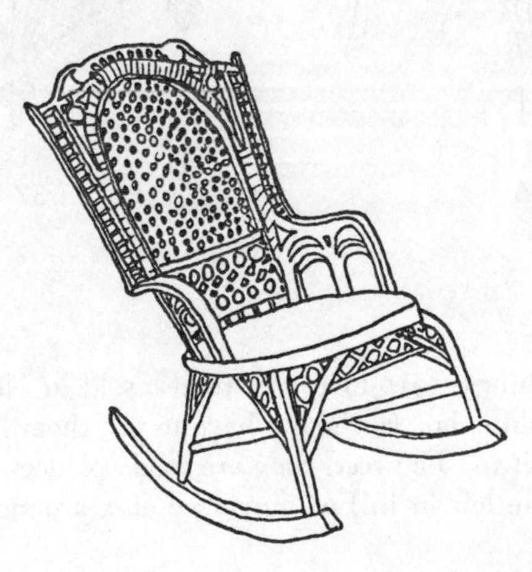

59 Another, but a considerably better-constructed gem. Lots of luck with it at $35.

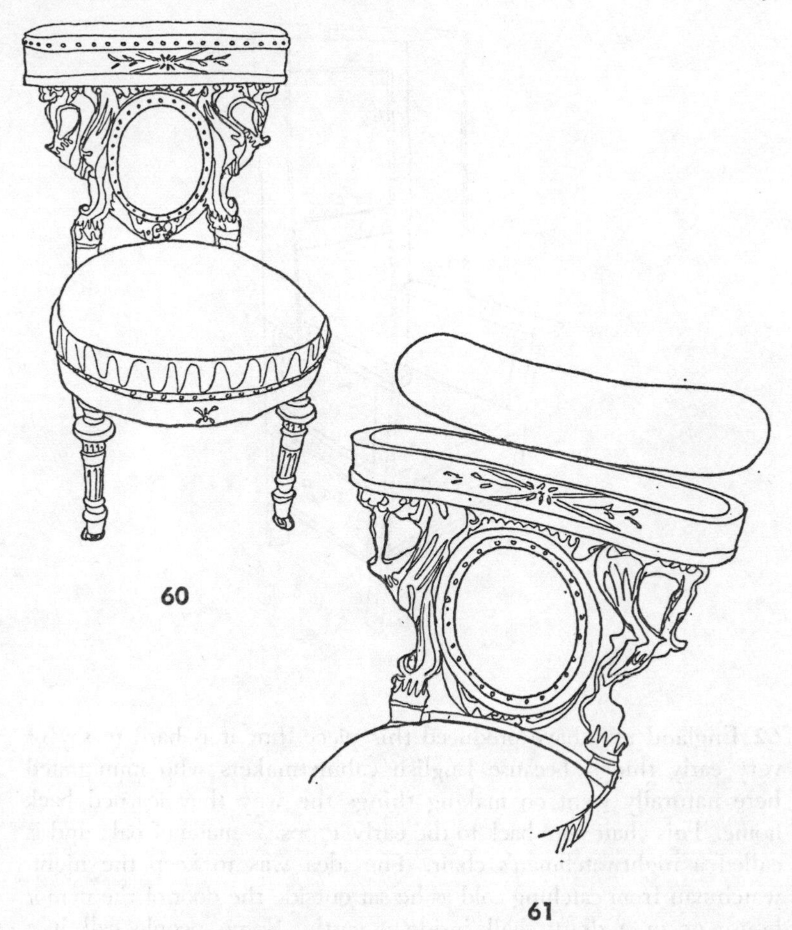

60, 61 Here is a gem that Caleb Davis dug up for the Dove and Distaff shop in southern Rhode Island at a place called Peacedale. The idea, he claims, is that you straddle the chair and lean your arms on the back to watch cockfights. And you keep your betting money in the box at the top of the back. At any rate, it looks like a Victorian fantasy to me. The front legs are quite Eastlake—1870 to 1890—and the wild carving is typical of the Jacobean revival of the same years. It may have come from England, and is a bargain at $135.

62 England may have produced this piece, but it is hard to say of very early things, because English cabinetmakers who immigrated here naturally went on making things the way they learned back home. This chair goes back to the early 1700s, is made of oak, and is called a nightwatchman's chair. The idea was to keep the nightwatchman from catching cold as he sat outside the door of the manor house or in a drafty hall inside a castle. Some people call it a grandma's chair on the theory that Grandma used it to keep drafts off her while sitting in front of the fire. Only $225.

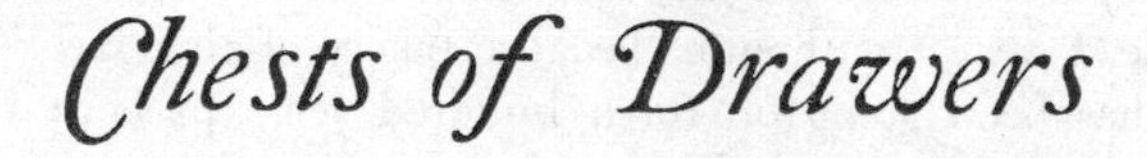

Chests of Drawers

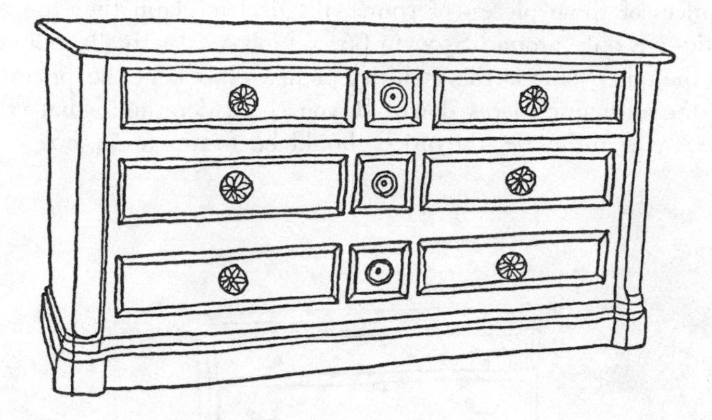

63, 64 For those of you who live in English manor houses, or want to pretend you do, we have these two English-flavored chests of drawers that are made of solid oak and stained almost black. If they are authentic, they were made in England and imported somewhere between 1650 and 1960. Cabinetmakers didn't work with oak in this country until around 1900, and then it was machine work, not hand-made. I say "if authentic" because fakery of this Jacobean sort of thing has been going on for a hundred years in both England and New York City, and the people who have been making the fakes were and are terribly good at their jobs. In fact, that is why the prices of these pieces–of course the dealers claim they are authentic–are only around $500 to $600. Nobody can really tell one from the other, and so the quantity of fakes has kept the prices of even the authentic pieces down. If you could determine that such a piece was authentic, the price should be $1200 to $1500.

65 I don't suppose there is anybody who would buy this book who isn't familiar with these pretentious masterpieces that so pleased the hearts of the bourgeoisie of the early 1700s. This Queen Anne highboy—a chest of drawers sitting on another chest of drawers—comes at the beginning of that century, the so-called golden age of furniture design. Hand-crafted with consummate skill out of mahogany, the duck-footed legs identify this as Queen Anne, although a better example of these legs is seen in the following illustration.

Minus the fan and with claw-and-ball feet and fluted columns running up the sides, this would be called Chippendale, which gives you a slight idea of how creative *he* was about highboys. In either case, highboys run from $1700 to $3500 and actually have no place in a book like this except that, by gosh, they are for sale.

66 This is what a Queen Anne lowboy looks like, although this one is actually the bottom of a highboy, as you can tell by the lack of molding on the edges of the top. Because of this it was bargain-priced at only $450.

67

68

67, 68, 69, 70 For his smaller chests, Chippendale adopted the kind of legs shown here and sometimes retained the Queen Anne fan and sometimes not. These pieces, which also show a variety of brass drawer-pulls, are all over two hundred years old and naturally have been restored and refinished probably more than once. They are in the \$450 to \$650 class, and the fact that there are so many of them around has always bothered me. However, I am told most of them are real, and a lot of them have come back on the market these days through auctions of estates. They are not very popular in the modern trend of interior decoration.

69

70

71, 72, 73 Hepplewhite furniture brings us up to the end of the 1700s. It is a simplification of Chippendale and can be recognized in chests by the splayed legs. If anyone is interested in more details to identify this style, one of the best books on the subject for the beginner is Drepperd's *First Reader for Antique Collectors.* These pieces are in the $450 to $650 class.

Incidentally, in the section on chairs I have shown no Hepplewhite because I didn't see any for sale. Undoubtedly they were so flimsy that they are now all broken into little pieces.

74 This is a Sheraton chest, which brings us past the turn of the eighteenth century to about 1815, and is associated with the American Revolution and our founding fathers. It soon gave way to Empire, but the influence of the chairs was felt throughout most of the 1800s in the form of the Hitchcock and related fancy chairs. In this piece the round wooden knobs and lack of knobs on the top drawer already foreshadow Empire. Such a piece sells for $350.

75

76

75, 76, 77 In these three pieces from the last half of the 1700s and beginning of the 1800s we see the simplicity that occurred when the country cabinetmakers made up chests in the style that was popular in the cities. Such pieces seem to me to have more charm than the original and to fit in better with modern furniture. Not to mention that they are cheaper. Between $150 to $200 for no. 75, $225 for no. 76 and $125 for no. 77.

77

78 Wouldn't you like to own a campaign chest brought home from the Boxer Rebellion—or some rebellion? These pieces are very popular. If they were not made by Americans, they were made for them in many different parts of the world. For the English, too. The richly figured woods are unidentifiable, but they resemble cherry and rosewood. Recessed brass handles and, ordinarily, recessed handles on the sides. They usually separate into two sections for easier transportation, but this one didn't. Must have been made for a general. Only $255.

79 This chest of bulky blocks of soft pine covered with fine Honduras mahogany veneers is just about as American Empire as we can get. It was popular after the War of 1812 and especially in the South, which was in its heyday during the years preceding the Civil War. Because it was the style preceding the Civil War, it is still more popular in the South than anywhere else. You also find a great deal of it in the old whaling towns of New England. Nicely restored, they still go quite cheaply in New England. In fact, ninety percent of the ones that come on the market up there are shipped South, where they sell for $85 to $125. (Many's the one I have seen stripped of its veneer and curved protuberances and sold as "Early American pine." May the Lord forgive me, back when I was working for dealers in Connecticut I even participated in such crimes myself.)

80 From 1850 to 1890 this walnut furniture in what is called the Renaissance style—for no reason that I can understand—dominated the American scene. It was well and solidly built, very heavy, usually marble-topped. This is an early example and retains some of the lines of Empire. Today it is valued at around $85.

81 By 1890 the Renaissance style was degenerating and it became fussy. Teardrop pulls were revived from the Queen Anne period, and you had pieces like this with marble tops in the more expensive furniture of the period. These were solid walnut with panels of burl-figured walnut veneer. Today they sell for $145—and soon they will go up.

82 The cottage or poor-man's chests made during the fifteen years before the turn of the century, and shortly after, were simple pine chests painted with false graining and decorated with carved walnut handles of the type used on the walnut furniture of the period when teardrop pulls weren't used. Most of them have been scraped down, stained a nice brown, and sold as Early American. The fraud is easily detected in the machine-type construction of the drawers and side panels. (In really old simple pine chests, the sides are single planks.) Refinished in pine and the handles replaced by round wooden knobs, such a chest brings $45 to $55 in East Providence or southeastern Pennsylvania. It is $10 less with the original decoration, although it should be $30 more—and soon will be when people begin to notice how examples of this false graining and decoration are disappearing.

83 Along with the mechanical revolution of the early 1900s the United States got this entirely machine-made furniture of Golden Oak, decorated with cheap pressed-brass pull plates. With the old finish removed, they are then rubbed once over with linseed oil and sold in sophisticated shops to sophisticated suckers for $65 to $85 (depending on size), which someday they surely will be worth. The New York City demand for them has pushed the Providence price up to $15 before cleaning, about $35 after.

84 A commode of the same period as the preceding piece, which is also popular in New York City at around $55 when cleaned off and oiled. It goes at auctions in the backwoods of New England for $5 to $10.

85 Another gem in oak that is popular in the Greenwich Village antique shops of smelly, smoky, filthy-streeted New York City. (Did you know that even in the humblest little town in Mexico you get fined if you don't sweep the sidewalk in front of your house every day?) The price-tag on this one was actually $125, and the dealer moved furniture fast.

86 The dealer who was selling this piece of Golden Oak, just like the preceding ones, had had the nerve to put solid brass reproductions of Chippendale drawer-pulls and plates on it. Nobody was laughing at all, except the dealer, who laughed all the way to the bank after getting $85 for it.

Clocks

87 88

87 The tall case or grandfather clock was made in this country from around 1750 to 1830, and was all handmade, with brass movements driven by weights. This is a fairly standard model of the early ones, with a cherry case. A simple model, it is worth $350. With more ornate moldings and carving the price would rise to $500.

88 Dated around 1770, this grandfather clock is made of curly maple and has a painted disk that revolves over the face to tell the phases of the moon. A more expensive model when it was built, it still is —at $650. This and the preceding clock are "standard items." There are, of course, many special grandfather clocks that are worth far more to clock collectors.

89 90

89 Around 1836 the revolution in clockmaking began with standing mantel or shelf clocks like this one, and they were made for fifty years. Eli Terry started it, and he was widely imitated. One of his clocks with a reverse painting on glass on the bottom is worth up to $400, but similar clocks such as the one shown here may be had for as low as $120. Almost all these clocks had wooden gears.

90 The Empire design of this clock places it around 1830 to 1850. It has a wooden movement and is driven by two weights—one to drive the works and the other to activate the striker which rings the hours and the half-hour. As quite a few of them were made and the Empire style is not very popular, these clocks can be had for around $60.

91 This clock with a case of painted pine is slightly later than the preceding one—say 1860 to 1890. It is also run by two weights, but has a manufactured brass works that made it inexpensive for its day. Enough were made so that they can still be had for around $45.

92 **93**

92, 93, 94 Around 1860 the big break-through in making clocks standard household equipment began with the advent of cheaply made brass works driven by a spring and regulated by a pendulum. Clocks such as these three were manufactured in the millions, and went on about every mantelpiece in the country. You can still find plenty of them in the rough, from $9 to $12 in New England antique barns (meaning shops that sell in the rough out of barns). Refinished and put in working order, they commonly go for $22 to $27. These three most popular styles are called the beehive, the steeple, and the square-top.

94

95

95 Like the O.G. mirror, this standing weight-driven clock (about twenty-five inches high) originated in the Empire period, but it continued to be made long afterward and is very common. It is made of pine covered with mahogany veneer, has brass works, and strikes the hour and half-hour. Around $35, cleaned and in working order.

96 About nineteen inches high, this ornately carved and highly polished walnut shelf clock in a sort of Baroque-Renaissance style dates from about 1860. Around $85, and a bargain as far as futures go.

97 If a lot of mantel clocks were made in the second half of the 1800s (see illustrations 92–94), they became a mania by 1900. For fifteen years or so following that date a thousand versions of these Greek temple mantelpiece clocks were sold like the proverbial hot cakes on a cold day. They have only recently worked their way into antique shops, of course, and so are still reasonably priced at around

$15 to $20 in New England. They all work well and are easy to put in running order. They are run by two springs and strike the hour and half-hour. They are regulated by a pendulum and are built so that they should run another couple of hundred years.

98, 99 Two Victorian wall clocks, often called "regulators." The one with the ornate carving is a sister to the shelf clock in illustration no. 96; the case is made of the same beautifully polished walnut. Both are spring-driven and their pendulums can be adjusted to keep extremely accurate time.

100 Another regulator clock of the style found in commercial establishments, schoolrooms, and railroad stations. These ordinarily can be had for $30, but this one also told the days of the month and so was sold for $50.

101 French clocks were imported during the second half of the 1800s, as they still are. Unless of special interest to clock collectors, they are valued at from $85 to $115. These are around ten inches high, are spring-driven, and have eight-day movements.

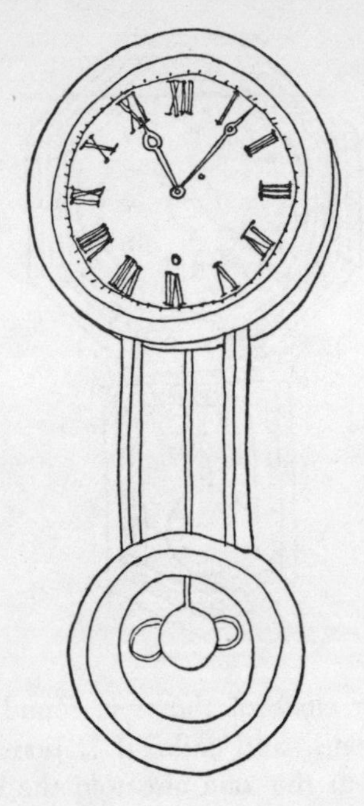

102 An odd and ugly wall-hanging regulator clock with a case of oak. It dates from the early 1900s and is valued at around $35.

103 A spring-driven wall clock of about 1915, valued at $25. It was finished in gray and certainly looked a lot better than it does in this drawing.

104 An oak-cased time-clock. I've punched one just like it, and there are plenty of them still being used in New England backwater factories. Cleaned and oiled in a New York City shop, it was priced at $65, and I would have bought it if I wasn't pretty sure I could pick one up for $15 or $20 in some junkshop around Providence or southeastern Massachusetts.

Copper, Brass, & Pewter

105 Usually with wooden handles painted or dyed black, the chafing dishes that are available date anywhere from the late 1800s to reproductions made yesterday, and it is virtually impossible to tell them apart, as they were not marked like early silver and pewter by Paul Revere, etc. In either copper or brass or combination they run only around $35 for old ones or good solidly made new ones. (Of course, all the ones you see in antique shops are old.) In case anybody doesn't know, they burn alcohol and keep your chafings warm.

106 107

106 Bed warmers these days are mostly hung on walls (or I suppose you could use them as silent butlers for elephants who smoke). Mostly the "not very old" ones on the market run to $35 or $45 in either copper or brass, depending on how fancy they are. Truly antique ones, say going back to the 1700s, will bring up to $125. Real age is seen in signs of wear and hand hammering.

107 Old more or less handmade kettles like this one—pre-1900—run from $15 to $25 as they rise in size from six- to twelve-quart capacity. In copper they run from $25 to $35.

108 An around-1900 or post-1900 kettle—holding eight quarts—goes for $15 in brass and $20 in copper.

109 Wash boilers of the early 1900s were at first semihandmade of copper, later really mass-produced of galvanized sheet metal. In copper they are around $15 "as is," $25 when polished and lacquered to keep their shine. Galvanized ones are worth only $3 to $5 as is. Painted or decorated they usually sell for around $15. If the decorator had some talent, that price could go up considerably, of course.

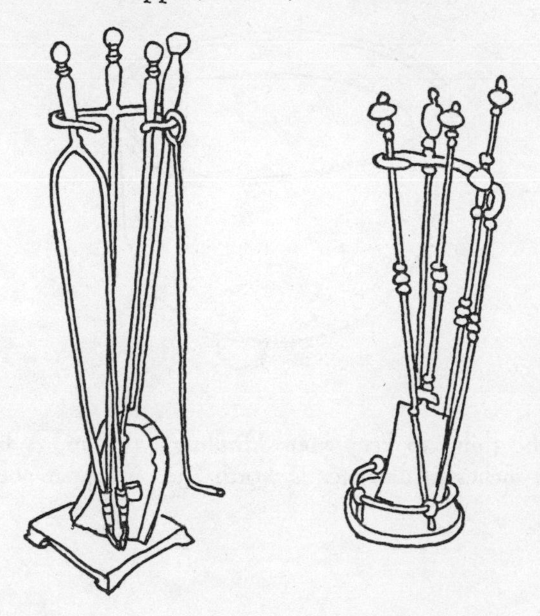

110, 111 The first set has brass handles, base, and shovel, the rod pieces being of iron—which gives the set a value of $25 to $30. The second set is all brass and $45 to $50.

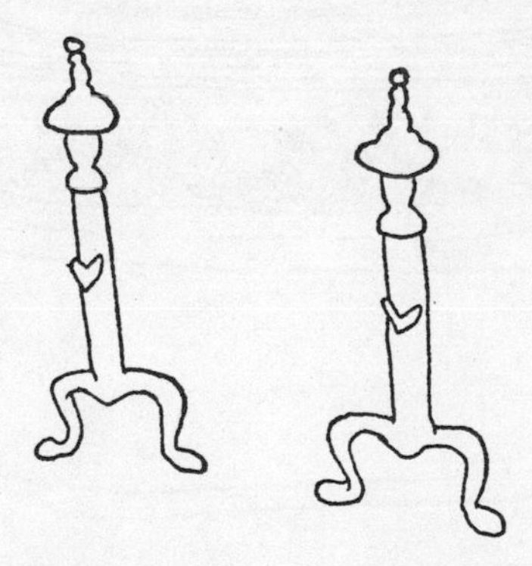

112 About fourteen inches high, of polished brass, these andirons sell for around $30 the pair. Fancier, and up to twenty-five inches high, they can cost $55.

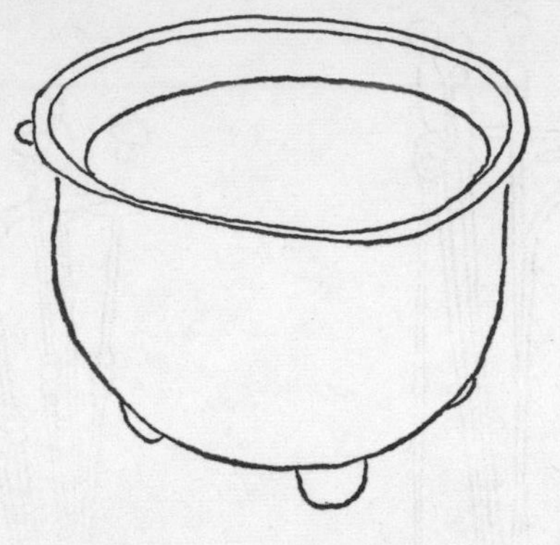

113 Just the thing to keep your kindling wood in. A brass one twenty-four inches in diameter is worth $30. A copper one is hard to find.

114 A hand-decorated, galvanized-iron wash boiler selling on Cape Cod for $22.50. Naturally you have to go to places like Cape Cod to get the decorated ones. Undecorated, they are $3 in junkshops.

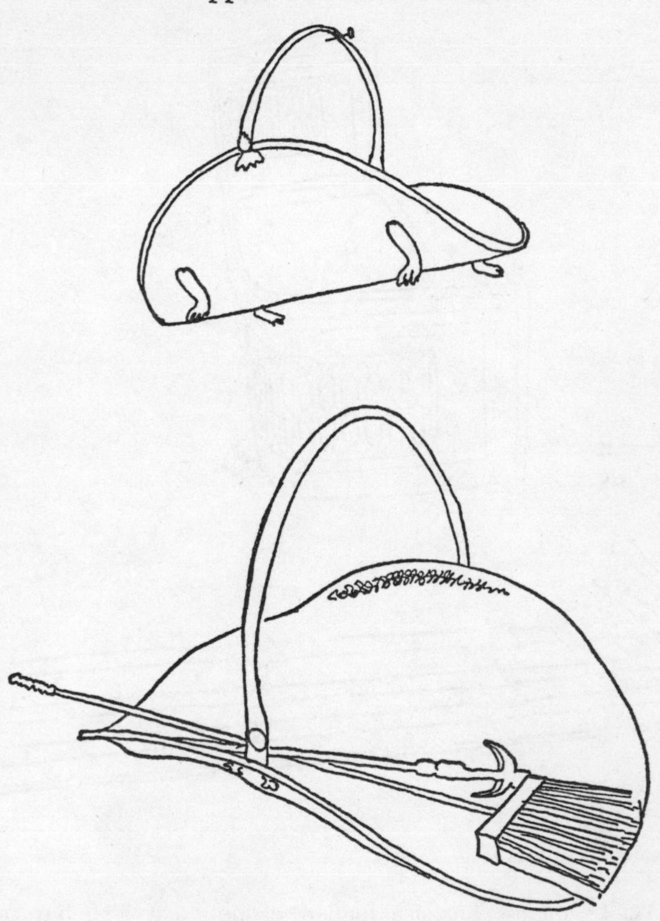

115, 116 Log-carriers is what I call them. This one is of hammered brass—not made in copper, too soft—and has nice little claw feet. With the broom and poke, the set is worth around $25.

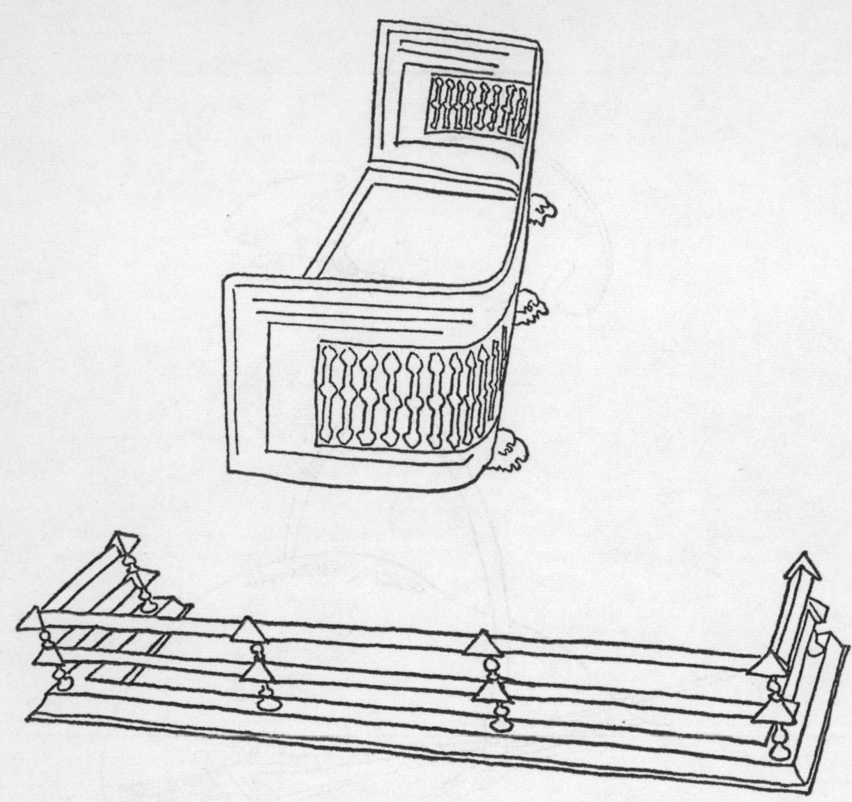

117, 118 Two brass fireplace fenders of no great age, but frequently found in antique shops. The sheet one sells for around $27.50, and the rod-construction one for $42.50.

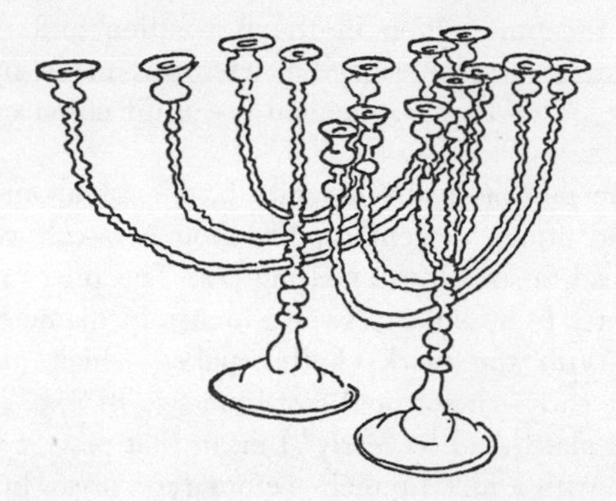

119 I once saw Liberace at the Coliseum in New York City, and guess what he was carrying out? These things, of course. Besides putting them on pianos, he has a roomful at home. Eighteen inches high in solid brass, these are $45 each or $90 the pair. A pair of twelve-inch-high brass candlesticks will cost you around $28.

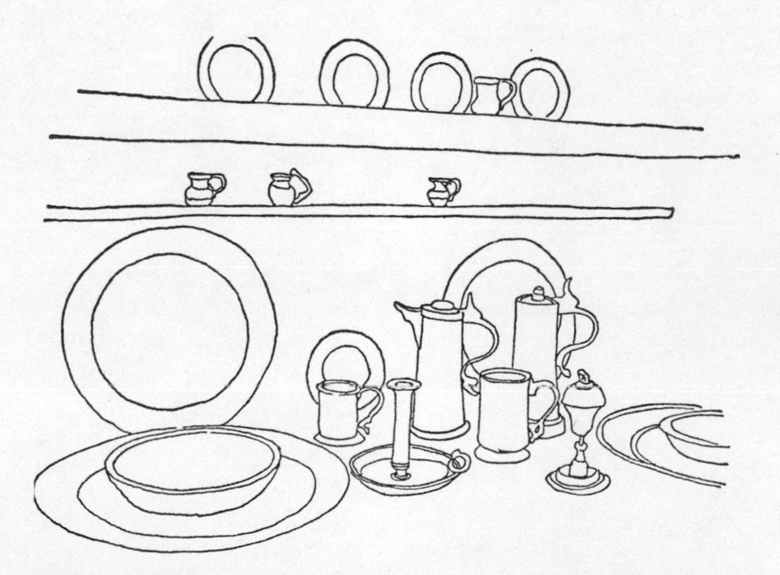

120 Pewterware was made in this country during the 1600s but none of this signed rare stuff is on the market anymore. It's in museums and private collections. One theory is that most of it got melted down for ammunition in the Revolution and the War of 1812. However, a lot of unsigned pewter was made by tinsmiths from around 1740 to 1850 for general use until china came on the scene.

The early metal was really a white bronze of about eighty-five percent tin and fifteen percent copper, though rascals were known to add some lead to stretch the melting pot. The prices go like this. Unmarked plates from eight to twelve inches in diameter run from $15 to $25. With the mark of the maker—which automatically means they are early—they would cost from $50 to $75. That's right, for each single plate. And by "early" I mean that pewter was marked —i.e., "signed" with a metal punch—before 1790 or so, but not after.

More sample prices for unmarked pewter are: spoons $6, candlesticks $25 to $35, pitchers $35 to $75, mugs $25 to $30, teapots $40, platters eighteen inches long $65.

Couches & Benches

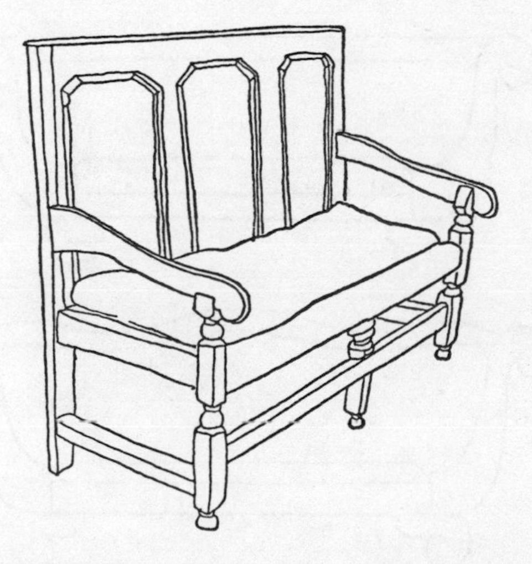

121 A paneled settle of very dark solid oak that dates back to around 1690 or 1920, depending on whether it is authentic or not. If it is, you could pay $750 for it—if not, it was still hard to make and is certainly worth $195. Besides, you can lie to your friends about it and how much you paid. Beautifully fitted together, all these pieces.

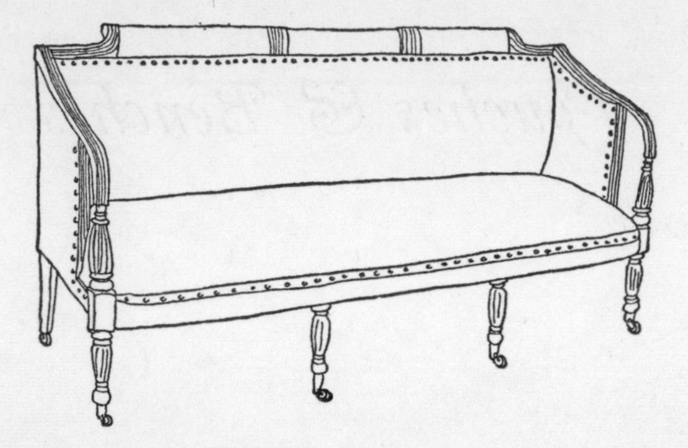

122 A lovely Sheraton sofa. These things have to be completely rebuilt and reupholstered, as they date back to 1800 and perhaps before. Beautifully hand-carved mahogany, even if the construction leaves a lot to be desired. After regluing, refinishing, and reupholstering, we come out at about $1100. Sorry, but that's the price of real class.

123, 124 Two versions of the very popular Empire sofa—of which a great many were made between 1820 and 1850. As they answer a pretty specialized need or taste, they are still available at a quite reasonable price—only $30 to $50 in the rough. After regluing, refinishing, and reupholstering (plus stocking in an antique shop) we come out at about $185 for the one with the curved back, up to $265 for the one with the straight back because it is much rarer.

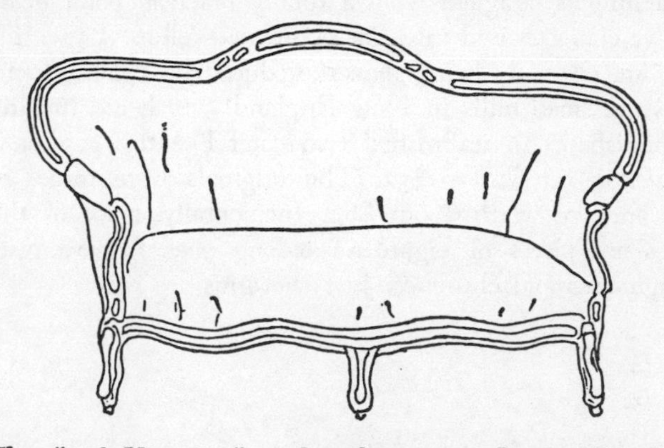

125 The "real Victorian"—early, that is—or Louis XV, this sofa reglued, refinished, and reupholstered is selling for around $265 these days. The technical difference between a sofa and a couch appears to be that a couch has only one arm and a partial back—in the Greek manner—but this distinction seems to have faded out of common English usage in the last twenty years.

126 Of the same breed as the captain's chairs shown in the chair section, these benches have also been made since around 1840, quite separately from any styles that were popular. They are cottage or country furniture, and are one of many such country pieces that demonstrate the principle of functionalism in design—the idea that if something is designed from a totally practical point of view, it will have character and integrity of line as well as of use. These, of course, are currently being mass-reproduced by the big factories as well as the small mills in New England, which are turning them out unfinished. An unfinished two-seater like this can be had in reproduction for $24 to $32. The originals were three- or four-seaters and are worth about $64. Incidentally, a lot of the "old" benches are pieces of eighteen-foot-long ones that were used in meetinghouses and churches. Just the arms are new.

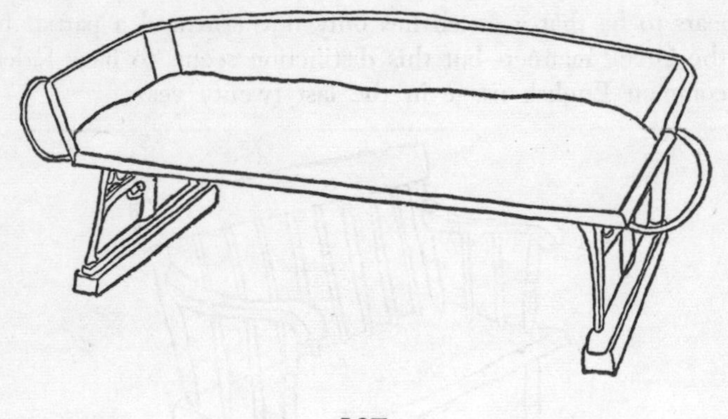

127

127, 128, 129 Mounted on various leg arrangements, but usually as shown here, buggy seats don't go back many years, but they have great appeal to people who had grandfathers riding in them right up to the day they bought their first Model T. Usually painted or lacquered a dull black with a red cushion—$45 to $65. In the words of my friend Monique, that cushion should be "as red as three lobsters."

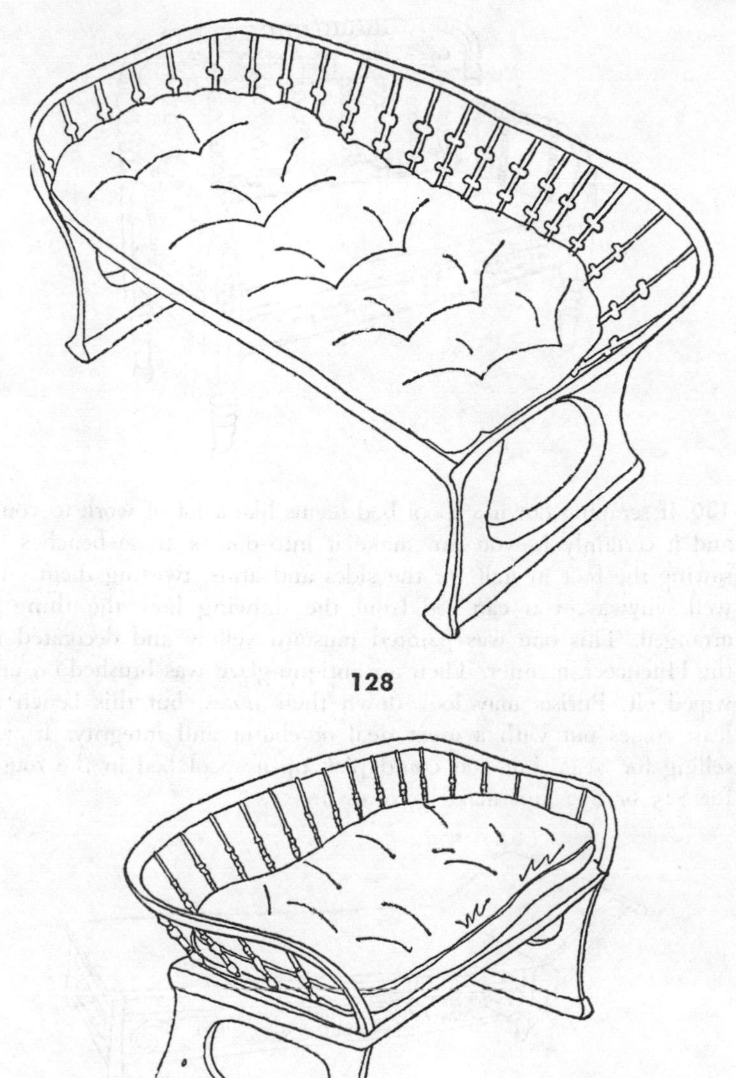

128

129

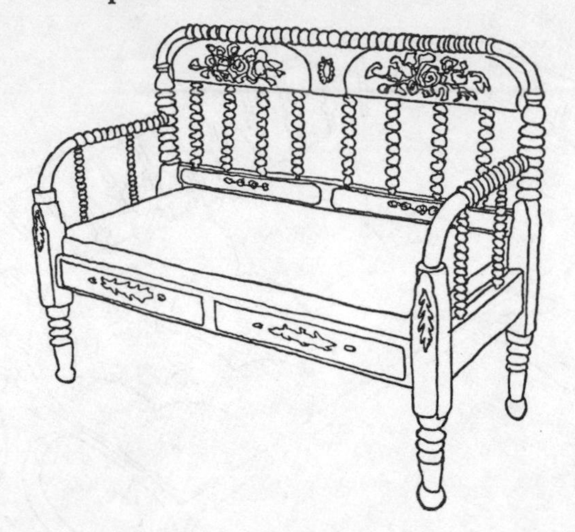

130 If scraping down a spool bed seems like a lot of work to you—and it certainly is—you can make it into one of these benches by sawing the foot in half for the sides and arms, twisting them . . . well, anyway, you can see from the drawing how the thing is arranged. This one was painted mustard yellow and decorated in the Hitchcock manner. Then an antique glaze was brushed on and wiped off. Purists may look down their noses, but this bench at least comes out with a great deal of charm and integrity. It was selling for $145, but you could pick up a spool bed in the rough for $25 or $30 and make your own.

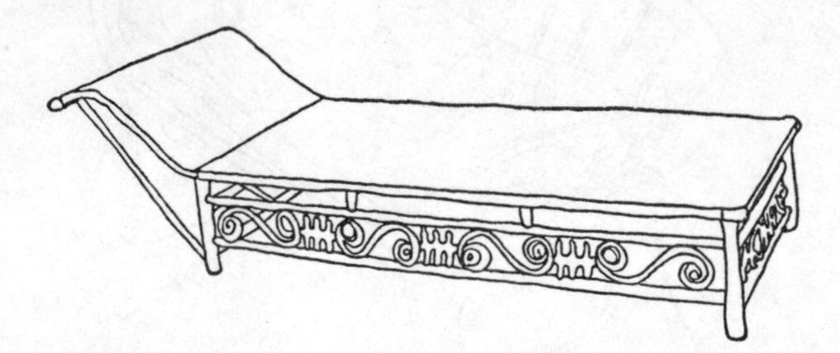

131 You don't see many of these bent-wood true couches (see caption to no. 125). It is definitely "camp," and if you don't know what "camp" is, it's really not for you anyway. East of Providence on good old Route 44 it was going for $35 without any cushions. About six and a half feet long.

132 Two nice little pine benches about twelve and eighteen inches high from Pennsylvania. They were and still are handy for reaching high shelves in old-fashioned kitchens. I don't think these had ever been painted, and someone had rubbed the old wood with linseed oil, which gave them a lovely patina. They were nicely priced at $14 and $18.

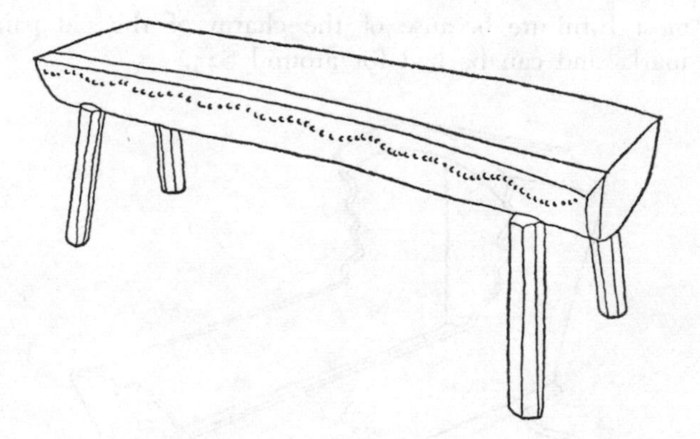

133 This is an authentic example of a piece that is reproduced a lot up in Vermont and Maine. The seat is half a tree-trunk segment. All kinds of trees are used, and sometimes the bark is left on the underside of the seat. Usually four to five feet long, the reproductions cost $35 to $45 and the old ones $5 to $25. It seems that when it comes to anything as rustic as this, people would rather have a strong new one than a rickety old one. *Chacun à son goût.*

Cradles, Cribs, & High Chairs

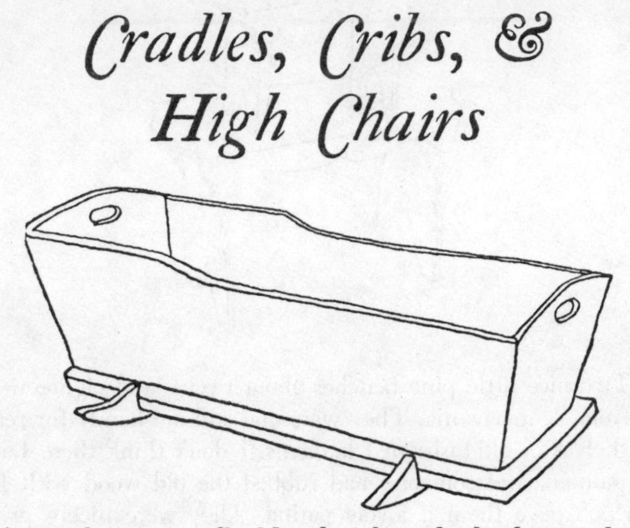

134 A simple pine cradle like this dates back about a hundred years and is very "country." These are left "as is" more frequently than most furniture because of the charm of the old paint and wear marks and can be had for around $25.

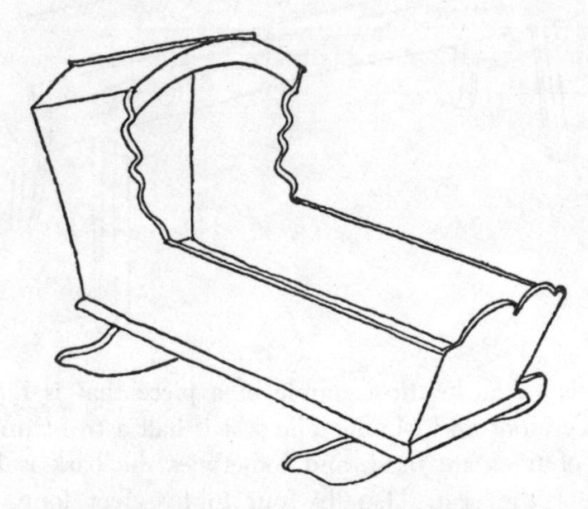

135 Cherry and mahogany were used for this lovely hooded cradle, which had a clear finish to begin with that was worth saving, and so, oiled and waxed up, it was sold for $85. Fine cradles like this will go up to $125 refinished.

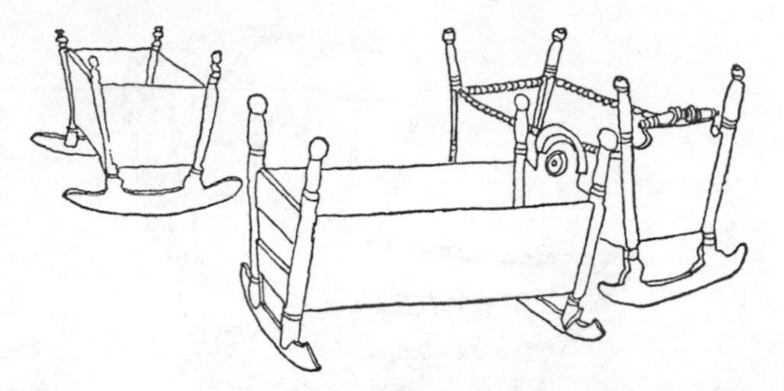

136 About fifty miles east of Montreal and throughout the eastern townships, Victorian cradles like these are to be seen everywhere. If they are simple and need regluing they sell for as low as $5. The more ornate ones, even in good condition, rarely exceed $10. They are pine with hardwood posts, and dealers can make a reasonable profit importing them, refinishing them over those long winter months, and selling them for $45. (I know that $5 to $10 sounds awfully cheap, but these things are a drug on the market up there.)

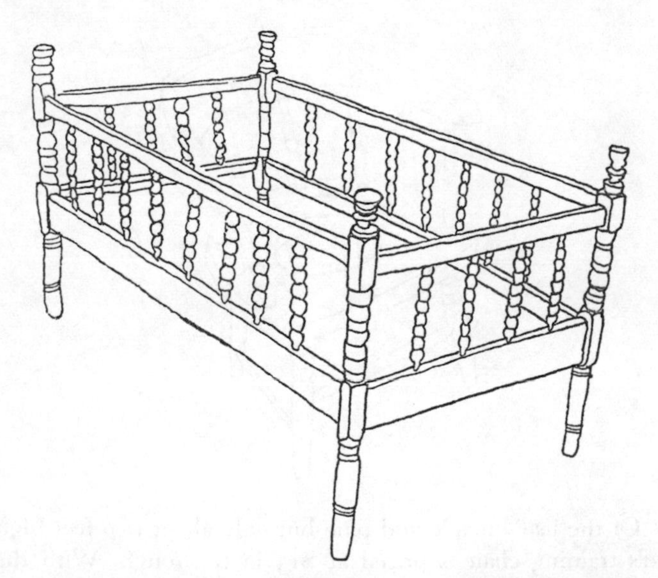

137 A Canadian spool crib of all-maple turned posts will cost you under $10. They were originally finished clear, so they are not too hard to refinish, but a refinished one costs $35, even in Canada.

138 Since wicker can stand up under the wear and tear of a nine-pound baby, these pieces of wicker are usually in good condition for holding magazines or knitting or something. Usually priced at $15 in the rough. Painted and antique-glazed, around $25 to $30.

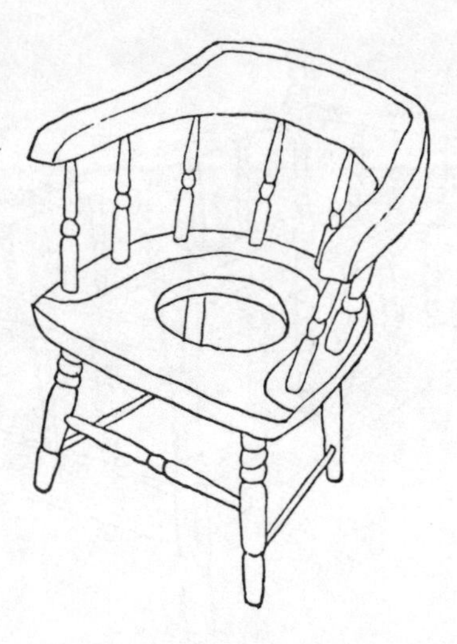

139 Of the usual maple and pine but only about two feet high, this child's training chair is priced at $15 in the rough. With the seat filled in and refinished, they should go for $45, considering the labor involved, but most dealers can only get around $32, and that is hard.

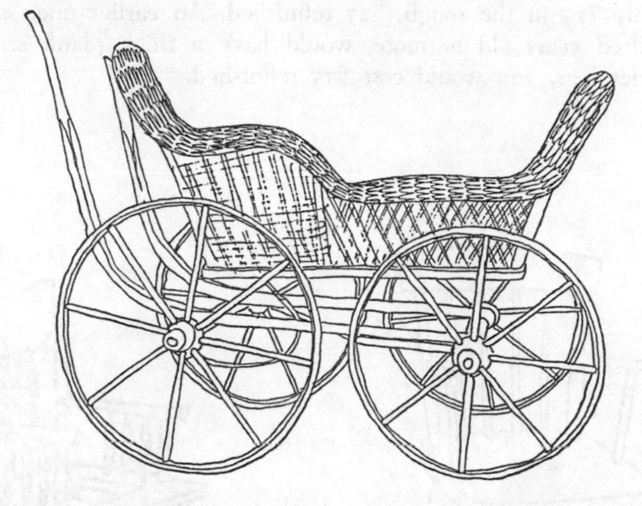

140 Wicker baby carriage in good condition. Victorian, of course, maybe 1900 to 1910. Very decorative, and hard to find in good shape. About $45 for this one, $65 with a parasol. These will skyrocket in price.

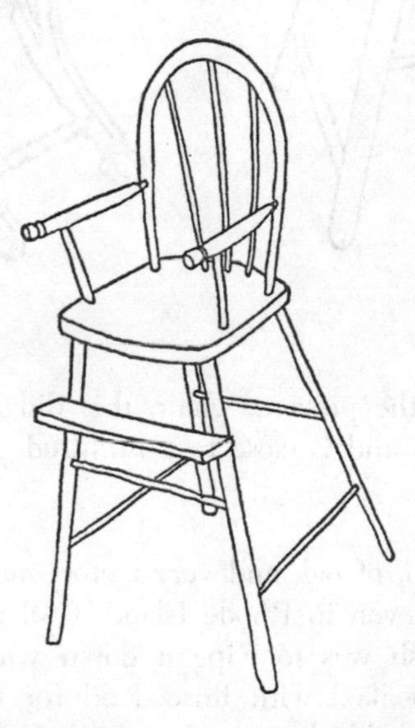

141 Simple, charming high chair with a bent back, this is nevertheless Victorian—as indicated by the thinness of the seat—and so is only $15 in the rough, $25 refinished. An earlier one, say one hundred years old or more, would have a thick plank seat and heavier legs, and would cost $55 refinished.

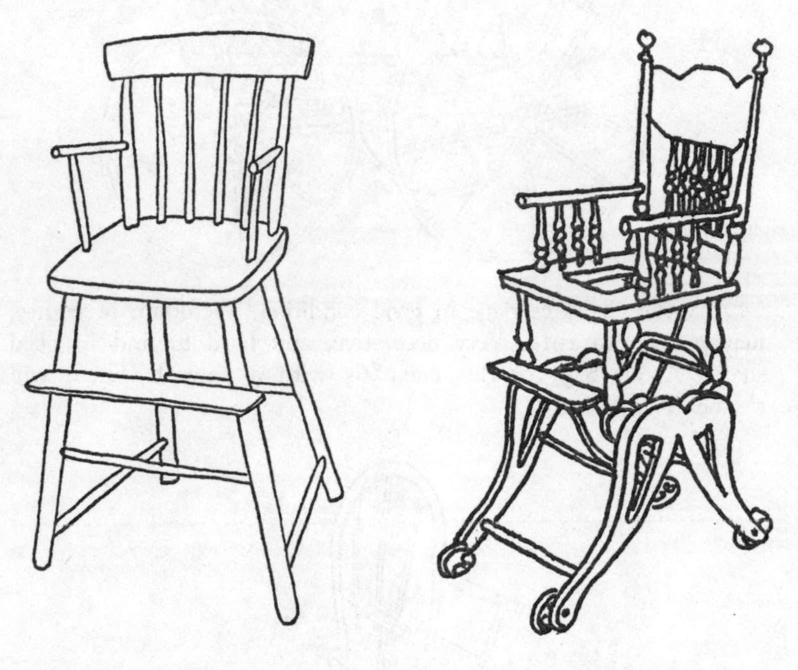

142 **143**

142 Earlier than the previous chair, this did have a single plank seat and pine legs, and is close to a hundred years old. Refinished for $45.

143 Late Victorian, of oak and very factory-made, this gingerbread gem is worth $25 even in Rhode Island. (All the dealer had to do to restore the finish was to wipe it down with lacquer thinner.) Cleaned off and soaked with linseed oil for the New York City trade, it would probably be priced at $125 in Greenwich Village—and they would probably get it.

Cupboards & Armoires

144 The cupboards that are on the market today appeared throughout the 1800s in hundreds of styles and designs because they were made by local cabinetmakers for small-town and country people. Because of that they are difficult to date. One fellow might have been doing in 1880 what somebody else stopped doing in 1810, and the nature of the tools and methods of putting wood together didn't change much throughout that century, so it is hard to find a cupboard that isn't supposed to date from around 1820. (You'd think they stopped making them in 1821!)

This one was made of pine and poplar in 1822 and, refinished, is so imposing that it is easily worth the $350 the dealer wanted for it. With scraped sides and scraped down but not finished, these open-shelf cupboards are a standard item in Lahaska, Pennsylvania, at $125. About $150 finished. They are not as deep or old as the one shown here, which accounts for the lower price.

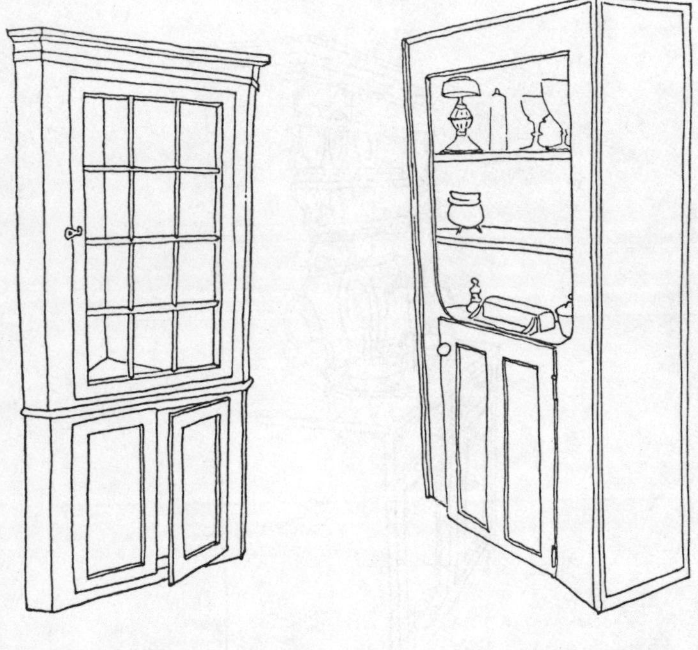

145 146

145 Corner cupboards with glass windows were made from, say, 1775 to 1875. I mean commonly made. They are usually pine and were painted—as was all the woodwork in the finer houses they were made for. The minimum price for a refinished one—a simple one such as is shown here—is $225. With carved arches on top, it would be reasonably priced at $375 to $450. Examples dating from the Revolution and before, large and carved, can go as high as $750.

146 Found in Pennsylvania, this piece dates from around 1850 and is valued at $225.

147 Rhode Island produced this style from 1840 to 1870. In pine, refinished, $125. On Route 44 east of Providence.

148 Called a floor cupboard or jam cupboard, this one from Pennsylvania is only $45 refinished in that area. It stands about three and a half feet high, is of pine and poplar. After 1850.

With a sheet of pierced tin in the door panel, it would be a pie cupboard and worth more—say $65.

149 Quite typical in the paneling and "stocky" overall lines, this piece is from the Province of Quebec. Such pieces are of soft northern pine, were painted with blue or yellow milk paint, and date from 1750 to 1850. Construction is mortise and tenon, held together with wooden pegs. All small-town-made, they come in infinite variety, and are still inexpensive. Scraped down and waxed —as is the mode in Canada—this six-foot-tall piece was only $110.

150 Corner cupboards sell for far less in Canada than in the United States. Taken down to the pine, this one was only $125

in the Laurentians—only about half as much as one of comparable quality would go for in this country. (If you want to get some of these bargains before they are all gone, see chapter "Where to Buy Them.")

151 With the original blue paint on it, now faded to almost a pale robin's-egg blue—and which only a Visigoth would remove—this piece was $65. I felt like a thief when I paid them the money in Defoy, P.Q.

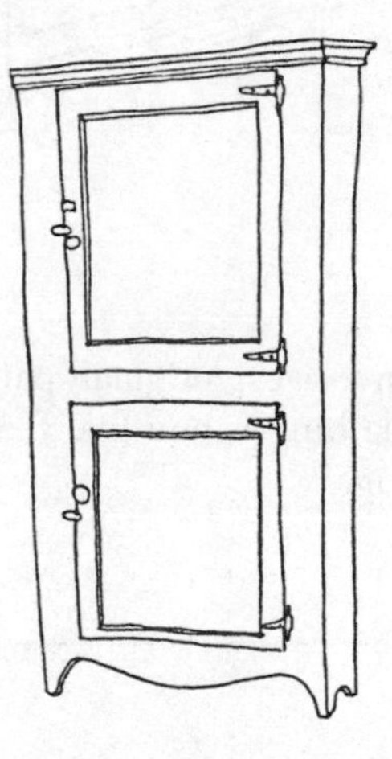

152 With hand-hammered hinges—real ones, not reproductions—this six-foot-high cupboard sold for $35. Original paint was in bad condition. In Defoy, and you'll cry all the way home if you don't bring a truck, as dealers from all over the States do.

153 Back in the Laurentians, original paint falling off, all pine, pegged, with handmade hinges, and five feet high, this armoire was $30. It needed regluing.

154, 155 Although Canadian, these closets, or armoires, as they call almost everything up there, were painted and decorated in a semi-trompe-l'oeil fashion that brought their price up to $135 and $165 respectively.

154

155

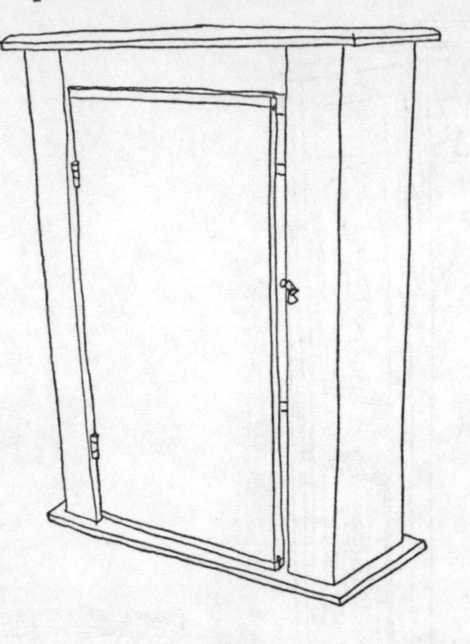

156 Note that the door is re-enforced on the ends the way breadboards are. There must have been a million of these made just before 1900. Four feet high, pine, refinished, at $45.

157 Circa 1850, this pine imitation of the finer mahogany sideboards or servers has some of the Empire style about it still. Around $65 refinished. In mahogany, $150.

158 Solid oak of 1915, this once was an icebox, but now is a home bar. About $10 from your junk man. Scraped down and linseed-oiled, $125 in expensive old Manhattan. I wish I had a dozen of them.

159 Two of the finest oak sideboards of the late Victorian era, so big and ornate that they really are unusual. In one of the Golden Oak shops of Greenwich Village they sell for around $200.

Decoys

160, 161 Although decoys are a collector's item—for men, of course —they are also extremely popular for those sophisticated decorative touches dear to the hearts of the decorators who create the American housewife's taste through the slick-paper "home" magazines. So in spite of the enormous number that were carved and whittled—most hunters made their own throughout the 1800s—demand is beginning to exceed supply and the price is going up. Old and unusual ones like these from a private collection run from $25 to $65 each.

162, 163, 164 Speaking of the demand exceeding the supply, why should anyone be disappointed now that reproductions of these standard geese and ducks have recently come on the market? With the original paint in good condition, the ducks are about $12 to $15 and going up fast. The geese would be $25 to $35 depending on the quality of the decoration. But reproductions of the ducks sell for $2.50 and the geese for $6 in Canada, unfinished, of course. Either decorated or stained an antique brown and then varnished, the ducks go for as high as $7.50 and the geese for $15 in a U.S. antique shop. In case you want to pick up a couple of hundred unfinished ones, they are made in a five-man shop in Daveluyville, Province of Quebec, only about three miles from the fabulous Defoy antique dump, about halfway between Montreal and Quebec city. Both towns are close to the new highway between those cities.

165, 166 And even Mexico has gotten into the act with papier-mâché decoys of great charm, though they are not very authentic. The ducks sell for around $2, and the geese under $5.

Desks

167 A classic of American furniture is the slant-front desk, which was made in the Chippendale, Hepplewhite, and Sheraton styles in all the woods from mahogany to pine and by all the cabinet-makers from the finest craftsmen in Philadelphia to the "carpenters" in every small town. Therefore prices vary widely. Most commonly available are desks of the native hardwoods—cherry and maple. These start at $400, but when the wood is figured interestingly, like curly maple, the price soars to $750. The occasional pine desks will go for around $200, because they are not really very old (around the 1850s) and the workmanship was not very good. Good craftsmen just didn't use pine in those days.

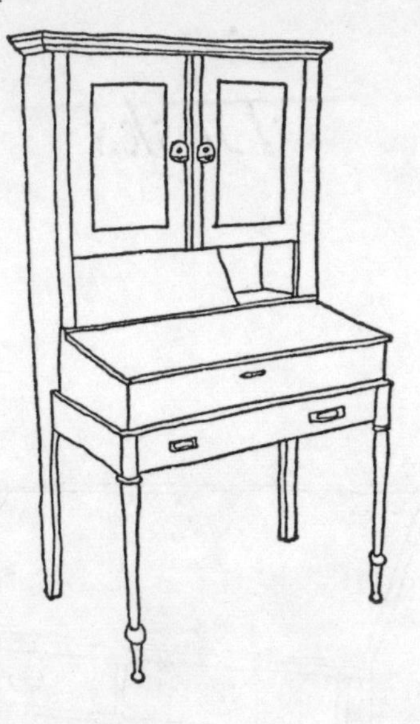

168 Desks—or whatever you call these things—of the Empire period didn't come off so well. But then, nobody is asking much money for them. This is a late one, about 1850, made of part solid mahogany and part mahogany veneer on pine. Desks like this sell for around $145.

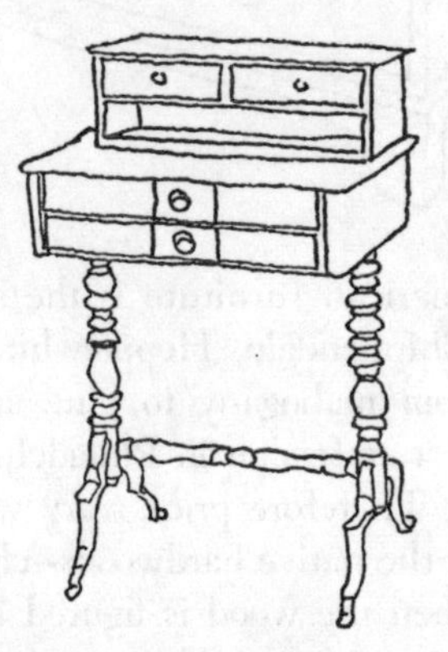

169 This popular Sheraton-type lady's desk, of cherry, was made a little later than it should have been—in the early 1800s—and so sells for only $145.

170 The lift desk was made in many variations of style throughout the 1800s for use by schoolmasters, businesses, and factories. Naturally today they are all called schoolmaster's desks regardless of their original use. Almost always made of pine, as they were not considered fine furniture, they can vary from $65 to $125, depending on how old they look.

171 Made late in the 1800s and derivative of the Empire style, this box on legs was originally a melodeon. Like most melodeons it has gone to its just reward of having been made over into a desk. Mahogany, $55. This is high, considering the availability of such cases, but women are so crazy for desks that they are all priced relatively higher than other pieces of furniture.

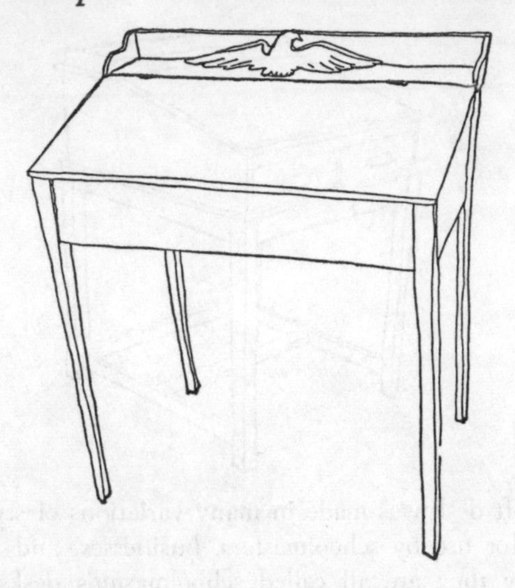

172 Here's a really early lift-top of pine with the eagle just resting on it to give it that Revolutionary air. Notice that the legs are integral with the box and nicely tapered. This piece goes back to the late 1700s. Refinished, $165.

173 Roll-top desks were one of the really worthwhile inventions of the Golden Oak era of Victorian, 1900 to 1920, and almost everybody wants one. That is why they sell for $45 to $50 even out in the hinterlands where people don't think of them as desks, but second-hand furniture. In New York City, cleaned and oiled, $145 to $165.

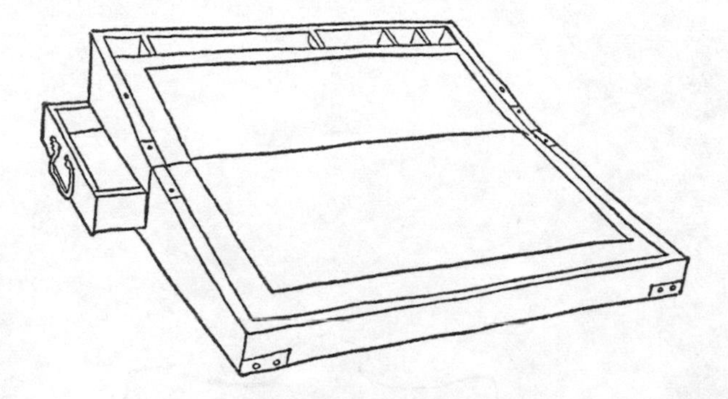

174 Lap desks were made from around 1820, and as the century wore on it seemed that everybody had to have one. Made of solid mahogany or pine with a mahogany veneer, they are virtually useless today, so they go very cheaply to anyone who wants one. For $5 to $15, depending on size more than anything else.

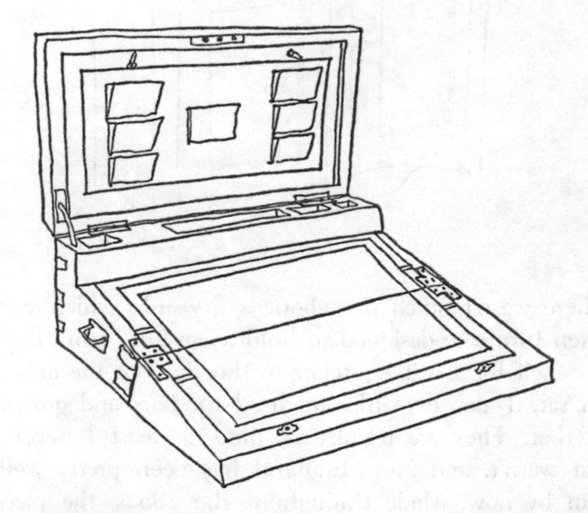

175 The inside of an especially fine lap desk valued at $45. Unlikely, if you ask me, to find a taker at any price.

Dry-Sinks

176 There wasn't much dry about a dry-sink, which was a piece of kitchen furniture designed to hold a washing pan. This one has a handy shelf for a water pitcher to the right of the area in which the pan sat. Today dry-sinks are used for bars and growing plants and all that. They are usually of pine, at least I never heard of one that wasn't, and New England has been pretty well combed for them by now. Made throughout the 1800s, the piece has its value determined by amount of character rather than by age. One like this should bring $130 to $150.

177 For the drawers on top, push the price up to $175. The reason these cost more than the open-shelf cupboards of approximately the same size is purely that women are willing to pay it because they want them something fierce.

178 This poor old thing was no bigger than a commode, yet sold for $85.

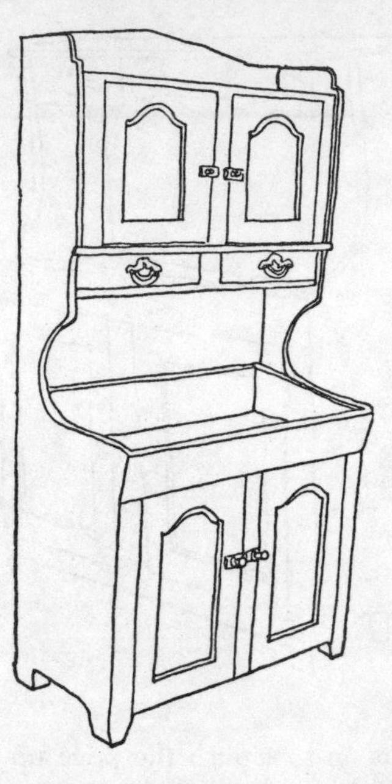

179 Pure Victorian and only a decade or two before indoor plumbing. But it *is* a dry-sink, and that is enough to push the price up to a crazy $125 anyplace (refinished). This one was pine, covered with the dingiest kind of depressing orange-brown false graining, and it sold for $65 that way.

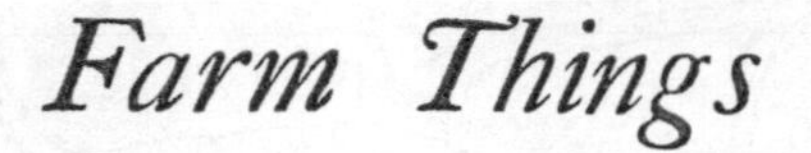

Farm Things

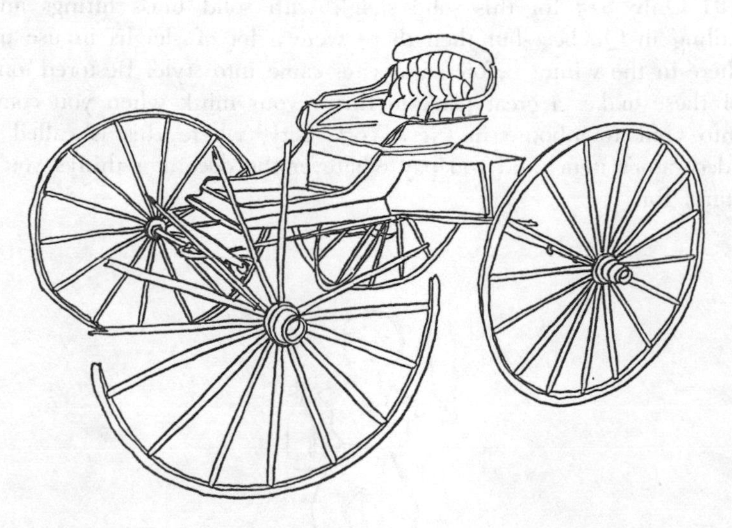

180 I thought one fellow was clever when he told me he had found a use for old buggies. He ran a nursery, so he put them in people's front yards and filled them up with plants. But he wasn't half as clever as the fellow I met up in Defoy with a truck that could hold eight of them. He took them down to Pennsylvania and sold them to the Amish, who use them as buggies. It's against their religion to own automobiles. In Defoy they go in surprisingly good condition for $35. In New England you might get a run-down one for $25, but they are usually scrapped for the wheels and the seat. That way a dealer can get $3 or $4 a wheel and $12 for the seat in the rough.

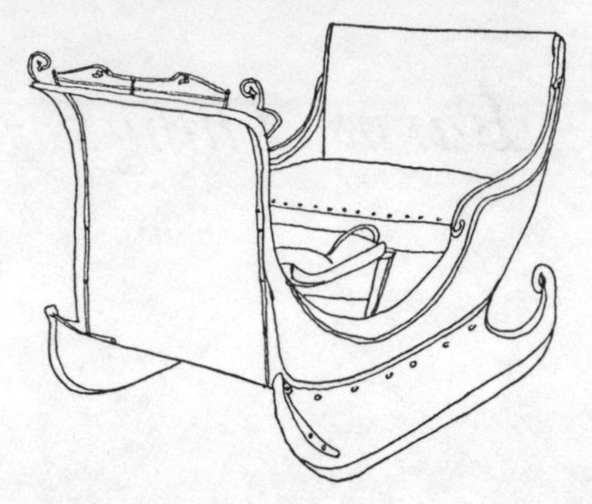

181 Only $25 for this solid sleigh with solid brass fittings and railing in Quebec—but then there were a lot of sleighs in use up there in the winter before snow tires came into style. Restored, one of these makes a great place to throw your mink when you come into your townhouse in New York City, where this is called a "decorator's item" and you pay whatever the decorator thinks you'll stand for.

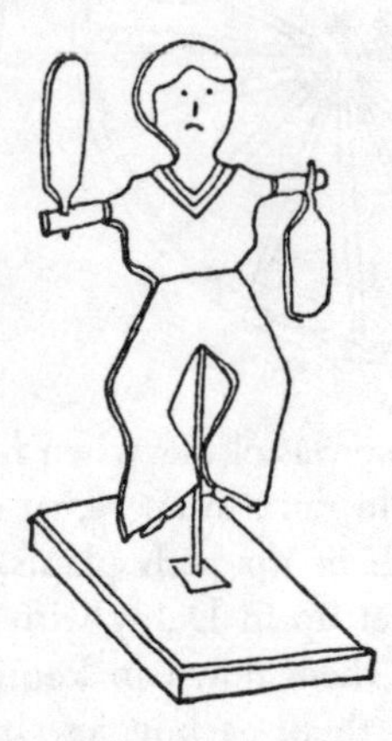

182 Only about a foot high, of painted pine board, these little fellows were popular around the turn of the century. You put them on barns, or any roof, just to see their arms spin in the wind. Depending on the amount of paint left on them, $15 to $25.

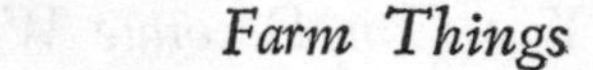

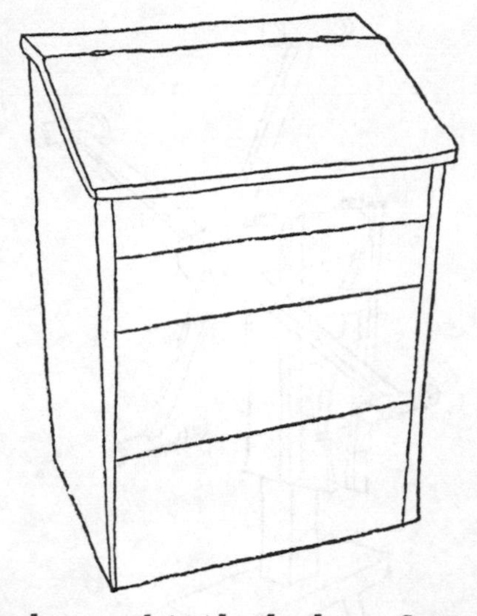

183 It's a grain box, used inside the barn. Originally it was not finished. Linseed oil turns such wood a beautiful brown. Priced around $35 in Pennsylvania.

184 Refinished, dough boxes are priced around $45 to $65. This one came from Pennsylvania, but most come from Canada, where they sell for $5 without tops and $12.50 with tops—in the rough.

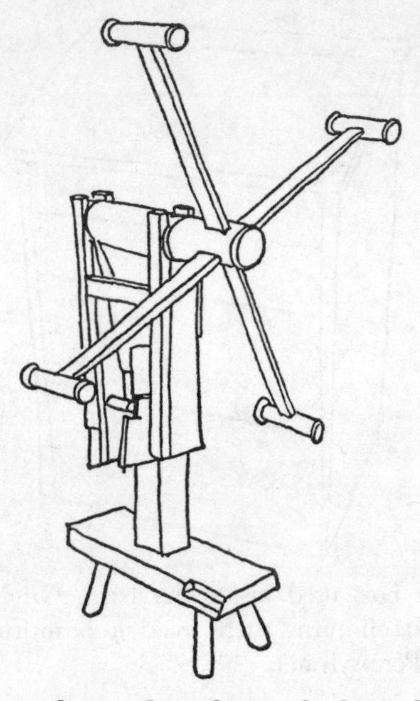

185 As a drug on the market, this perfectly useless yarn winder can't be beat. Made of maple and pine, these items are thought by dealers to be big enough—about three feet high—to be worth $12 or $15, but they're not.

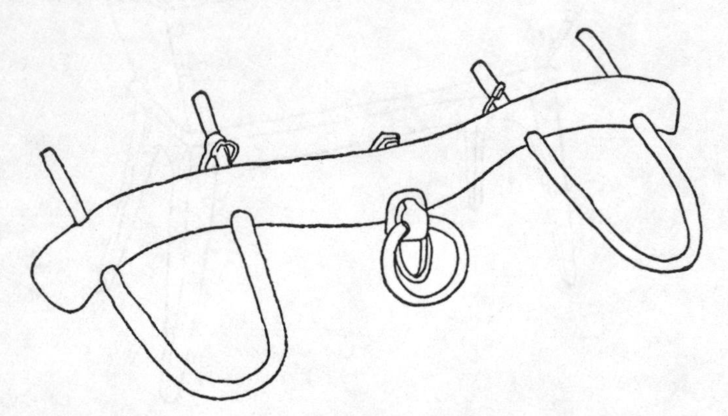

186 Now all you people in Texas hear this. Those oxbows that you are paying $45 for—and I've seen them in many a highway antique shop out there—are another Canadian import, and you can fill up your station wagon with them for a standard $9 apiece from dealers anywhere in the Province of Quebec.

187 Cranberry scoops are a specialty of Cape Cod, but they sell all along the New England seacoast for $35 refinished. Some of them aren't very old.

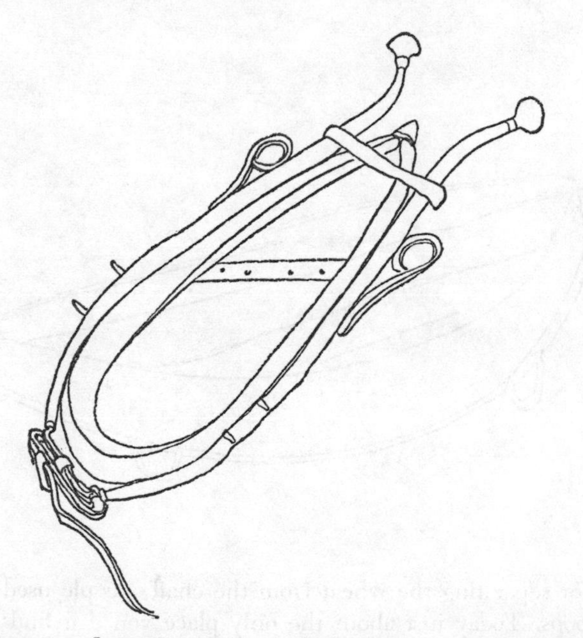

188 What you do with a horse collar is hang it on the wall or put it on a horse. A nice one like this with brass fittings is only $12.

189 I don't know why we're running this second picture of a buggy. Maybe it is because the first one we showed had a broken wheel.

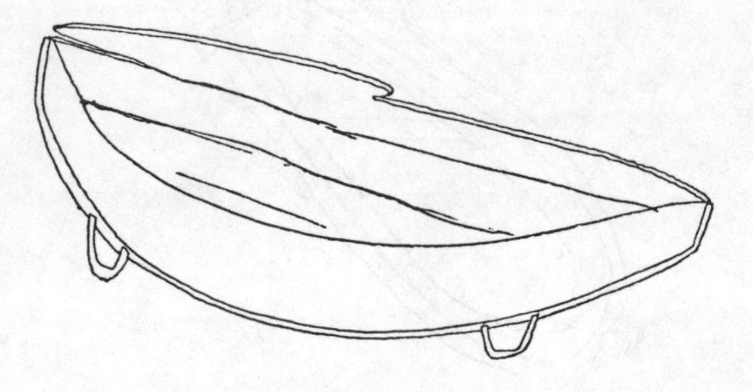

190 For separating the wheat from the chaff, people used winnowing scoops. Today just about the only place you can find one is in Quebec—for $5 to $10 in the rough. Refinished for hanging on walls, they sell for around $35 in the States.

191

192

191, 192 Shaped copper weather vanes such as these two examples run to $125 or more.

193 A Pennsylvania-style weather vane. Virtually all the ones on the market today are forgeries, so don't pay over $25. They are about thirty inches high.

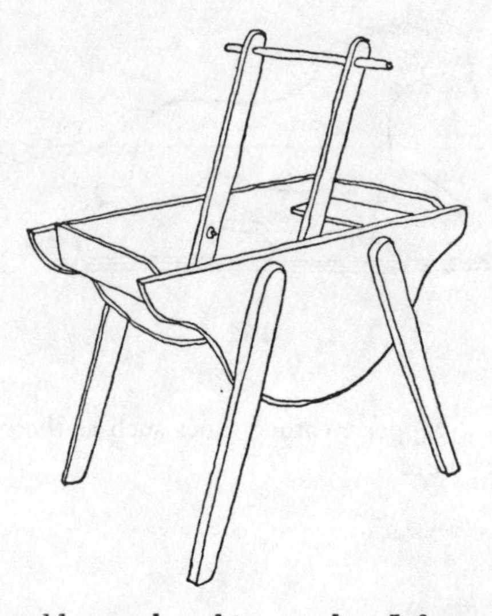

194 Somebody told me what this was, but I forget. Anyway it is typical of all kinds of factory-made wooden devices that began to come on the market around 1900—butter churns, mixers, washers, well-pump covers, etc. They are still lying around New England farms and can be had for $5 to $10.

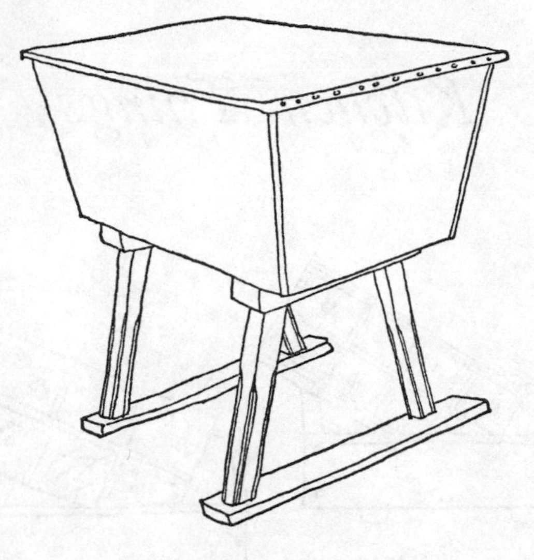

195 No, it wasn't a dough box, but you could claim it was if you wanted. It was a wash tub, because that's what the printing said on the side. In a shop, $15.

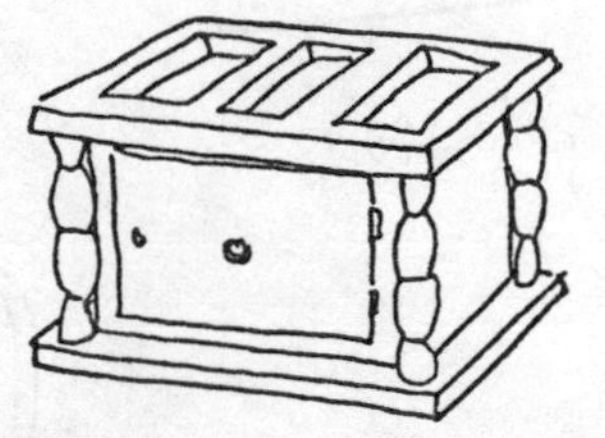

196 A foot warmer. It went with your buggy, under your robe to keep your feet warm in the winter. A tin box with a maple frame, you filled it with hot stones or bricks—not burning coals as most people think. There must have been an awful lot of foot warmers, because they are all around at $12 and less.

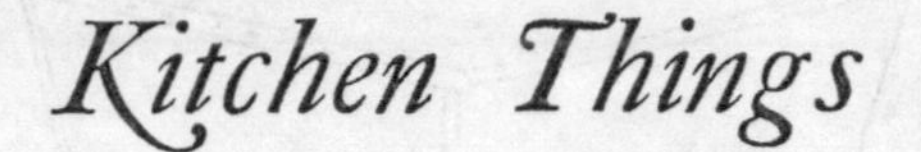

Kitchen Things

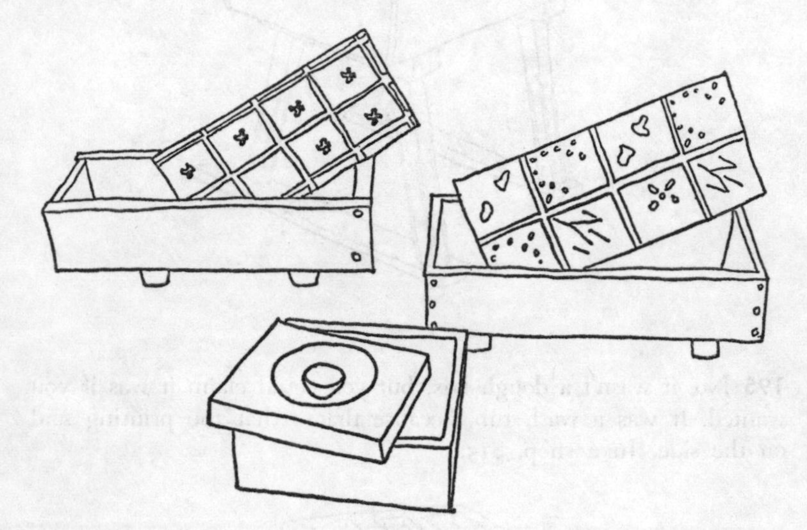

197 Wooden butter molds, $5 to $7.

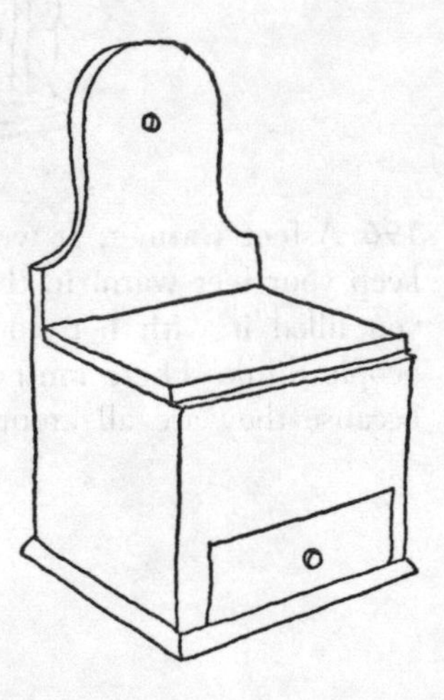

198 Wooden match-holder that hung near the old iron stove. The top lifts, drawer opens. Price, $8.

199 Assorted wooden kitchen implements. On top, a lemon press for $3.50. The paddles, forks, and mashers are usually $1.50 each. All these, of course, were made after 1900. Older ones were worn out and thrown away.

200 Another press and some stirrers. The long wooden bowls were and are standard items, ranging from $10 to $15, depending on size.

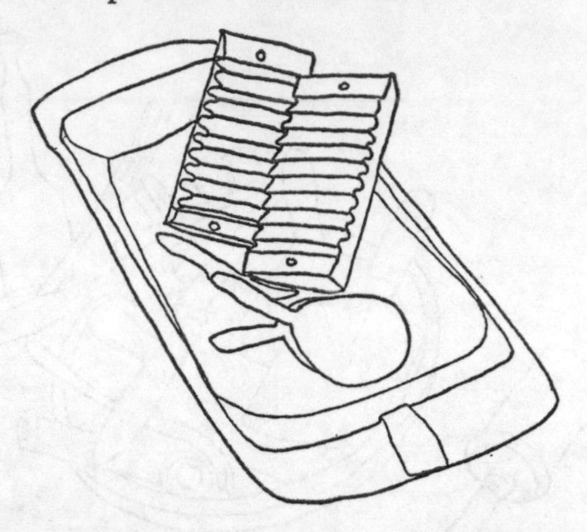

201 From Connecticut comes this cigar mold in two pieces (sitting in the bowl). The mold $7, the paddles $1.50 each, the large bowl, $14. But remember, these are eastern Pennsylvania prices.

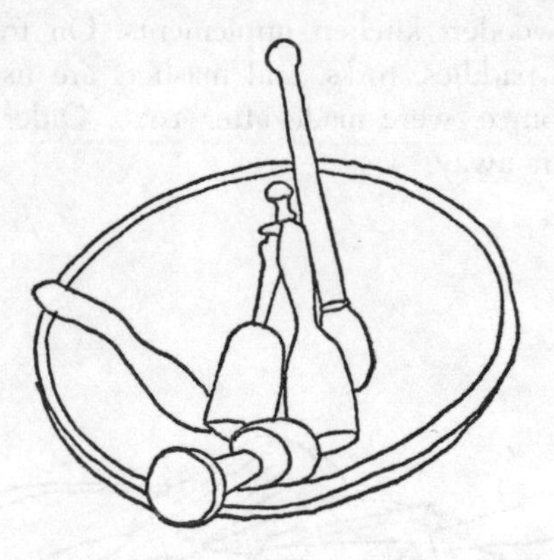

202 Round bowls are not likely to be as old as the long ones, which were chiseled out of pieces of split log. The round ones came in when machine-turning became practical, so round bowls are usually worth only $5 or $6. There are exceptions, such as the bird's-eye maple bowls of central New York State, which seem cheap to me at $18 for twenty inches across.

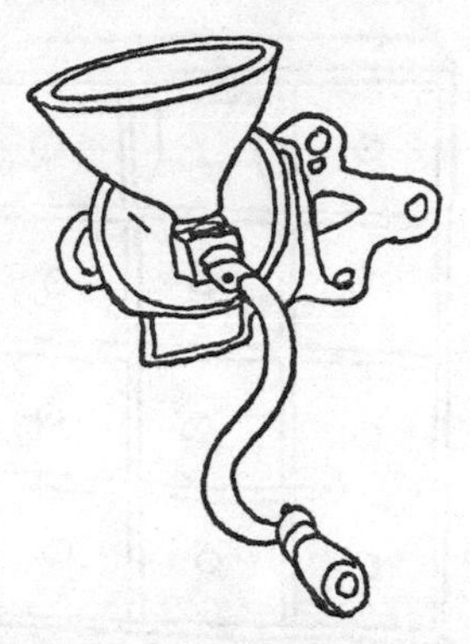

203 Many varieties of cast-iron coffee grinders that screwed onto the wall were made in the early 1900s. Since they can still grind coffee —and fresh-ground coffee is great—these have recently had a big upswing in price. From $2 or $3 a few years ago to $10 and $12 at summer auctions.

204 All kinds of molds used to be popular in the kitchen. This one is eleven inches high, and is half of a maple-sugar mold, according to some authorities. I think it was used for making big cookies.

205 Five-inch-high mortar of brass, with pestle, $15. For grinding spices, I am told.

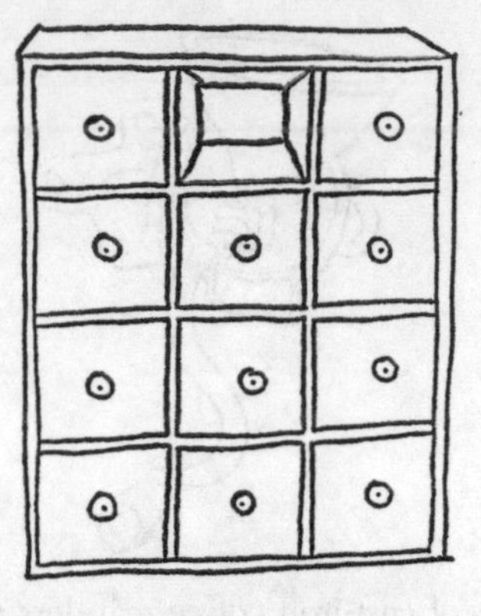

206 With five-inch square drawers, pieces like this are called spice boxes, but they were also used for pieces of string, pencils, notes to the milk man, etc. You can figure almost $2 a drawer when pricing these very popular items.

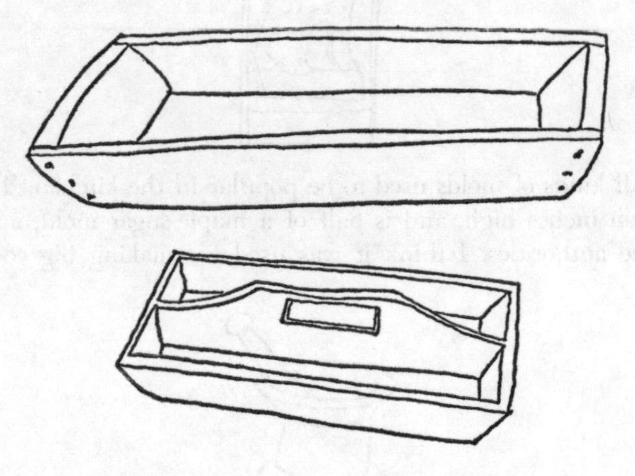

207, 208 The simpler knife box here is the older. Even refinished, these go for under $5.

Lamps

209 Made famous by the motion picture *Gone With the Wind,* these lamps actually weren't made until around 1880. Brass and decorated milk glass, they originally burned "coal oil," as it used to be called. Electrified today, a completely authentic one will bring $95. You see them for less, but there are many complete and partial reproductions. The easily breakable globes are widely reproduced, so check to see that the globe really matches the base.

210 With brass bases and clear glass shades, these common table lamps sell for $15 electrified. The figured base marks it as Late Victorian.

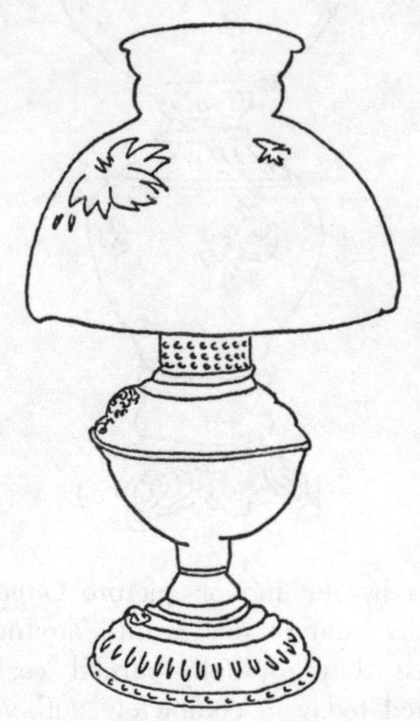

211 This milk-glass shade with a touch of color is a reproduction. On the brass base, this lamp, somewhat earlier than the last one, is priced at $16.

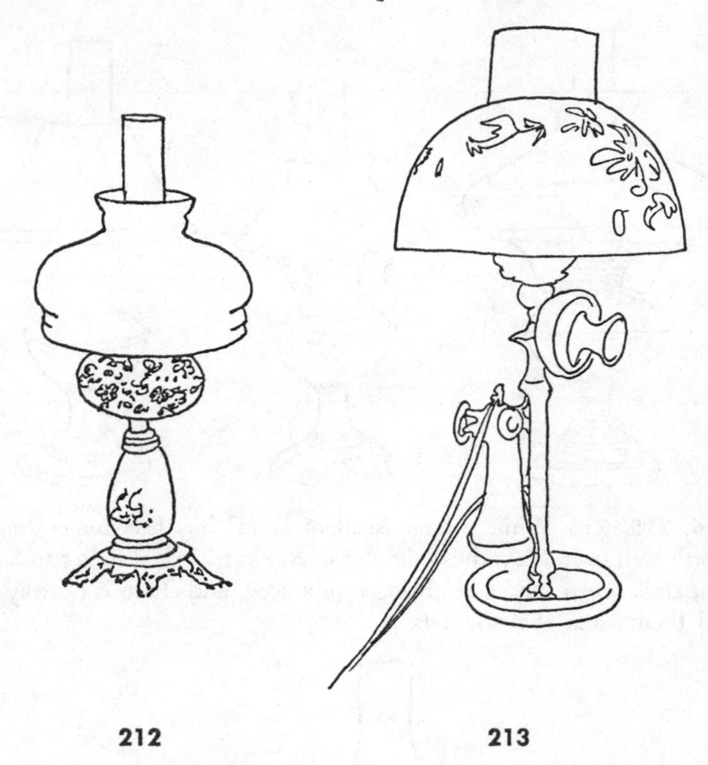

212 213

212 Made before 1900, this lamp has metal feet and rings and decorated glass base, and is a cousin to the *Gone With the Wind* lamps. The plain milk-glass shade is a replacement, which cuts the lamp's value from $65 to $25.

213 You can't stop Americans from inventing things. So, with reproductions of fixtures, chimneys, and shades easily available these days, this lamp wasn't too hard to put together. But all the parts cost something, including the old phone—about $3—and you come out in the end with a price of $35.

214, 215, 216 While a true "student lamp" has become rare and worth well over $125, these simpler ones, electrified, run $25 to $45. The dark green shades are being reproduced, and there is no way to tell them from the originals.

217 These lamps are all over, and does it really matter to you if the bracket is a reproduction? Around $2.50 for the lamp separately, $3.50 for the bracket whether real or reproduction. But $8.50 for the combination. That's $2 for bringing them together.

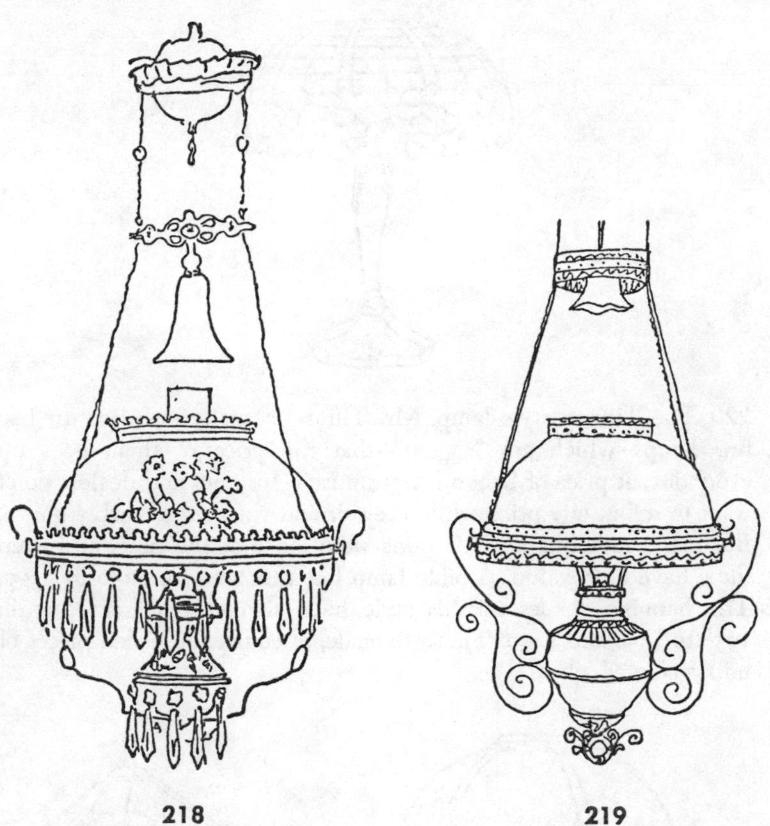

218 219

218 All those sparkling pieces of glass bring the price of this hanging monstrosity up to $125, but I wouldn't pay it.

219 Only $45 to the extremely interesting person who would want one of these in his house.

220 The Tiffany *style* lamp. Mr. Tiffany actually manufactured so few lamps—which are "signed"—that the price of them goes up every day. A price of $1200 is not unusual for one, and dealers don't want to sell at any price while they sit and watch the market go up. But many high-quality imitations were made at the time, and even these have high value. A table lamp like this goes for $250 to $300. The hanging shades in this style have skyrocketed from $35 in 1958 to $350 and $400. They are made, of course, of leaded pieces of milky colored glass.

221 **222**

221, 222, 223 Made of pieces of glass fitted into a metal frame, these lamps came after the Tiffany ones, were produced in much

223

greater quantity, and are often ugly. Nevertheless they have climbed in the last ten years from $3 to $45.

224 A kerosene-burning lamp of tin, painted black. Probably a primitive flashlight. The hinged tin flap on front was either to keep you from breaking the glass or for signaling. Ten inches high and $9, not electrified.

225 Outdoor hanging or post lanterns were a pretty rare thing, and about ninety percent of them on the market today are fakes, handmade or artificially aged reproductions. They run from $35, electrified. If the edges of the glass are beveled, you just might have the real thing at $125.

Lift-top Chests & Commodes

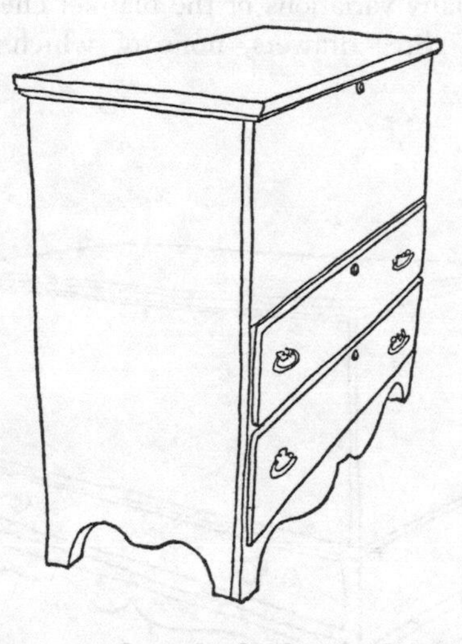

226 Blanket chests are relatively high-priced because they are intriguingly different as well as useful. This is an honest one with a lift top and two drawers below the chest space. (What I mean by calling this an honest one is that in many cases blanket chests are made to look like four-drawer chests, but the two top drawers are dummies.) Refinished in pine it is $110, the same in poplar, as much as $168 to $185 in cherry or maple.

227 There are many variations of the blanket chest designs. Here is a pine one with three drawers, none of which work. Refinished, $85.

228 The one drawer works, and the whole chest rests on a separate base. Probably made before 1800, this is of special value. Solid maple, refinished and restored, $265.

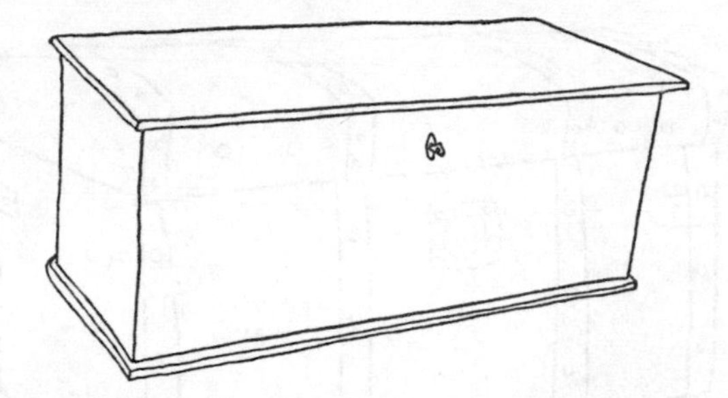

229 Any lift-top box is called a blanket chest, and it is appropriate for such use. This four-foot-long pine box is delicately made and was probably designed for such use in the first place, that is, not as a traveling or sea chest. With the original dark green paint looking very old but in good condition, it costs $55; refinished, the same—so wouldn't that be a lot of work for nothing?

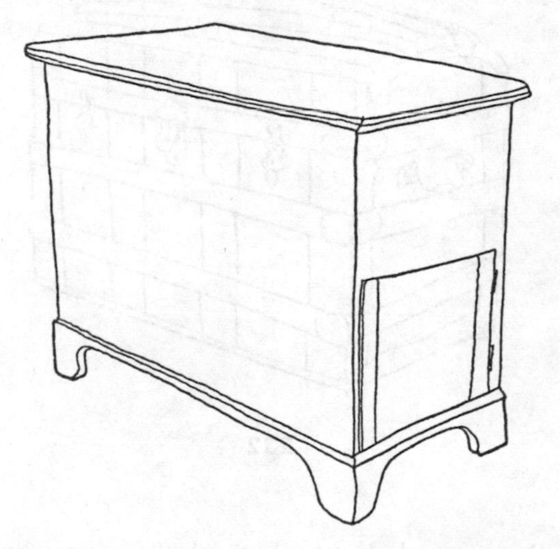

230 Well, the only explanation for this variation is that it came from a Pennsylvania farm, and down there they were always trying to figure out a better way to do something. The mystery is what they were trying to do. The top lifts and the area revealed has a bottom just above the side door. No door on the other end. Refinished in pine, $70.

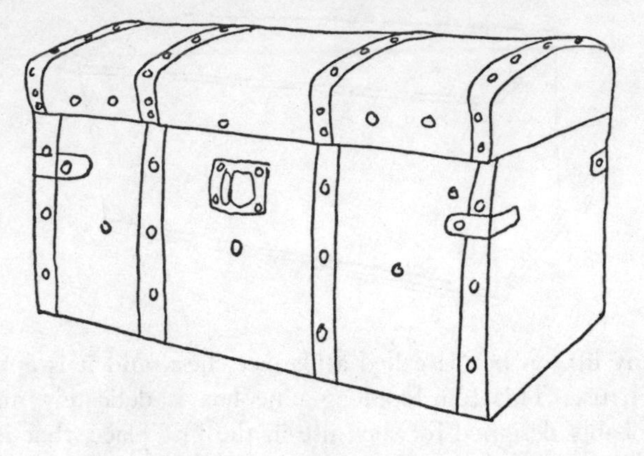

231

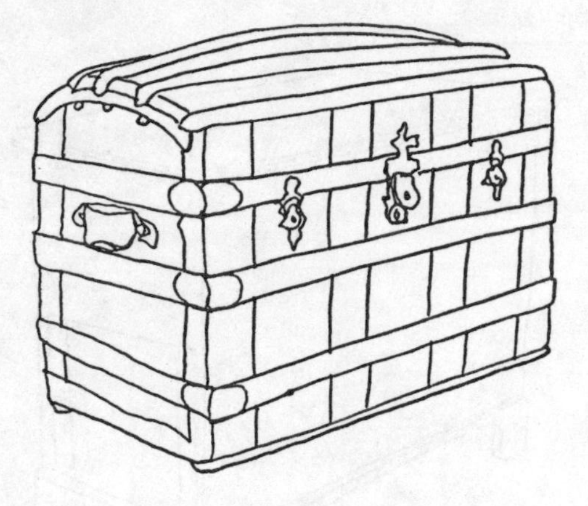

232

231, 232 Business picked up in old trunks a few years ago. Anything made of wood, even if covered with paper, oilcloth, or leather. That was when some genius figured out a new way of using the gullibility of New Yorkers to make a fast profit. Any metal is left just as it was, but the covering is soaked off the wood, which is then stained an antique brown and linseed-oiled. The resulting "antiques" are then sold as blanket chests for $65 up.

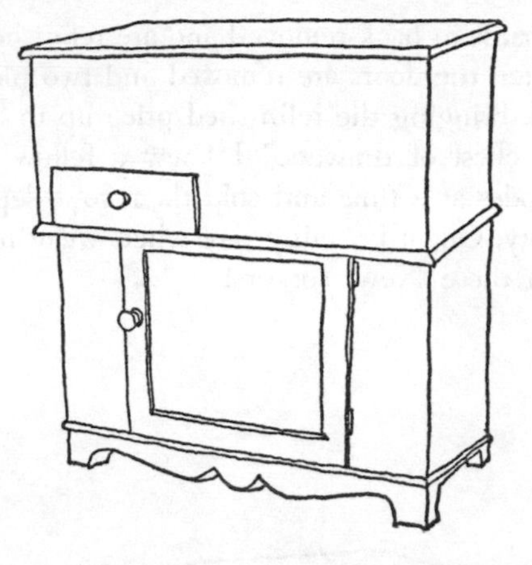

233 Another popular classic: the lift-top commode that used to hold a pitcher and washbowl in the top, toilet articles in the drawer, and I can't remember what in the bottom, but I'm sure it must have been something nice. These were made from around 1850 to 1910, of pine, painted with false graining and designs in panels. Refinished, $45 to $65. They are also being reproduced in unfinished pine—easy to "age" in a hurry, but costing $35, which is more than they cost "in the rough"—which is $25.

234 Before the lift-top commode in no. 233 was scraped down, it was decorated like this standard pine commode of the early 1900s. Pitcher, bowl, etc., were kept in the bottom. These commodes have their splash boards in back removed and are refinished in the natural pine—$25. Often the doors are removed and two pine drawers fitted into the space, bringing the refinished price up to $45 for "such an unusual little chest of drawers." I knew a fellow who did this to twenty commodes at a time and sold them to a department store in New York City. Oh, it's a rainy day when we're not putting something over on those New Yorkers!

235 They made them in oak, too. These sell for around $7.50 in junkshops and Good Will stores around New England. Cleaned and oiled, they are $30 and up to New Yorkers.

236 Going back to the Civil War, commodes were made of solid walnut and usually had white marble tops. These are "real antiques" by now, and bring about $65 with the marble top. Only $35 if walnut was used for the top.

Marine Things

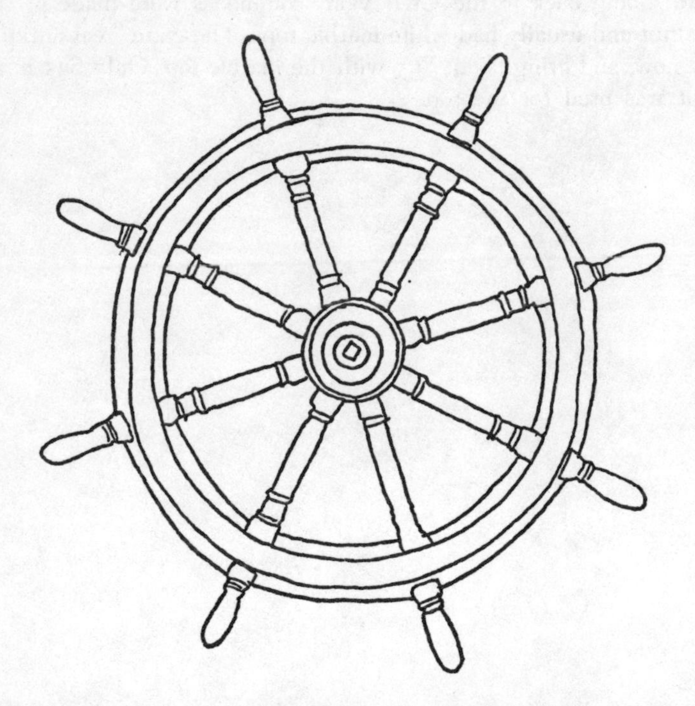

237 Usually with brass trimmings and not in need of any refinishing, these items run from $45 for two and a half feet across to $175 for the large five-foot ones. That's the measurement of the wheel itself, not including the handles.

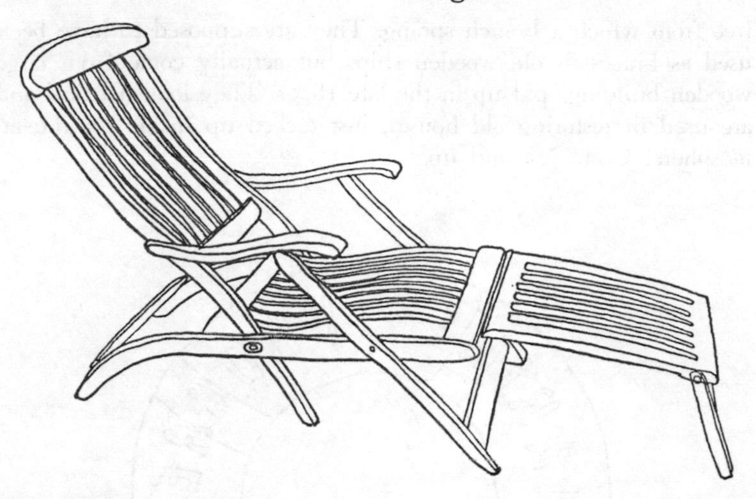

238 Deck chairs are very strongly constructed of hard wood, usually maple, and average $25 as is. You have to refinish your own, and a long job it is.

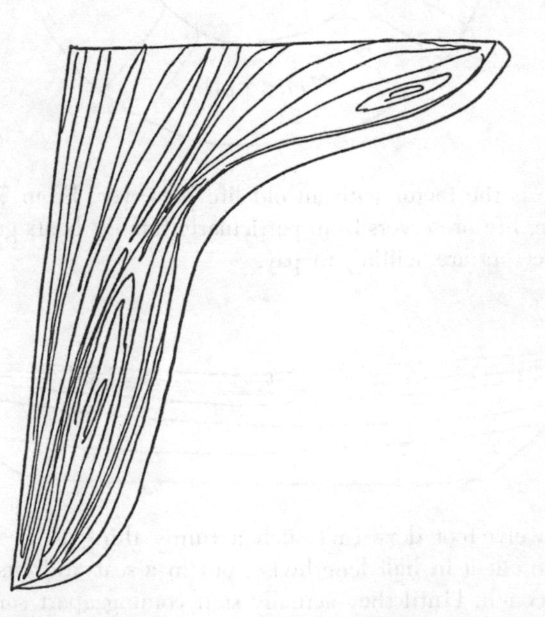

239 Ship's knees are bulky pieces of pine measuring about two and a half feet along each straight side and were cut from the part of a tree from which a branch sprang. They are supposed to have been used as braces in old wooden ships but actually come from large wooden buildings put up in the late 1800s. They look nautical and are used in restoring old houses, just tacked up inside for the atmosphere. Cost, $25 and up.

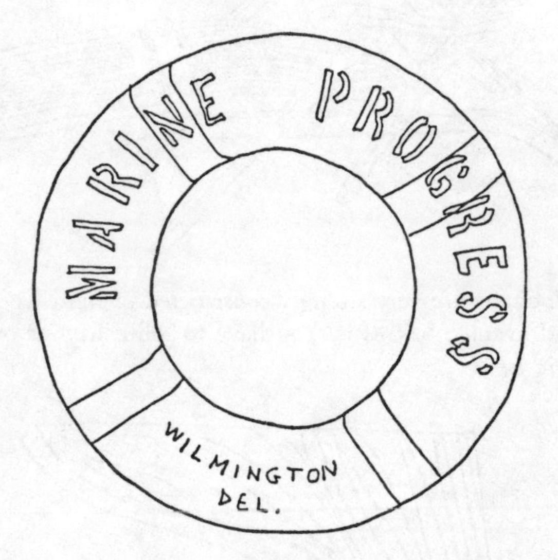

240 Size is the factor with an old life preserver. From $10 to $25. Of course, life preservers from particularly famous boats go for whatever collectors are willing to pay.

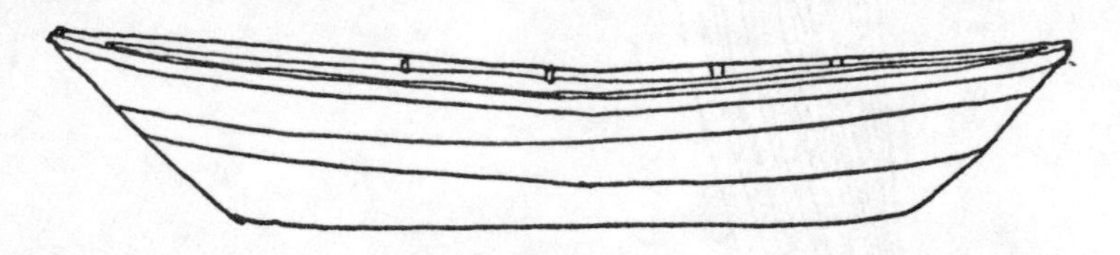

241 A twelve-foot dory isn't such a funny thing to decorate with when you cut it in half lengthwise, put in a seat and cushions, and call it a couch. Until they actually start coming apart someone will think he can save it, so to get one intact, you will have to pay around $25.

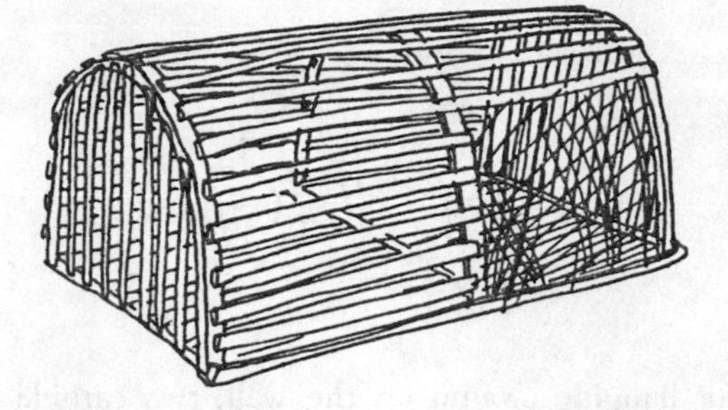

242 There comes a certain time in the life of every lobster trap when it has gotten too rickety to use anymore but still hasn't begun to break up. At that point a lobsterman will be glad to get $3 or $4 for it or give it to you if he likes you. In shops, $6 to $8. If you can think of something to do with lobster traps besides hanging them around for atmosphere, you can get to be a rich man.

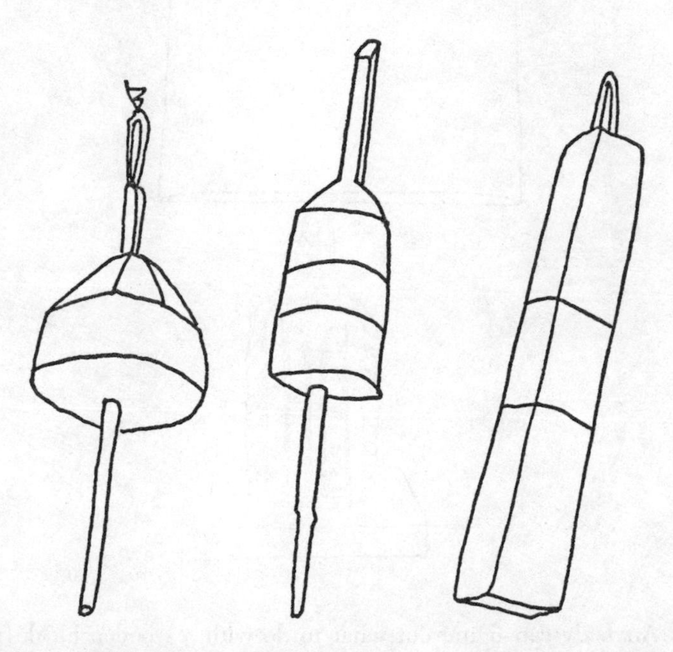

243, 244, 245 Wooden floats for lobster pots can still be had for $1.50 to $3 for ones with real "character."

246 Just for hanging around on the wall, two carbide lamps used on an early naval vessel will cost you $12.50 the pair.

247 Anybody can figure out what to do with a wooden block from a block and tackle. You make a lamp out of it. This block was eighteen inches high. The assembled lamp, $45.

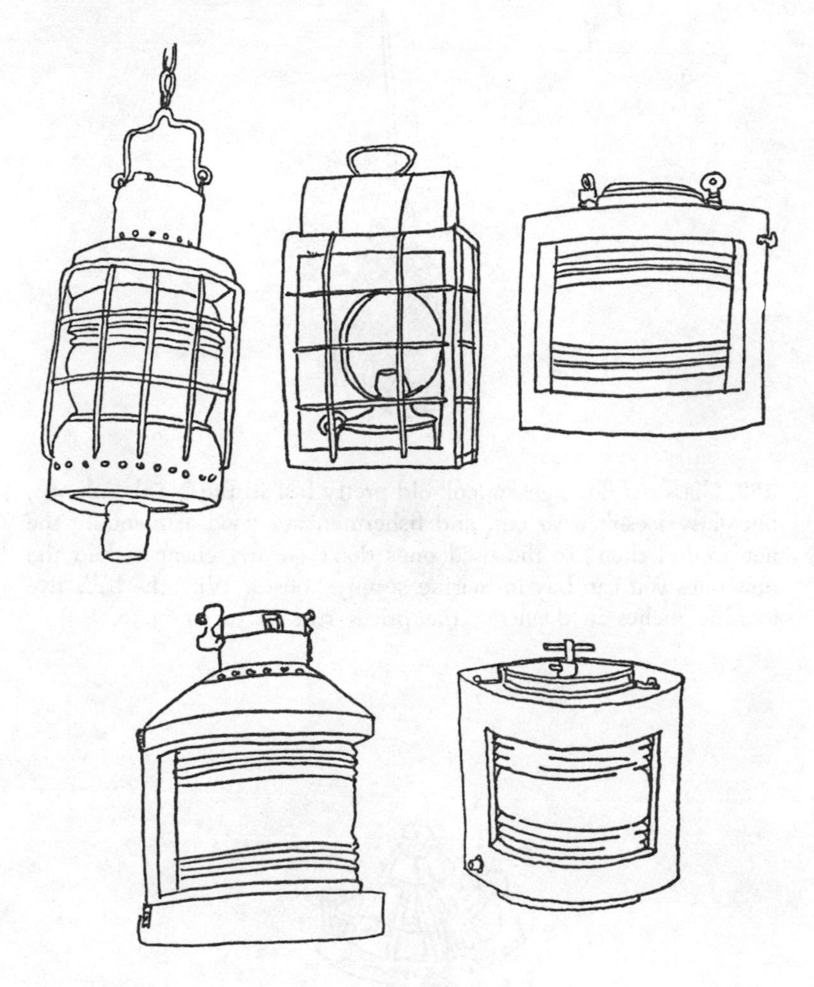

248, 249, 250, 251, 252 Hanging deck lights and running lights are available along the New England coast. Many a boat is wrecked or abandoned, but somebody always saves the lights. In galvanized iron, they are around $15 each; in brass, $35 for one about ten inches high. These are usually from fishing boats and yachts. For big ones off ships—twenty to thirty inches high—the price will be $135 to $200 in brass, which is what the big ones seem always to have been made of.

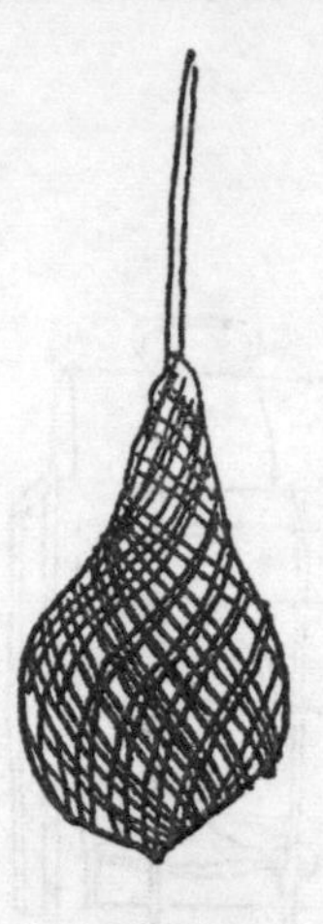

253 Glass net floats get to look old pretty fast in the North Atlantic, but glass doesn't wear out, and fishermen are good at mending the net around them, so the used ones don't go any cheaper than the new ones you can buy in marine supply houses. With the balls five to nine inches in diameter, the prices run $1.50 to $3.50.

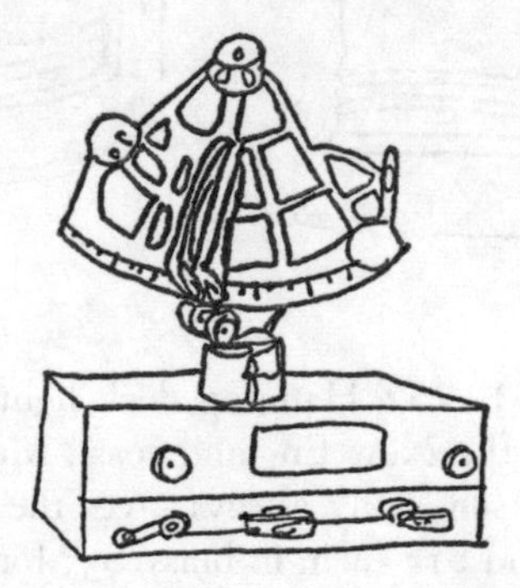

254 A fifty-year-old sextant, still perfectly usable, eighteen inches high and in a polished mahogany brass-fitted box—$200 and up.

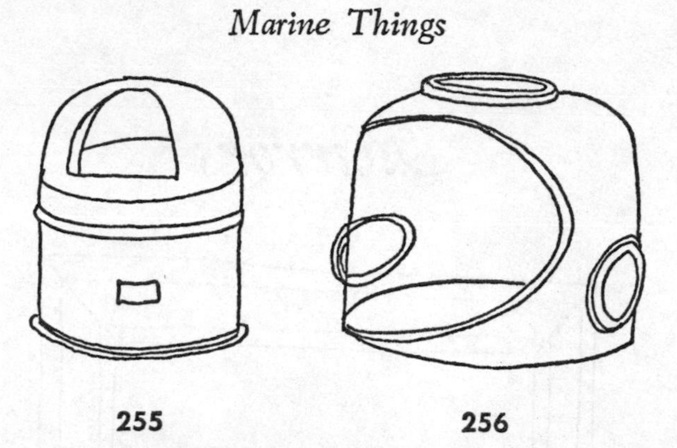

255 **256**

255, 256 Binnacles or compass covers in brass for putting all sorts of things under. Around $35.

Mirrors

257 Mirror frames of mahogany veneer on pine, with the austere lines of the American Empire style, can date from 1815 to the Civil War. The commonest size is two and a half feet high or wide, depending on how you hang it. The front surface usually has what is called an ogee curve but sometimes is flat. These sell for $12 to $16 as is, and all you have to do is wipe them down with denatured alcohol to "refinish" them. However, ninety-eight percent of the ones that have come onto the market in the last thirty years were soaked in tanks of water to remove the veneer, then they were oiled or shellacked and sold as "Early American" pine. These are now selling for $18 to $22 for the two-and-a-half-foot size.

258 About two feet high, this mirror with reverse painting on glass is of the same era and construction as the preceding one. About $35, with veneer and picture intact.

259 From the late 1700s or the early 1800s a gilded frame and reverse painting on glass, about eighteen inches high. $55.

260 **261**

260, 261 Fancy mirrors like this were made to more or less "go with" your Hitchcock chairs. From the early and middle 1800s. Mostly black and gold. About $35 plain and $55 with reverse painting on glass.

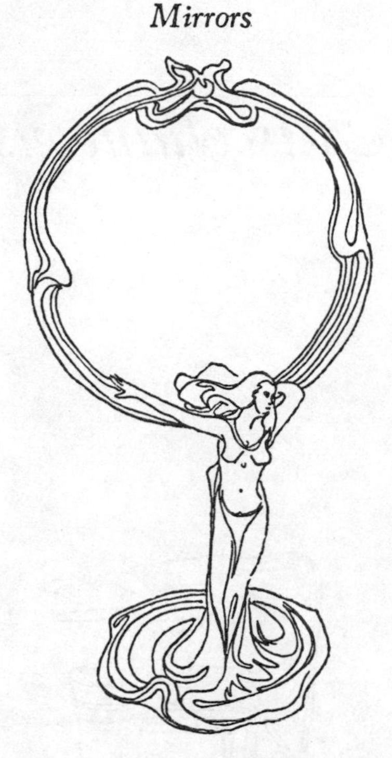

262 An art nouveau standing dressing-table mirror of cast metal, enameled white with antique glaze, $25.

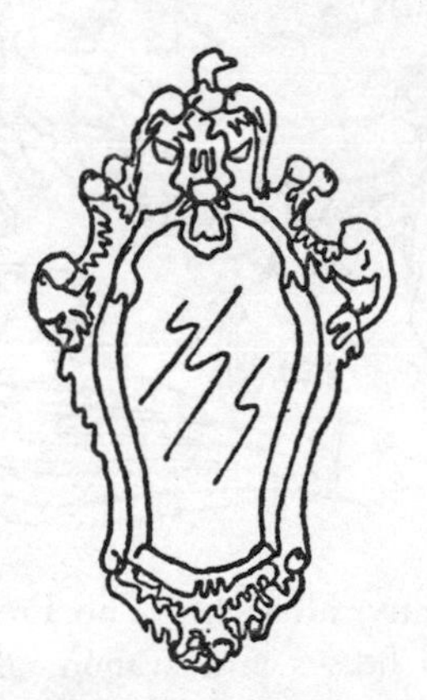

263 Ornately carved and gilded mirrors, about two feet high, very French-looking and probably imported from France sometime in the last hundred years, can be had for around $45.

Miscellaneous

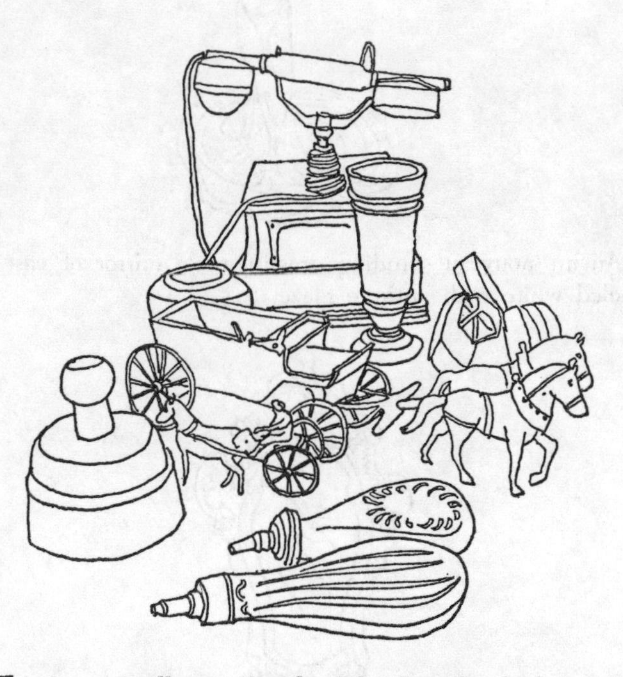

264 This is a miscellany, all right. The French telephone, $22.50. The cast-iron team of horses and wagon, about $50. Fire engines go to $65, but are being reproduced, so watch out. Tin horse and sulky, $14. Powder flasks, $8. Round object on left is a wooden butter press, $6.

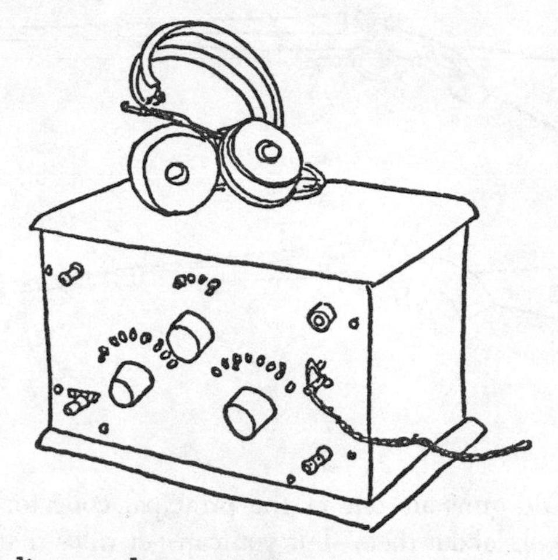

265 Early radios are about as young an antique as you can find, but they are fun, especially when they can be fixed up to work, or when new sets are hidden inside the old cases. Nobody is throwing them away anymore, and this one is worth $15. I suppose early television sets will be the next thing.

266 A collector's item and for use in interior decoration, early phonographs with brass horns run, depending on how big the horn is, from $65 to $125.

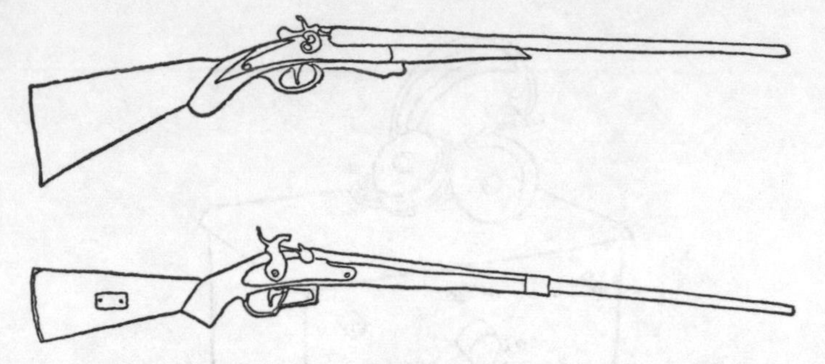

267, 268 Old guns are one of the principal collector's items—there are many books about them—but you can get rifles that aren't special but "just look old" for $15 to $25.

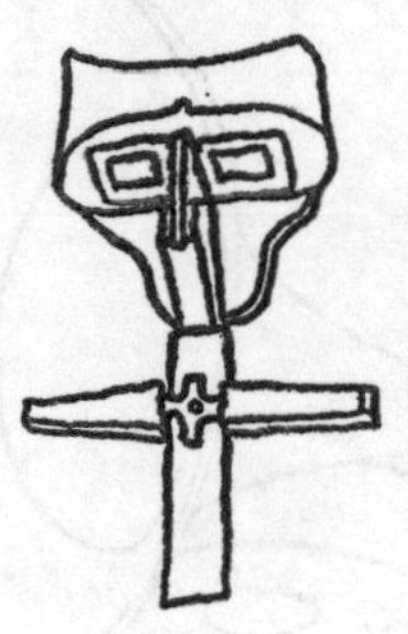

269 Stereoptical viewers were the Cinemascope of yesterday. Depending on the quality of the wood, from $6 to $15. The cards, five for $1.

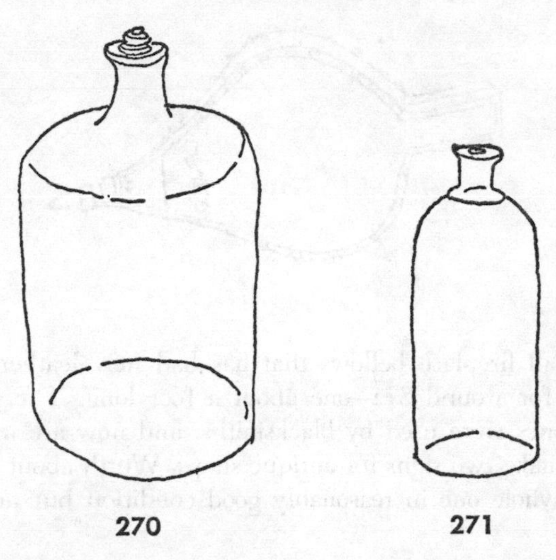

270 Early five-gallon water bottles of greenish glass with bubbles in it are plentiful from the early 1900s—about $7 each.

271 Everybody is collecting bottles these days, even digging around in old dumps. But the average pint to quart bottle with a ground-glass stopper is worth only $2. The ones with black and gold glass labels that come from old drugstores run around $5 to $10, depending on how intriguing the name of the drug is on the label.

272 Bell jars are still being made and sold to the antique trade. Dealers pay from $1.50 for one four inches high to $7 for one eighteen inches high.

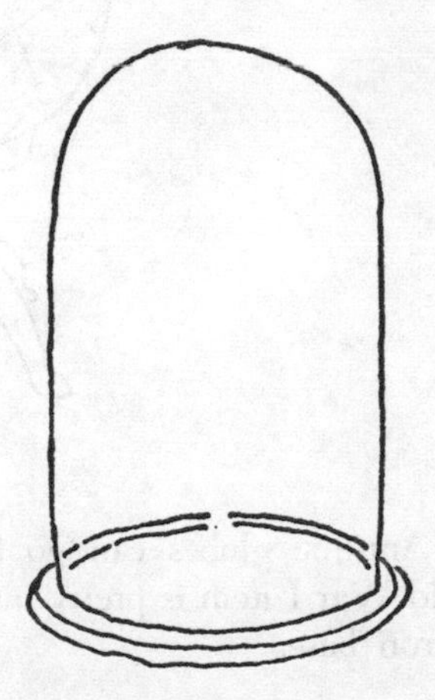

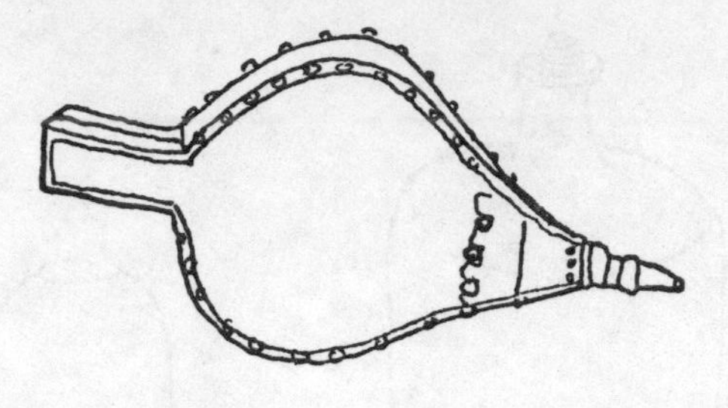

273 A small fireplace bellows that has had new leather put on it should go for around $12—one about a foot long. The giant four-foot-long ones were used by blacksmiths, and now are usually split in half to make two signs for antique shops. Worth about $20 a side, $50 for a whole one in reasonably good condition but not restored.

274 Antique globes can go for all kinds of prices, but this pre-World War I item is pretty interesting for $25—stand two feet high, cast-iron base.

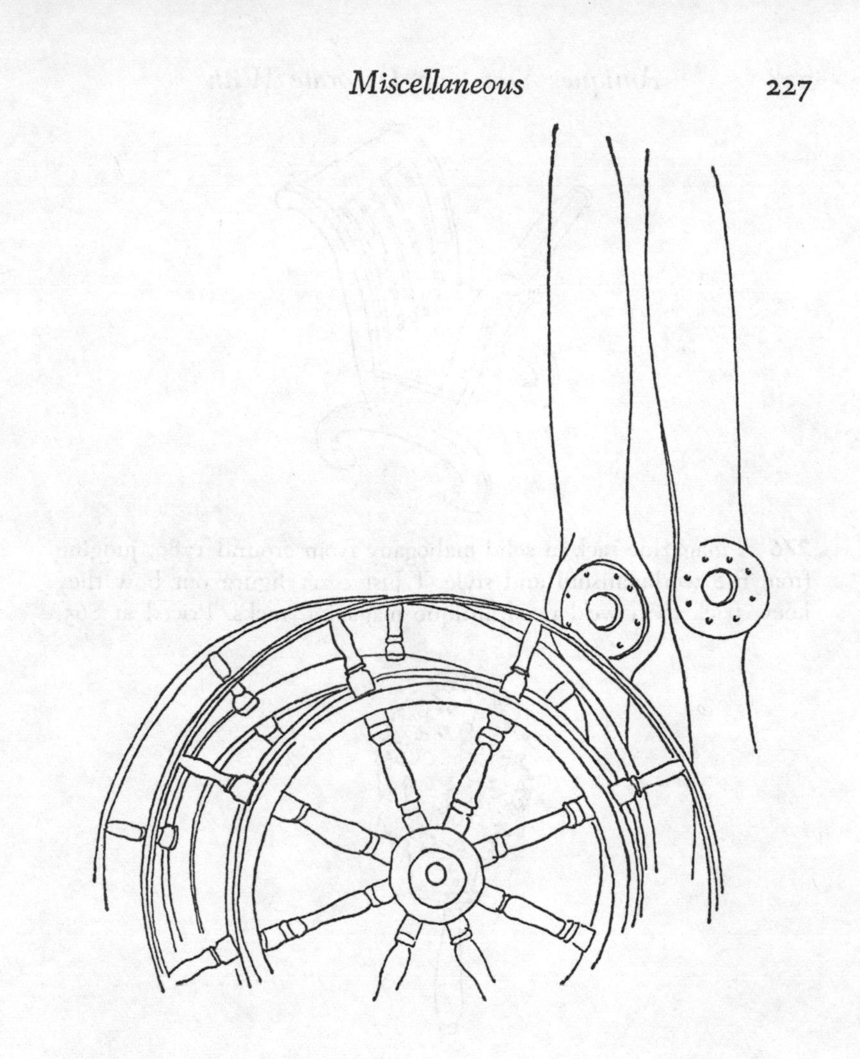

275 Wheels from river boats in good condition or refinished are around $125, the early wooden propellers, $85.

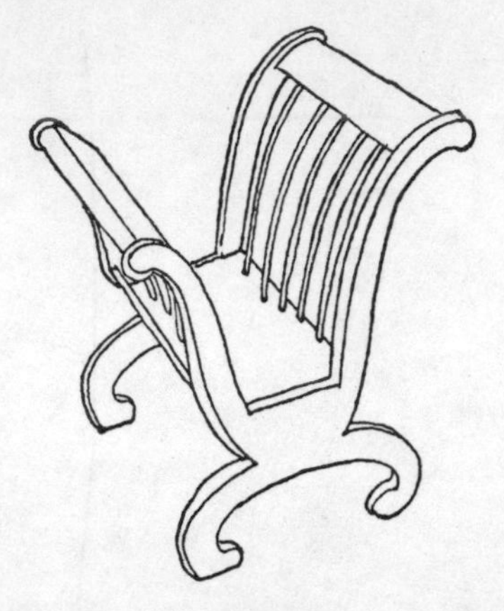

276 A magazine rack in solid mahogany from around 1780, judging from the workmanship and style. I just can't figure out how they knew back then we'd need antique magazine racks. Priced at $65.

277 From the late 1700s, this device was designed to keep the glare of the fire out of your eyes. That's a bowl of flowers painted on the shade at top, which raises and lowers about ten inches by means of a rachet on the back. Finely made and a good painting—$160.

278 279

278 Whenever old mansions are torn down, all kinds of architectural bric-a-brac comes on the market. The longest dimension of this piece is ten inches, and if you can think of something to do with it, it's yours for $3.

279 Without one of these on your house, the fire company would stand there and watch it burn down. Widely reproduced in miniature, the real ones were eight to ten inches wide, and can be had for $25 to $35.

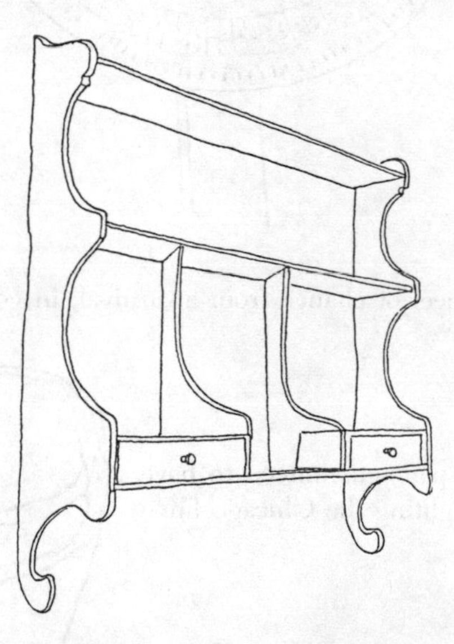

280 It seems that if you didn't have anything else to do between 1700 and 1900, you made the little woman some shelves. These *look*

very early, of thin pine, but it is impossible to date a hand-made piece like this within a hundred years without going to a laboratory. A good value at $35.

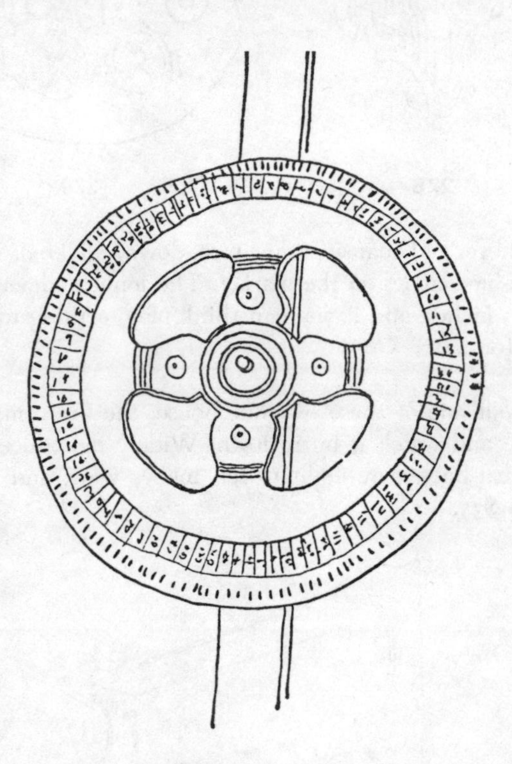

281 An old wheel of chance from a carnival, in good working condition—$25.

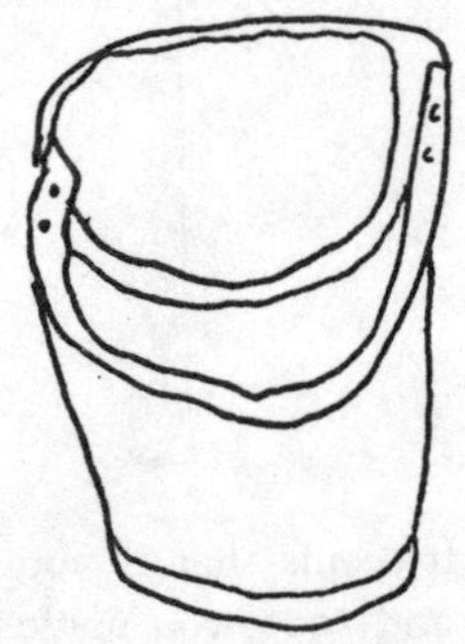

282 A leather pail—guaranteed to have been used in fighting the Chicago fire—$11.50.

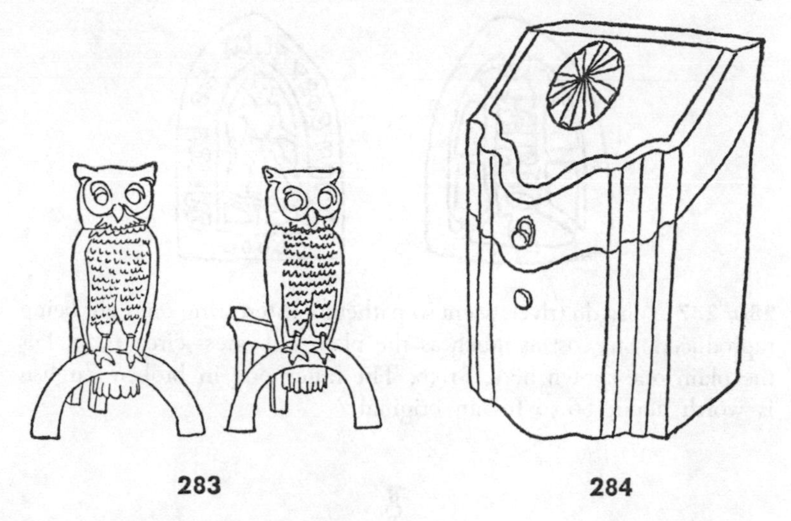

283 284

283 A pair of cast-iron owl-type andirons, $22. About $45 in brass.

284 A Hepplewhite knife box for your sideboard—$165. (How miscellaneous can we get?)

285 This miscellaneous? It's a 1933 Pontiac. What a buy for your game room at $850.

286, 287 Why do trivets seem so pathetic? Interesting ones are being reproduced, but cost as much as the plain old ones—circa 1900. For the plain one shown here, $1.50. The fancy one in broken English is worth about $6.50 for an original.

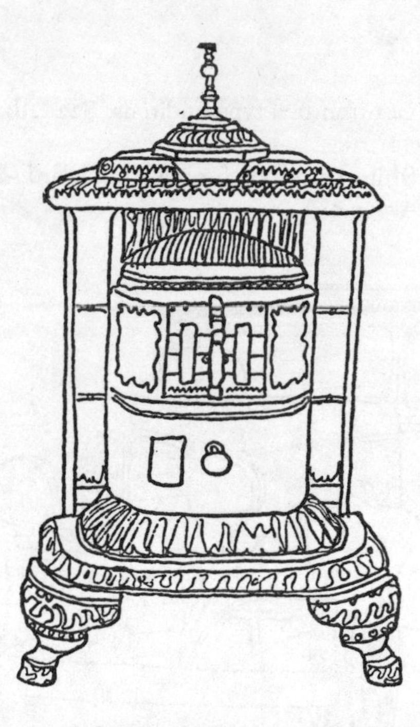

288 Cast-iron stoves of the Franklin type can be had all around New England for $40 to $65. The real thing is $100 to $115, which isn't any more than the exact copies of it that are being made and sold widely.

289 Everybody needs a couple of antique dolls in an old wooden box lying around for atmosphere. Of course, dolls are a big thing with collectors, and can go to fantastic prices. But ones that look real old—with bisque heads and arms attached to stuffed bodies—and are, say, ten inches tall can be had for around $35.

290 An early carbide lamp of tin painted black with gold stripes, $12.

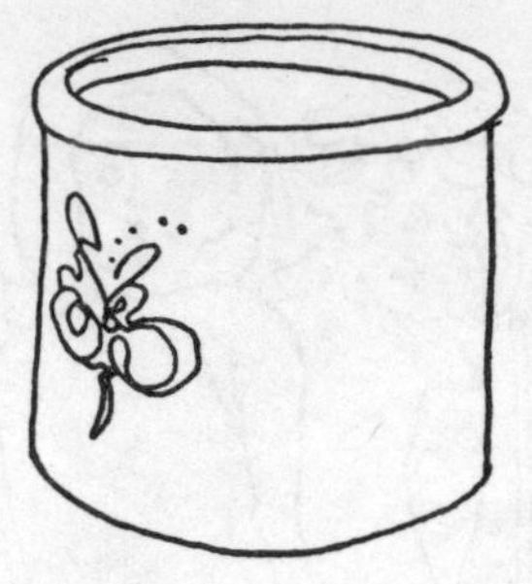

291, 292, 293 If it bears the mark or one of the designs of one of the five potteries that made Bennington ware, crockery like this runs in the \$30 to \$40 class, but there is a lot of the same kind of thing in the \$5 to \$10 class if you are not real fussy about brand names.

294 With a face that would stop a clock, this cast-iron bulldog only stops doors. Eight inches high, \$12.

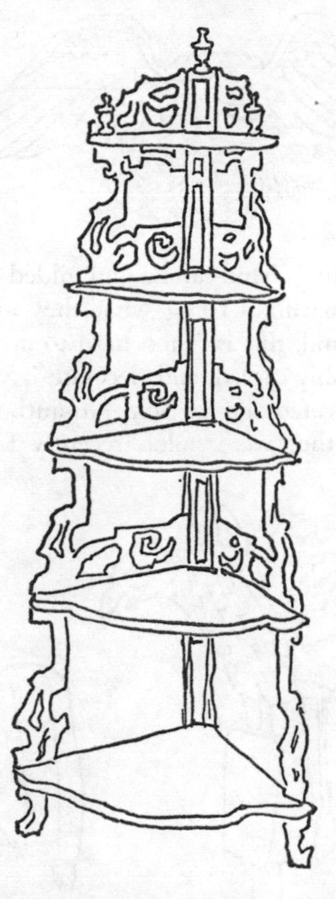

295 This is so miscellaneous that nobody ever figured out a name for it—it is called simply a "what-not." About five to six feet high, it stands in a corner, is usually made of oak—post 1900—and is something of a fad these days. That's why it costs from $45 to $55.

296 Everybody wants a hand-carved and gilded eagle from way back in 1776. Carving machines being what they are, and in operation all over New England, this isn't too hard to arrange. You can get a thirty-inch one, freshly carved, and decorate it yourself for $16, or a plastered and gold-leafed one for $65. No authentic old ones are on the market unless they were stolen recently from a museum.

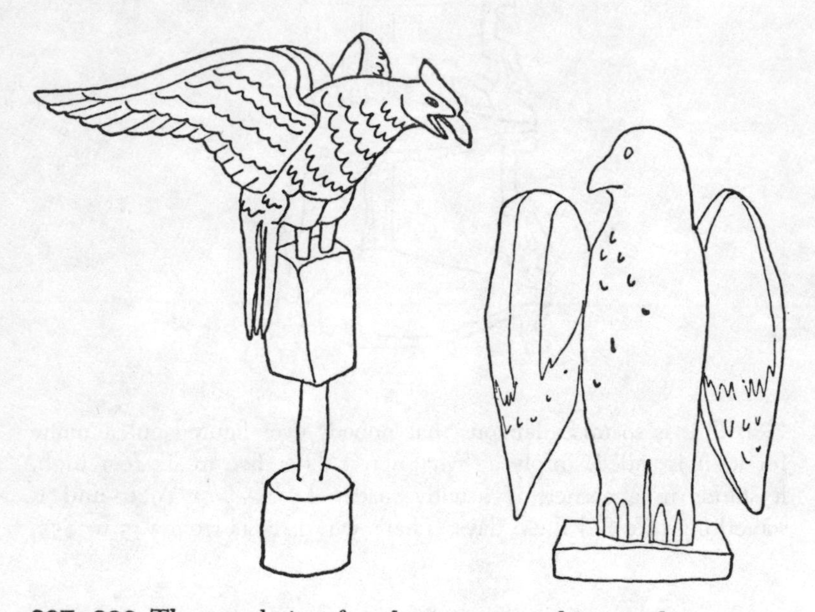

297, 298 The popularity of eagles is no new thing in this country, thus primitive eagles like these are not too hard to find. Prices are very irregular, and you can make many a "steal," as dealers strangely enough have little feeling for primitive art. The one standing on a post had a twenty-five-inch wingspread, and was priced in a shop at $65. The cruder one was $15. And I think both were worth much more.

299 A tisket, a tasket, and many an old basket eighteen to twenty-four inches long will go for only $2.

Secretaries

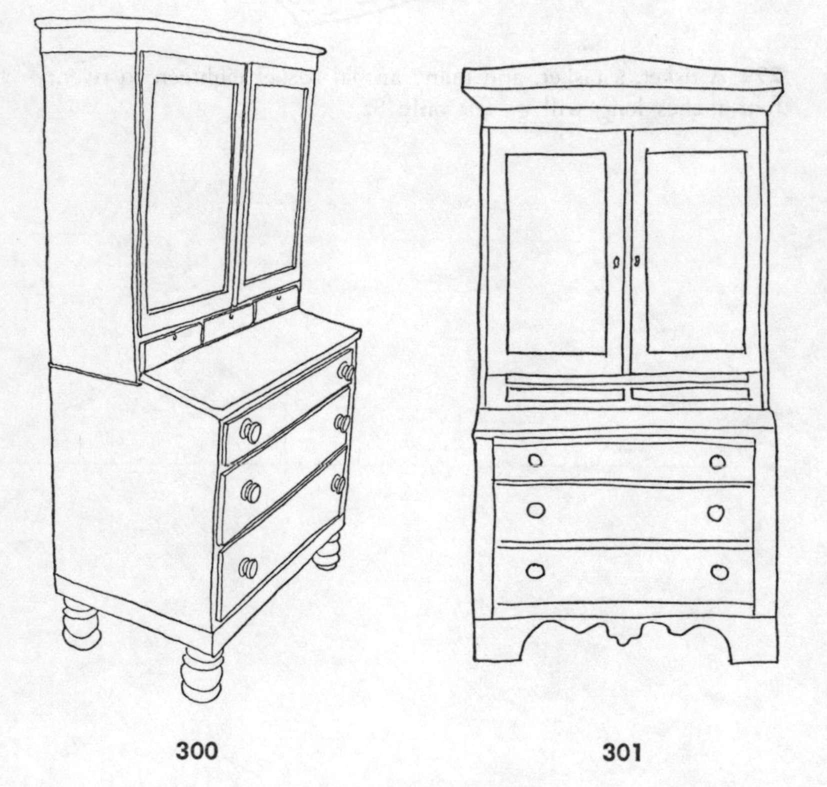

300 301

300, 301, 302 The secretaries that are still on the market are only those of the Empire period. There weren't many made in the earlier styles and the ones that were made are in museums or mansions. These three are of typical Empire construction, good Honduras mahogany on pine, and are in the $300 to $350 class. Empire is still a bargain, but don't count on this going on forever.

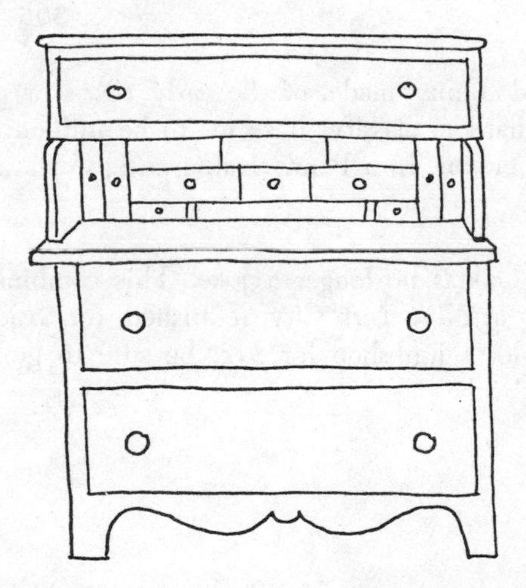

303 When the writing surface of this piece folds up and you push it in, the piece looks like a chest of drawers. The name is "butler's desk." About $225, restored and refinished.

304

305

304 Pine and country-made, of the early 1800s or possibly before, this piece is hard to classify. It seems to be influenced by Hepplewhite and Sheraton. In a Pennsylvania antique show it was priced at $650.

305 Golden Oak is no longer a joke. This combination desk and bookcase sells in New York City, refinished, for $140, so if you see one in your local junkshop for $15, be sure to grab it.

Shades

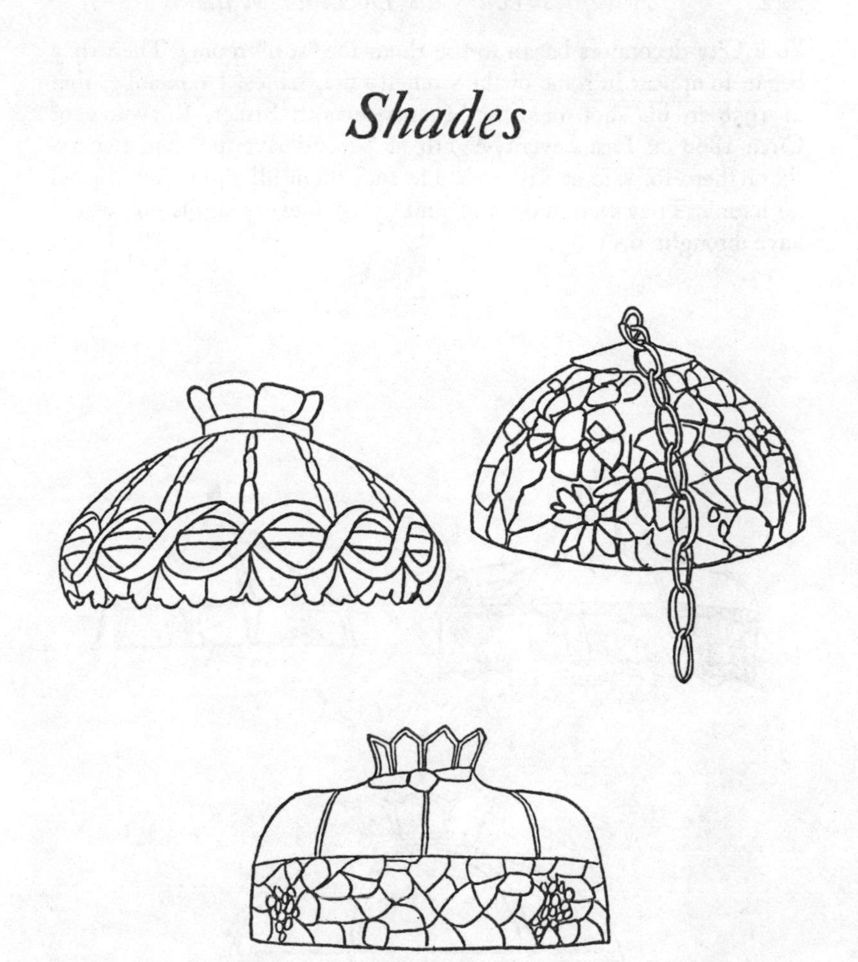

306, 307, 308 The biggest Cinderella story in the history of American antiques is that of the leaded-glass shades of the early 1900s that used to hang over just about everybody's dining-room table. No interest was shown in them at all until about 1955–56, when New

York City decorators began to use them for "fun" rooms. Then they began to appear in some of the women's magazines. I remember that in 1958 in his shop on East Seventy-seventh Street, Roy—now of Circa 1890 on East Seventy-eighth at Second Avenue—had twenty-six of them for sale at $35 each. He sold them all right, but wished he hadn't. They were nice ones, and by 1966 every single one would have brought over $300.

309, 310, 311 When the price of the leaded-glass hanging shades began to skyrocket, even these ugly things made of pieces of glass fitted into metal frames and behind designs in metal strips came onto the market. They now run $35 to $65. Will they go up spectacularly too? My guess is no, because they don't have the real beauty that the leaded glass ones do.

Statues

312 313

312 Victorian, cast in concrete, three feet high, of great charm for a garden—$150.

313 From the 1920s and for your game room—$2 apiece for the hats, and $12 for madam, who is very waxy.

314 Six feet tall, a thin lead shell filled with concrete, this thing weighs a ton, but it is yours for $65.

315 Twenty inches high and solid plaster, about fifty to sixty years old, this piece of storytelling statuary sells for $15. Those of the same breed made by the factory of John Rogers average $35, go back to the 1860s.

316 Plaster, twenty-four inches high, this bust of the Great Emancipator has neither signature nor manufacturer's mark. Age undetermined, price $22.

317 Hiawatha here is a product of the rather dull year of 1907. Of cast plaster and an assembly-line paint job, he is valued at $27.

Tables—Dining Size

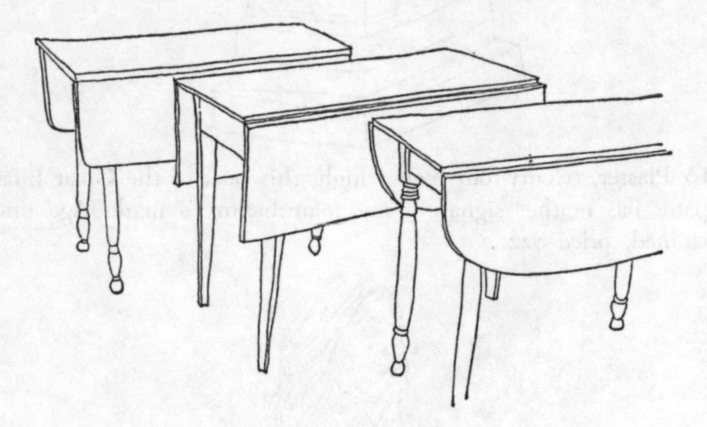

318 From around 1780 to 1850, drop-leaf tables were made as a staple piece of American furniture, the vast majority of them only hinting at the official styles prevalent in the cities. However, the tapered square legs–derivative of Hepplewhite–indicate that a table was made early in this stretch of years. The one shown here in the middle is an example.

The woods used were mainly cherry, maple, birch, and mahogany. In these woods they are about $90 to $100. If the maple is figured –curly, tiger, or bird's-eye–add another $25. For the square, tapered legs, add $20. In pine or poplar the price drops to around $50.

319 The round table was a classic of the Hepplewhite style and has been widely reproduced, or you might say continuously made since the late 1700s. Priced $350 to $750 depending on the age, condition, and quality of the inlay work, if any.

320 A Pembroke or breakfast table in solid mahogany, dating from before 1880. Priced at $350.

321 A fine example of a Sheraton drop-leaf table in solid mahogany with beautifully carved legs, this model is valued at around $225.

322 Ingenuity was never lacking. In this model, when the single leaf is raised, the whole top swivels around ninety degrees. Solid cherry of the early 1800s, $165.

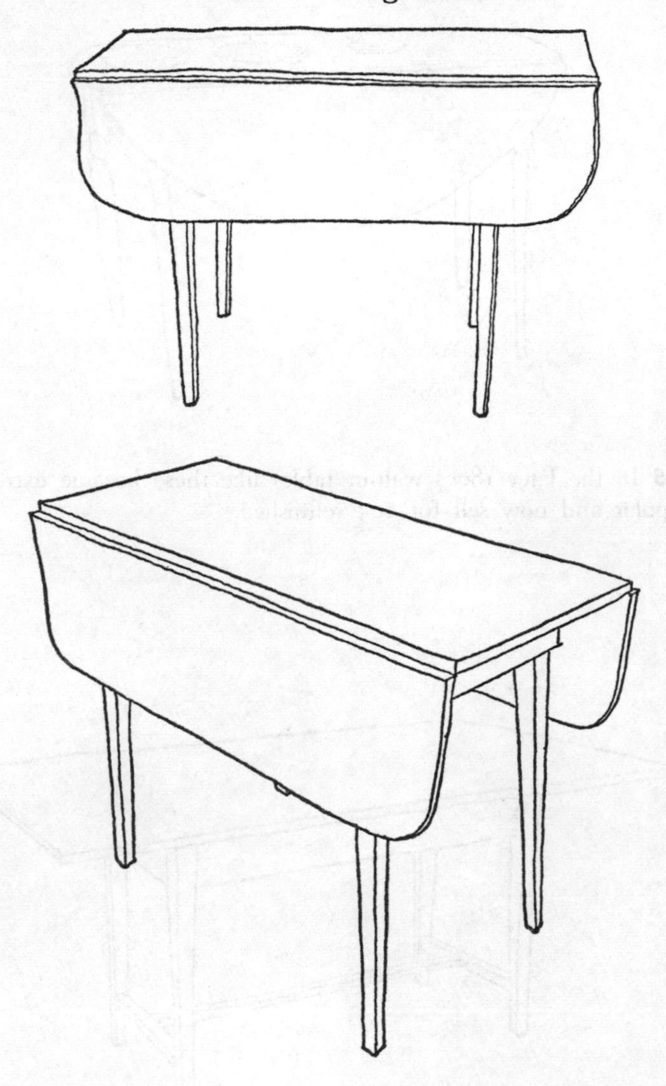

323, 324 Two simple pine tables that have had the corners of their leaves rounded to make them look better (?), and new square legs nailed inside the frames. Complete fakes, but the pine looks nice stained antique brown and shellacked—$35 to $45.

325 In the later 1800s walnut tables like these became extremely popular and now sell for $65 refinished.

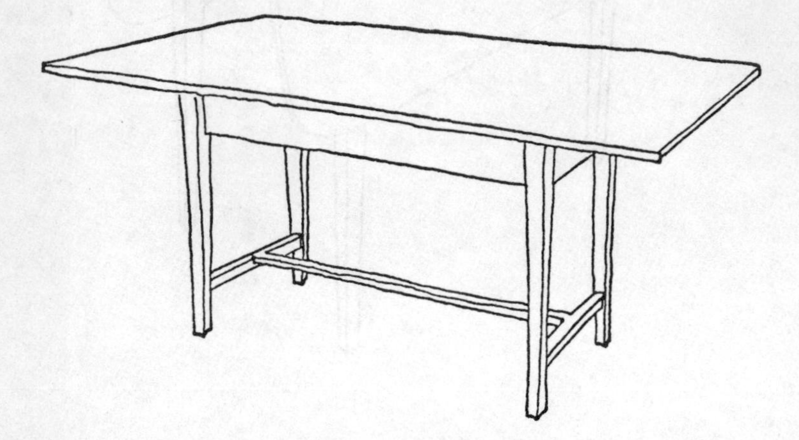

326 A rustic H-stretcher table of pine from around 1800 will sell for $175. With full stretchers—that is the tavern table—the price for the cheapest would be $250.

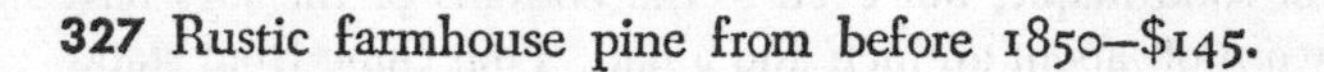

327 Rustic farmhouse pine from before 1850—$145.

328 Golden Oak, post 1910. In New York City, $165.

329 Only twenty-four inches across the top, this early 1700s butterfly table is of solid maple, but even so the bottoms of the legs have rotted and worn off about an inch and a half. That came from standing around on dirt floors. A bargain at $165.

330 An excellent example of a small tavern table of the mid-1700s, which are hard to find. This one was in walnut, but cherry, maple, pine were used. Original Chippendale pull, bottoms of legs restored, $250.

331 A full-stretcher or tavern table in pine from about 1800, and in remarkably good condition for one of these tables. Well worth $175.

332 Very rustic and very worn, this pine H-stretcher in the rough and falling apart goes even in this condition for $90.

333 A solid mahogany serving table from about 1840, about $85.

334 Those aren't Hepplewhite legs, they are just plain ones. This is a simple pine work table made not much before 1900, but stained and refinished it fools a lot of people. Actually worth around $45.

Tables—Small

335 Martha Washington is supposed to have been fond of these small Sheratonish tables. From the early 1800s in solid mahogany, this one goes for around $145.

336 A two-drawer bedside table in maple—$75. With only one drawer, it would be $60.

337 In the late 1800s pine bedside tables like this with the drawer on top, or bottom, as shown here, were everywhere. Refinished, $32.

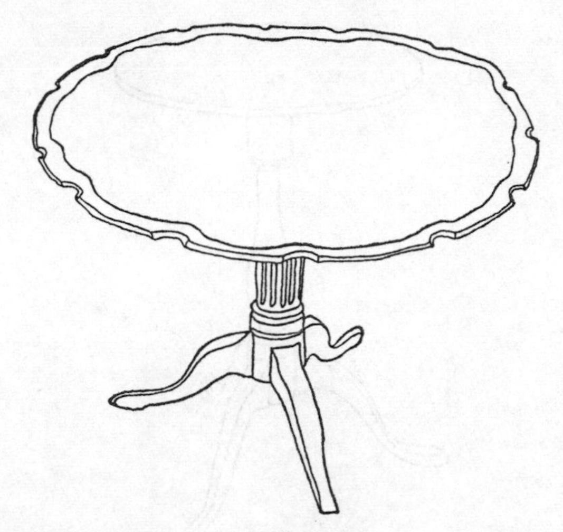

338 Chippendale pie-crust table in mahogany with matched mahogany veneers, about three feet across, $375.

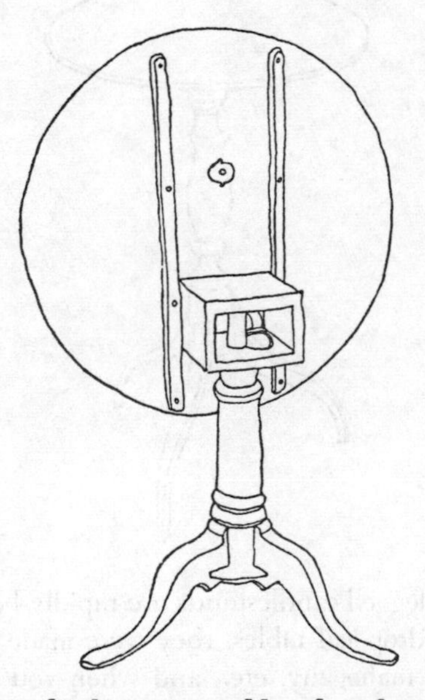

339 A more or less birdcage-top table, though usually the device that allows the top to tilt as well as turn looks more like a cage. In cherry, $165. Other hard woods were used.

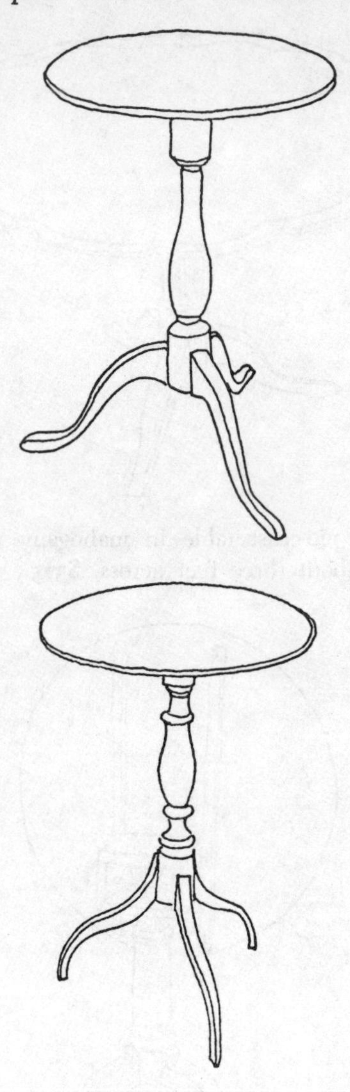

340, 341 Three-legged candlestands are rapidly being bought off the market. Like the drop-leaf tables, they were made from 1775 to 1850 of maple, cherry, mahogany, etc., and when you can find one, they are now as high as $85, which is a lot for such a small amount of table. However, reproductions, forgeries, and fakes will soon fill the vacuum, I am sure.

342 A fragile, lovely little Hepplewhite side table, authentic, mahogany—$125.

343 A very rare homemade back-porch table about two feet high. These were for hunching over and peeling potatoes or resting an ice-cream freezer on while you cranked it. Genuine pine, refinished $25.

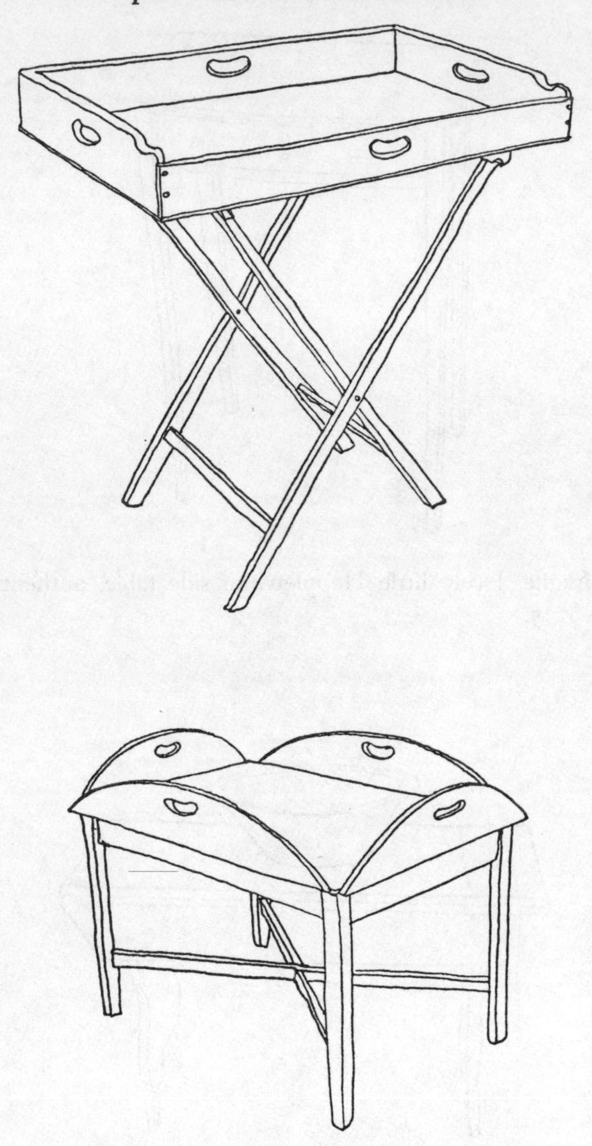

344, 345 Butler's trays high and low of solid mahogany. From the first half of the 1800s. High $85, low $145.

346 Princess of the late Victoriana—the post Civil War or Renaissance period—is the marble-top table. Worth about $20 in 1950, $165 today. Top, here, is about three feet across. The wood is walnut.

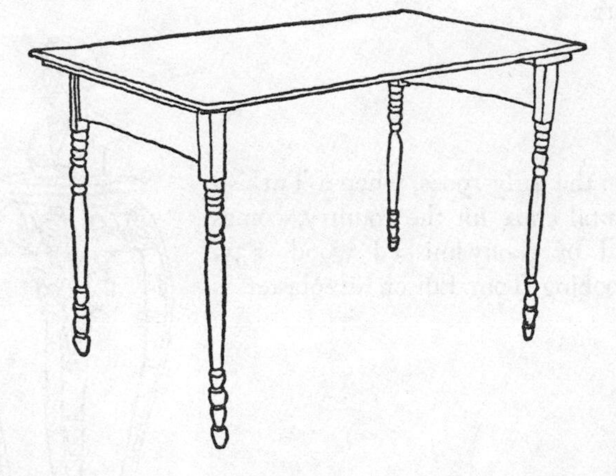

347 From around 1910 comes this sewing table of thin pieces of oak that is as firm and steady today as the day it was made. Refinished, $14 in the country. No telling what they will bring when they get to New York City.

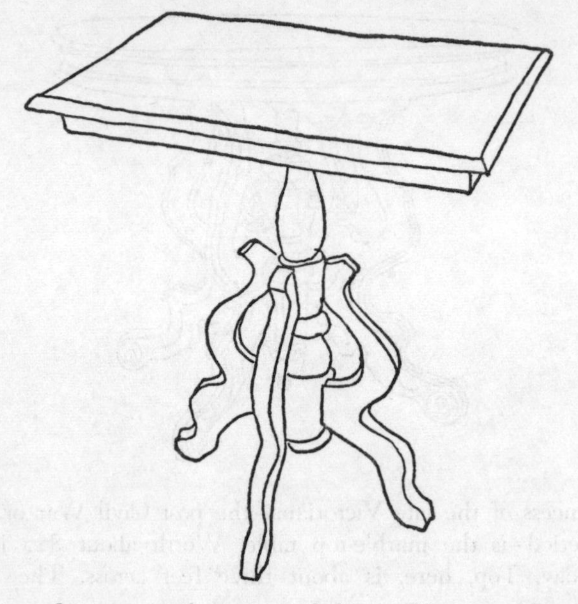

348 This is the poor-man's version of the marble-topped Renaissance style of the late 1800s. All pine, false-grained to what was probably supposed to look like walnut; usually flowers on the top. In the rough, $12.

349 From the early 1900s, when a Turkish and Oriental craze hit the country, comes this stand of ebony-finished wood, $35. Lonely looking Tom Edison in plaster is $12.

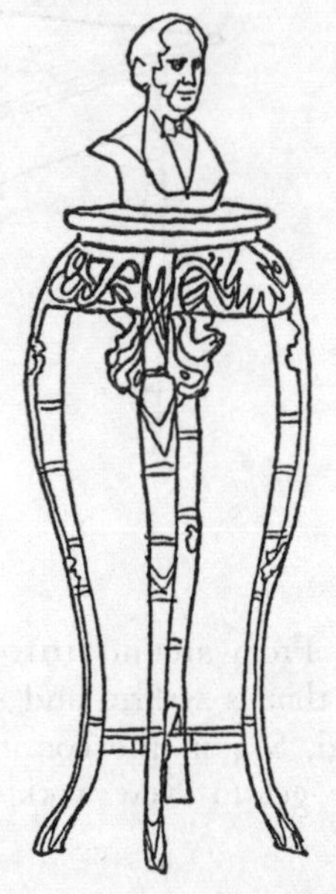

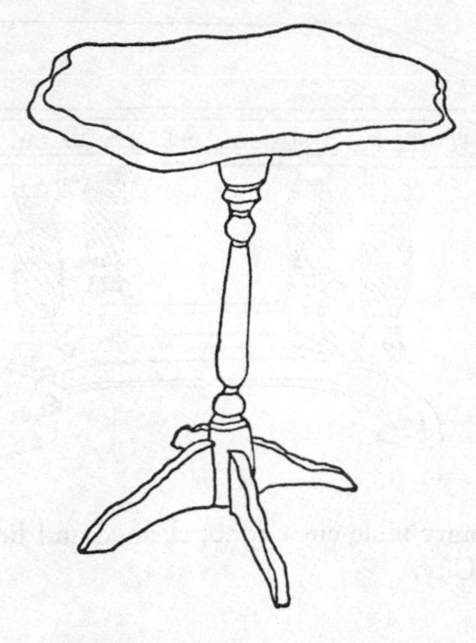

350 False graining on pine from just before 1900, this not very antique stand goes for $7 as found.

351 Another standard item of the American antique shoppe! Always of pine, from the late 1800s and early 1900s, these washstands are now up to $45 refinished.

352 An oak library table circa 1900, cleaned and linseed-oiled, $125 in New York City.

353 Darkly stained oak of the Mission period, circa 1915, refinished —$65 in New York City.

Tinware

354 Toleware—such as this fourteen-inch-tall coffee pot—is made of sheet iron and painted. The base color is usually black, but can be a simple red, yellow, or blue. Brushstroke decorations in the Swiss peasant manner. Dates from 1820 to 1880. With the original decoration in mint condition, you would have to hold an auction to determine the value of any given piece, but a coffee pot like this with about half the decoration remaining sells for $35; without enough decoration left to preserve, $20—in which case you sand it smooth and redecorate it.

355 Ten inches long, this piece of tole is called a document box, and *everybody* must have had one. With decoration excellent, $45; worth preserving, $25; ruined, $12.

356 Decorated tole trays are usually about two feet long. They are priced by the condition of the decoration: excellent condition, $65; enough decoration to be worth preserving, $35; decoration ruined, $10. And it goes without saying that the redecoration that is done could often pass for the original—and does!

357 Only six inches long, possibly a jewel or trinket box, this little toleware gem is valued in fair condition at $14.

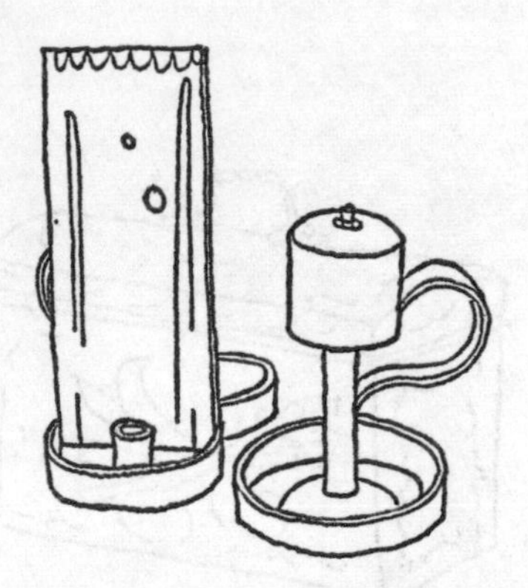

358 Tinware is the same sheet iron used in tole, but it was dipped in tin to give it a rust-proof coating. Lighting devices like this are from the first half of the 1800s, were handmade by the local tinsmith. Candleholder and reflector $14, whale-oil lamp $12.

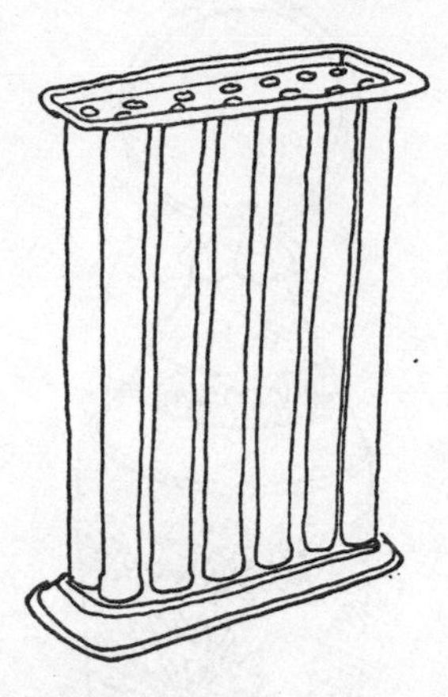

359 One of the most popular antiques ever invented! Even if they do date from 1850 to 1900. Early candles were hand-dipped and some farmers still made candles even after the new-fangled kerosene lamps came in. They are priced by the hole, and have skyrocketed in the last few years to $1.75 per. Will be up to $2 a hole any day now, making the best size to make a lamp out of—an eighteen-holer—worth $36. No wonder people have started making them up again to keep them busy during the long winter months while they wait for the tourists. (They charge the same price per hole, too.)

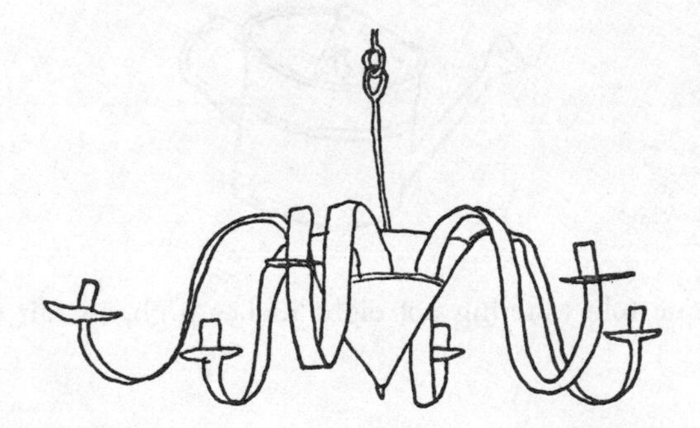

360 About thirty inches across, this tin chandelier for candles is authentic if fairly rusty. It can be had for $45, which is just about the price of one of the shiny new reproductions.

361 A lantern about eighteen inches high from the middle 1800s. Pierced sheet iron soldered together, $16. If it was ever tinned, none is left.

362 Antique tole watering pot eight inches high, in fair condition, $12.

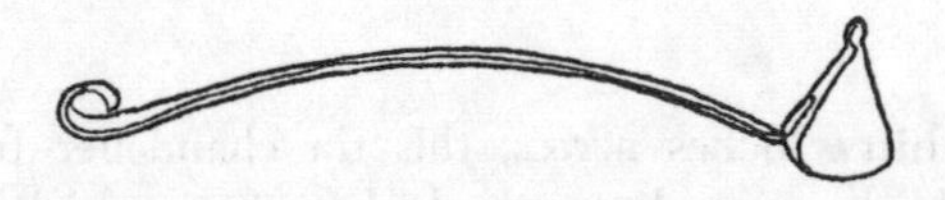

363 Tinned sheet-iron candle snuffer-outer, $6.50.

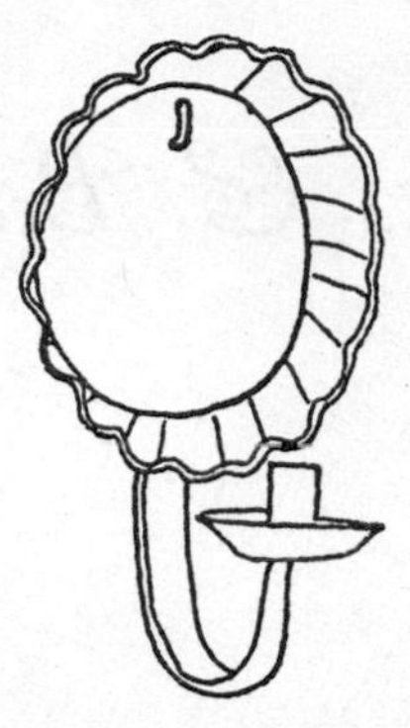

364 Tinned sheet-iron candle-holder and reflector that hangs on a wall. The rusty old ones and ones made last year both cost $8.50.

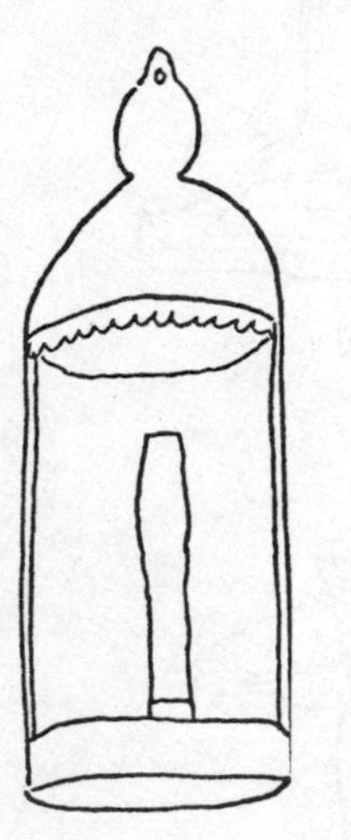

365 This one stopped the soot from collecting on your ceiling–$12.

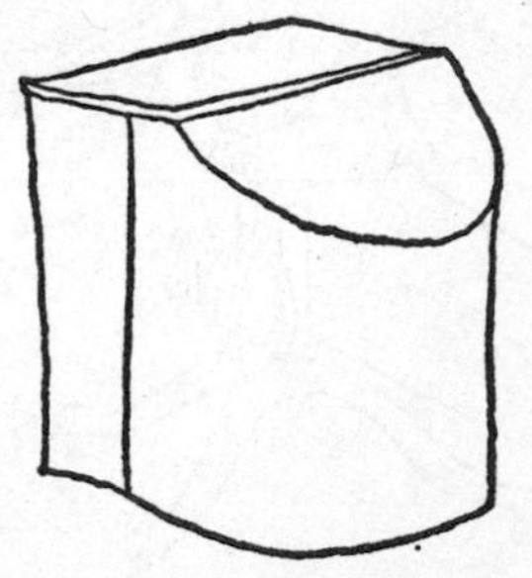

366 Tea canister from the late 1800s, about eight inches high, plain black, $8. Good commercial decorations on it, $12.

Toys & Banks

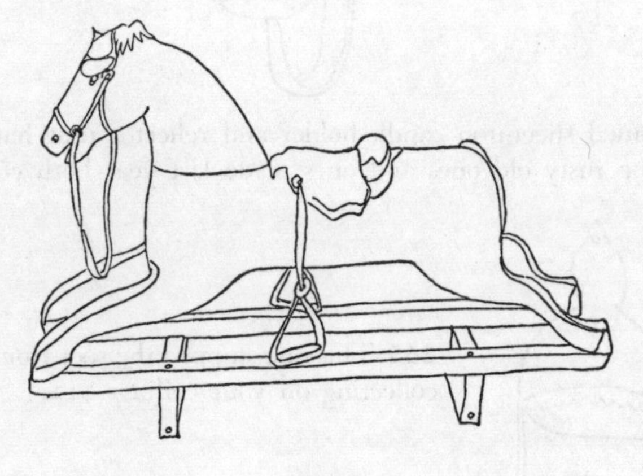

367

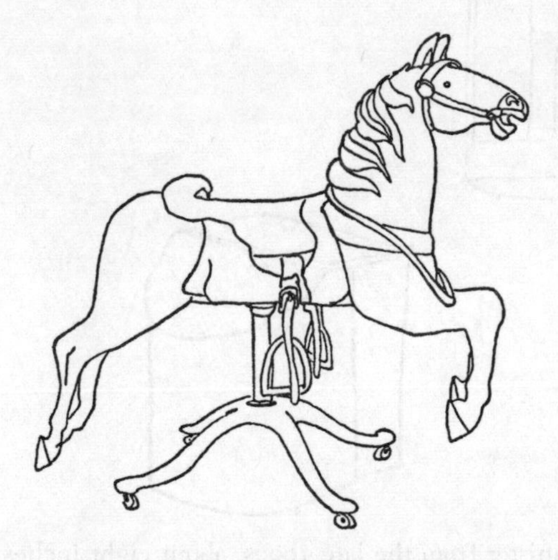

368

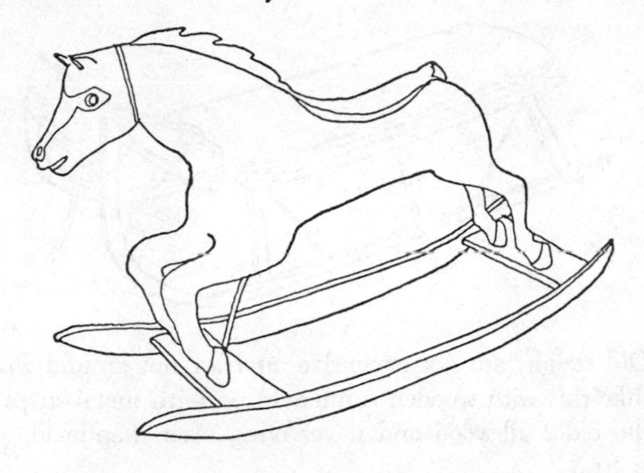

369

367, 368, 369 Rocking horses depend a lot on the condition of their surface for their market value. Each of these three has a different reason for being interesting, and all are worth about $125 each.

370 A pull toy, eighteen inches high and covered with cloth worn threadbare in places, $22.

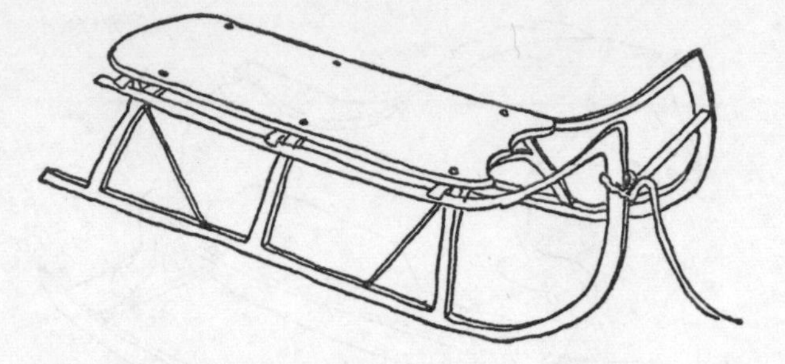

371 Old sleighs are not expensive, at least not around Providence. Ones like this with wooden runners faced with metal strips are only $9. The older all-wood and lower ones, often handmade, are only $12 to $14.

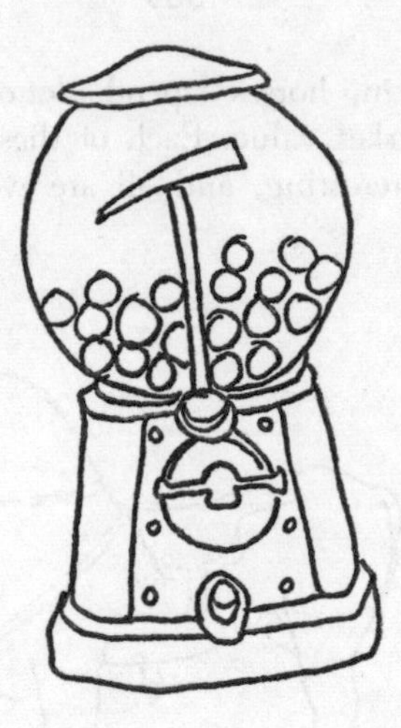

372 Gumball machines may not be old, but they are a lot of fun. In good working condition and full of fresh gumballs, a standard $16.

373, 374, 375, 376 Tin toys of the early 1900s have considerable charm and, like these, run from $7 to $17, depending on how interesting you and the dealer think they are. These are all under a foot high. A three-foot-high Ferris wheel might go up to $85.

373

374

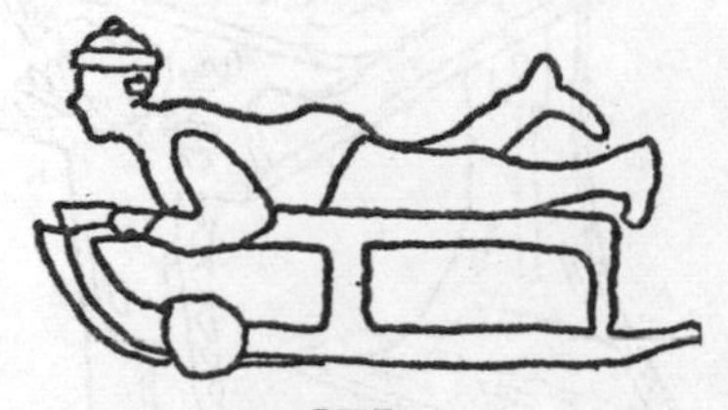

375

376

377 Cast-iron toys are earlier than the tin and go for much more. This oxen-and-log—about eighteen inches long—is $45. Fire engines and hook-and-ladders are $50 to $60.

378 School desks are a drug on the market at $7—unless decorated the way Peter Hunt did this one up in Orleans, Massachusetts, on Cape Cod. Then the price depends on the quality of the decoration.

379 Even this 1927 truck of far sturdier sheet metal than the tin toys will now bring $12.

380 In general, prices of toy action banks of cast iron have been driven sky-high by collectors' competitive bidding. There are a dozen items worth over $1000—one recently sold for almost $4000; a few of the commonest still sell for under $100. And forgery has become a big business, because it is easy: an original is used to make a sand mold. This is the way one company makes these banks, which it sells as "authentic reproductions" for $10 to $20. With a little clever aging . . . beware!

381 Weird things abound, and this is an all-wood tricycle priced and sold at $45.

382 Wagons with wooden wheels, sometimes metal-tired, are quite commonly available. With all wheels in good shape, one like this brings $25.

Trade Things

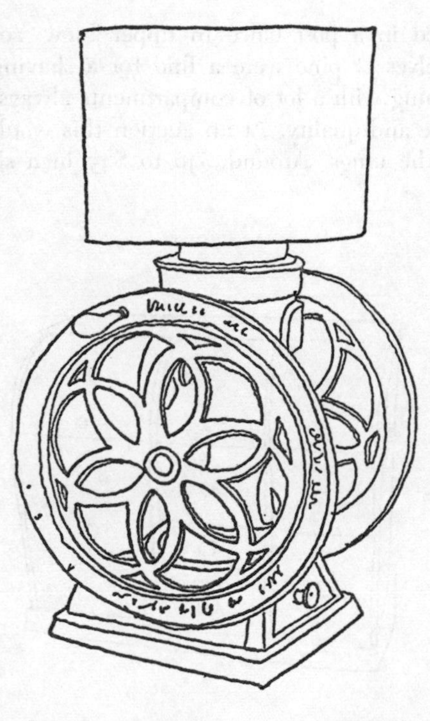

383 Coffee grinders from grocery stores invariably are made into lamps. It's something that just *has* to be done. Prices on these are standard and fairly stable. Two feet high $45, two and a half feet high $55, big three-footers $65. Made of cast iron and usually painted black, red, and gold, most of them can still grind coffee.

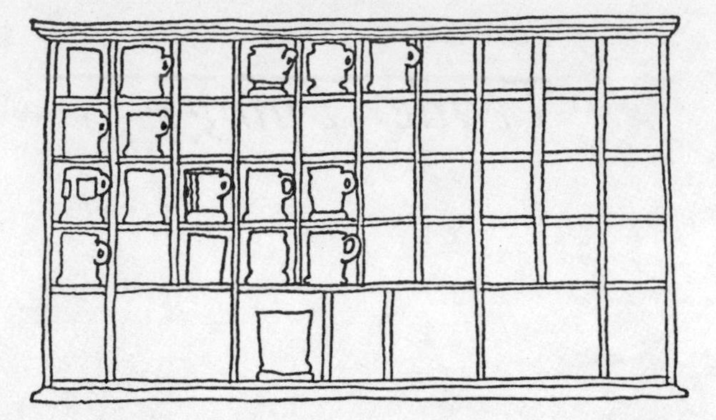

384 Once used in a post office in upper New York State, these homemade shelves of pine were a find for a shaving-mug collector I know. Anything with a lot of compartments always goes relatively high for its age and quality. At an auction this would bring $25 to $30—without the mugs. Around $40 to $45 in a shop.

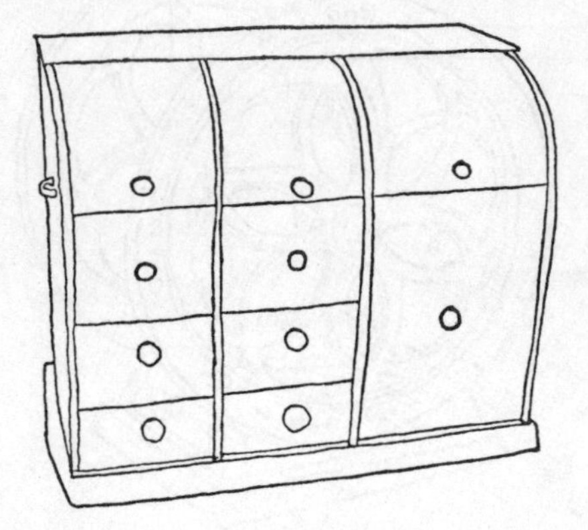

385 With the three top sections "rolled" back, the front sections pull out, except the one on the far right, which is a dummy in front of a deep bin. Anyway, the construction is a wooden frame with tin drawers, etc. As this thing, whatever it is, is three and a half feet high, dates pre-1900, it is worth around $65.

386 You can get into a lot of arguments about workbenches like this one of pine and some other hard, pale wood. It may even have come from an early factory. However, it makes an interesting piece for any informal room at $85, refinished.

387 Since this pine cabinet is fifty-six inches high and about three feet wide, one guess is that it held plans or patterns in the late 1800s. Cast-iron handles. Only $85, refinished.

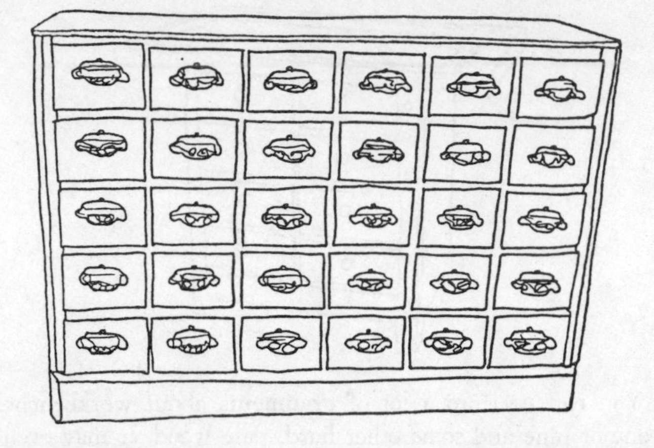

388 Even post-1900 factory things are desirable if they fill somebody's need to "get organized" by having enough drawers to put things in for once in their lives. This piece is three feet high, of solid oak, with cast-iron handles. In the rough, $35. Refinished, $65.

389 I forget whether Royal Society was ribbons or thread, but this item definitely came from a circa 1900 piece-goods store. All oak and in beautiful original finish and condition, only $32. It stands thirty inches high.

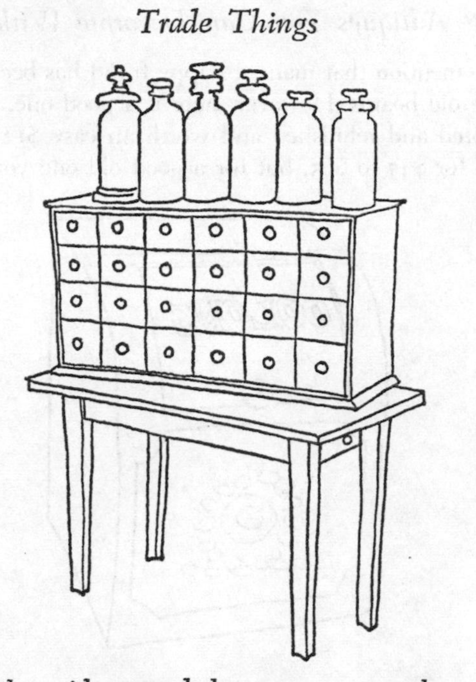

390 The bottles with ground-glass stoppers are about $2 for the quart size. The chest of small drawers, about twenty inches high, with white porcelain knobs and refinished pine is $48, or $2 a drawer. Good handworkmanship, though. The crude pine table, with dirty white paint on it, $6.

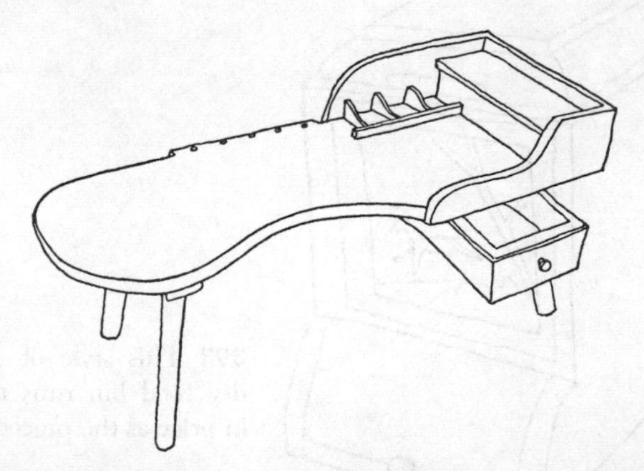

391 The reason there are so many cobbler's benches isn't because there were so many cobblers but because practically every farm had one. Not to mention that many a happy fraud has been put together out of some old boards. However, here is a good one, well-built and nicely restored and refinished and worth an easy $125. Crude ones can be had for $45 to $65, but for a good old one you have to pay.

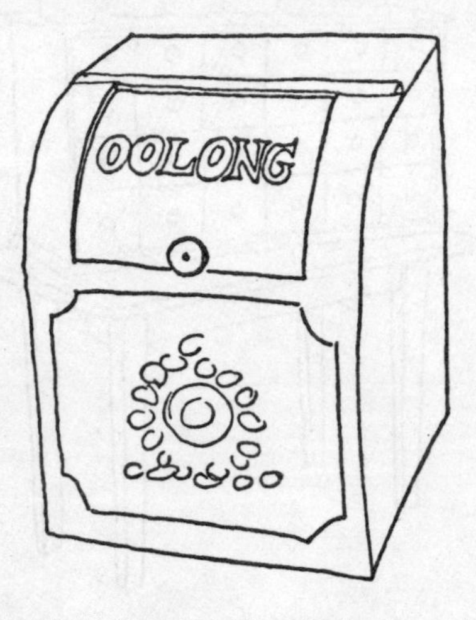

392 Standing around eighteen inches high, a tea bin like this with the decoration in very good condition is $35. Tinned sheet iron with black base paint on the outside.

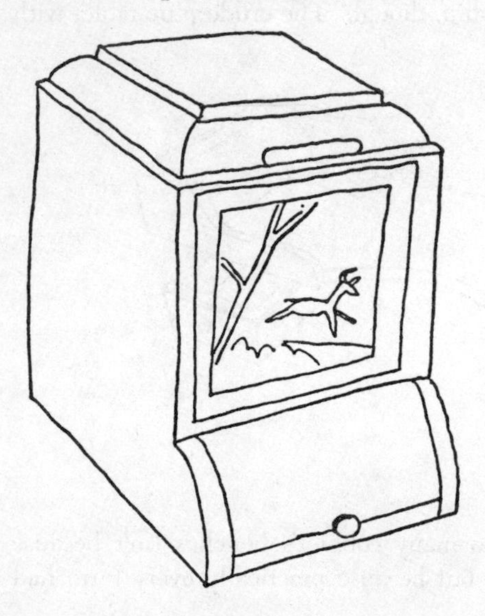

393 This style of caddy or dry food bin runs the same in price as the preceding one.

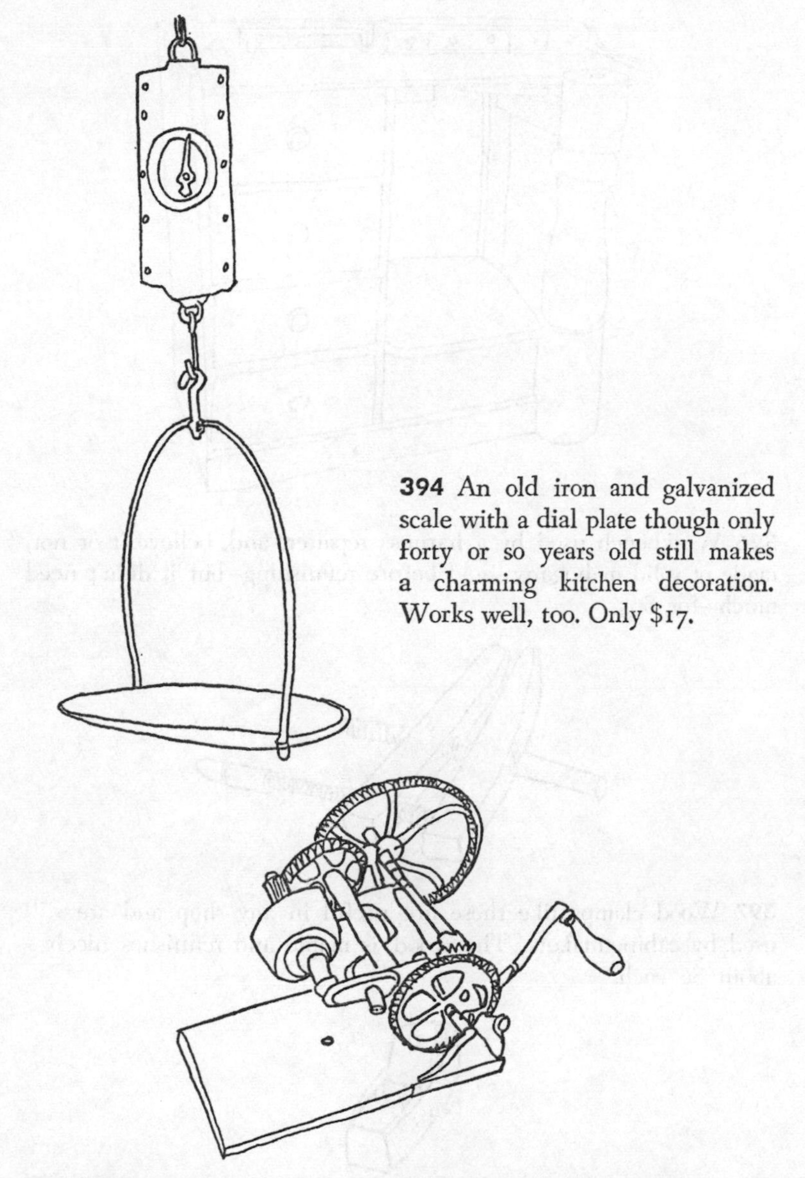

394 An old iron and galvanized scale with a dial plate though only forty or so years old still makes a charming kitchen decoration. Works well, too. Only $17.

395 Well, it isn't an apple-peeler, because we couldn't peel an apple with it. Nice piece of machinery, though. A lamp? Anyway, cast iron and only $11.

396 Workbench used by a harness repairer, and, believe it or not, made of solid mahogany. Sold before refinishing—but it didn't need much—for $65.

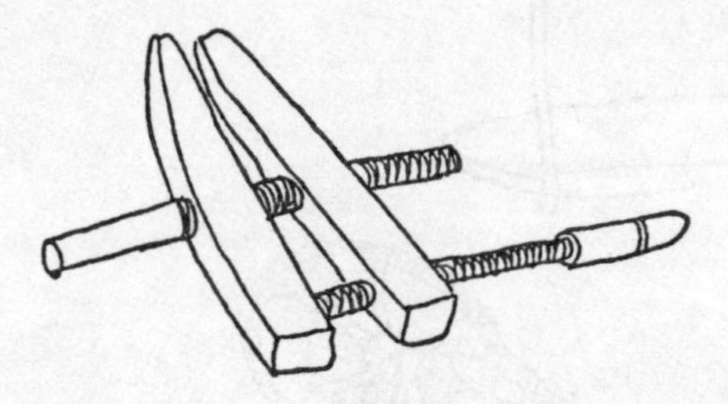

397 Wood clamps like these are useful in any shop and are still used by cabinetmakers. The wood is maple and refinishes nicely—about $6 each.

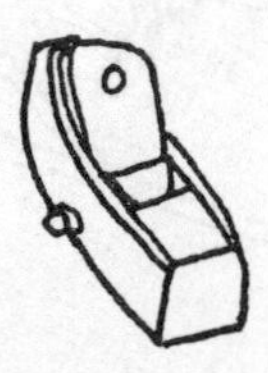

398 Block planes and molding planes about nine inches long usually go for $2 apiece. Maple.

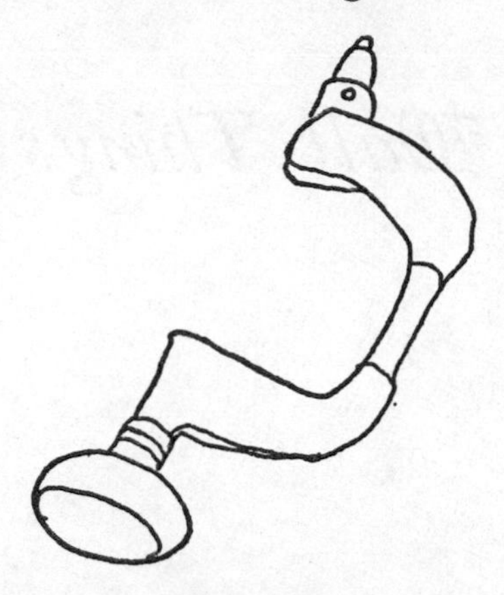

399 This brassbound bit of curly maple goes for $12. Looks good.

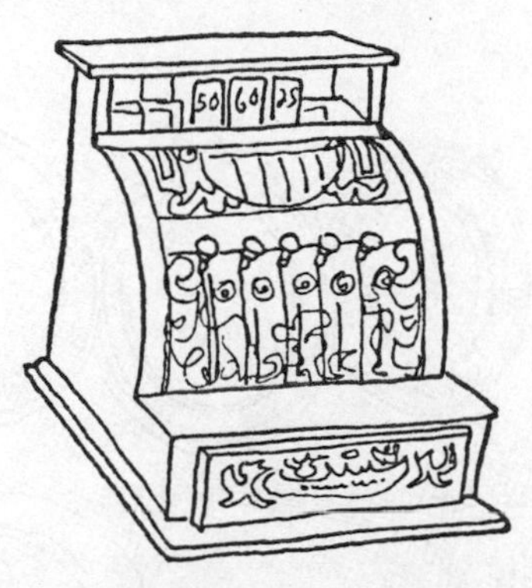

400 Stands eighteen inches high, cast iron painted silver, and is a knockout in any kitchen—$35 in working order.

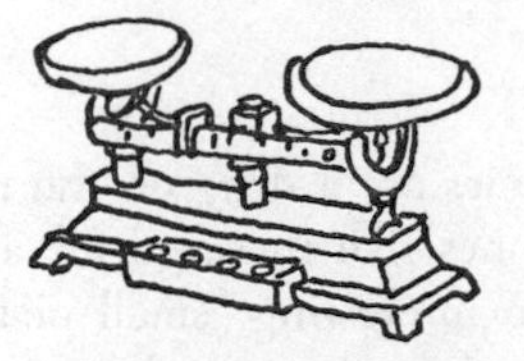

401 Another item for the swinging antique kitchen: scales that really work. About 1915, $17.

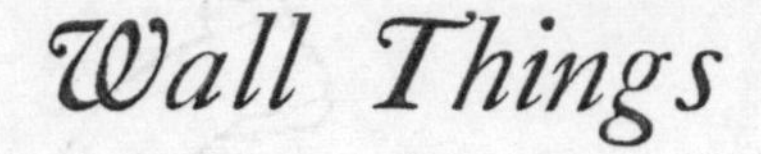

Wall Things

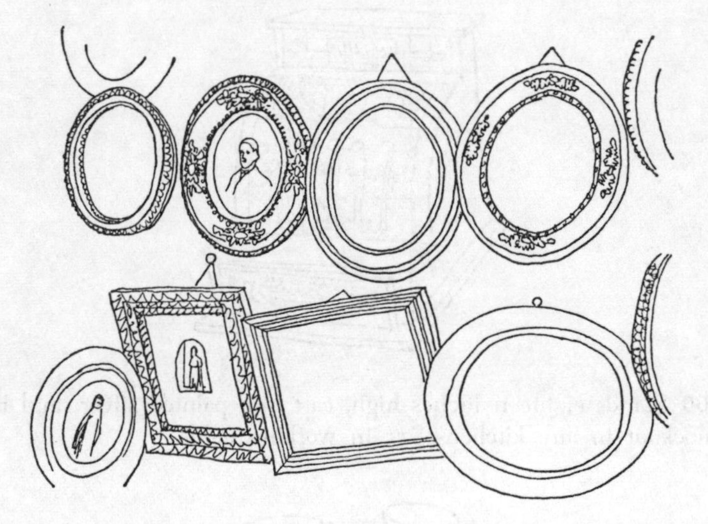

402 Big Victorian frames are a drug on the market and are hard to give away, but small ones like these go for a few dollars each, can be grouped to make an interesting "small picture" wall. Third from the left on the top row is a classic walnut frame with a white and gold inset, sometimes a black strip on the sides. These are about $8 or $9 apiece and often sold in pairs, which are not hard to find.

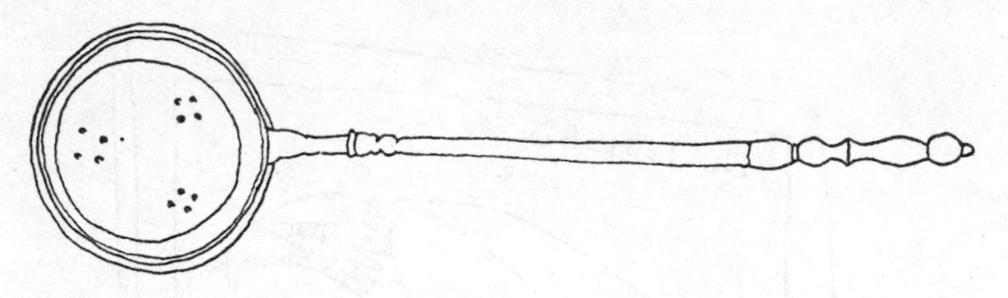

403 A bed warmer, about four feet long. See illustration no. 106.

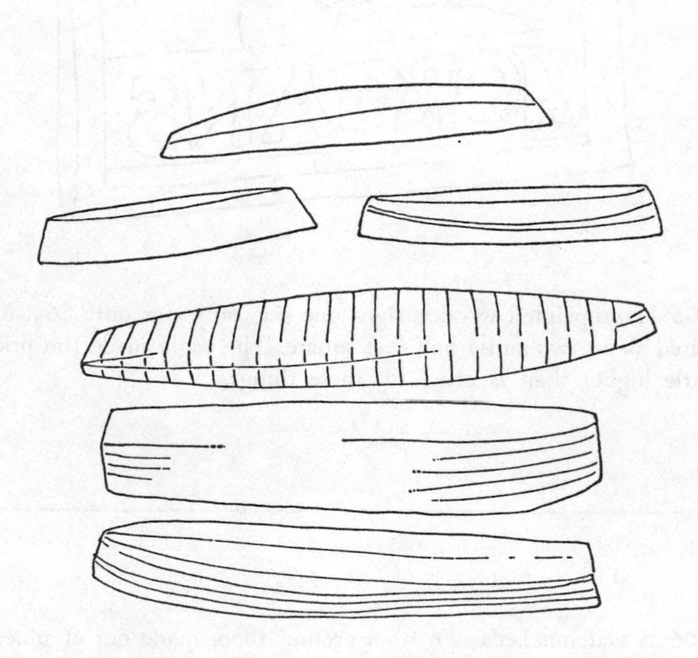

404 Builder's models used in planning the construction of ships and boats. They usually come apart to give the contours at different levels or cross sections. Pine or maple, eighteen inches to two feet long, they look wonderful on a wall or just lying around. They go for $15 to $35, depending on size.

405 Hand-painted wooden sign—one side only—for only $65. Measured about two and a half feet square. The eagle made the price a little higher than is usual for these things.

---

406 A watchmaker's sign from around 1870, made out of pine, six inches thick and twenty-six inches tall. Beautifully weathered black and gray paint—a real find, $125.

407 An old inn sign, good for covering up walls and other surfaces, about $25.

406

407

408 Just an old wooden street sign of the kind still to be found in many a New England village—$5.

409 Things that aren't really "enough" to hang alone can make interesting groupings like this one. The river-scene oil painting was just old and was bought for $9. The gilded letter "E" was $5. The notary public enameled sign was $3.50. The fruit prints from an early seed catalogue go for 50¢ to $1. The two frames were $6 the pair.

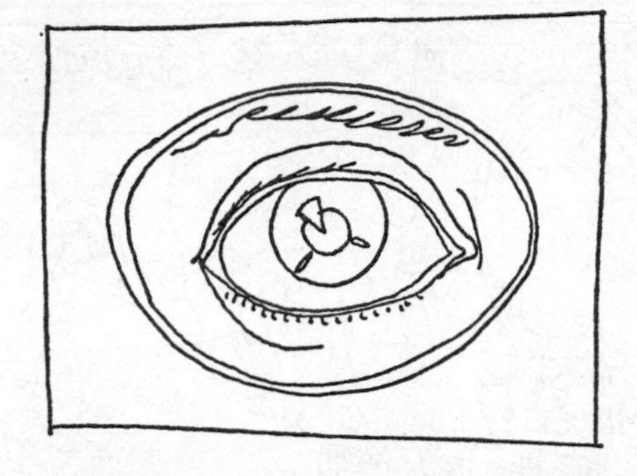

410 An antique decalcomania eye affixed to the back of a piece of glass. The oval measures about eight inches across. Last I heard, it was $3.50. Roy had a bunch of them at Circa 1890, Seventy-eighth Street and Second Ave., New York City. (Advertisement.)

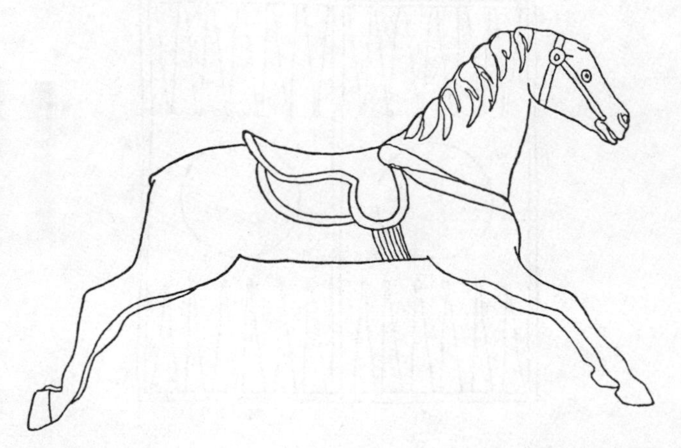

411 A very large early rocking horse–six feet long–of pine painted white. Nice for $165. And don't tell me you can't have a horse on the wall. In California they sell life-size rubber ones for practical jokers to keep in their swimming pools.

412 Lithographed in five colors, this circus poster may not be very old, but it has a lot of atmosphere for only $14. About four and a half feet long.

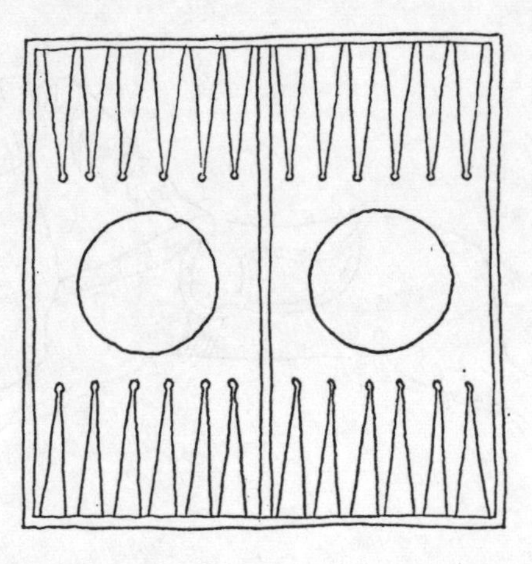

413 The weathered old paint on this backgammon board indicated it was used on a cool lawn on hot summer afternoons in some New England town in the 1880s. Faded red, black, and gray; a checkerboard on the other side. All this for only $2 in a junkshop, actually worth around $16.

414 Early catalogues used to sell fruit seeds to farmers were small books about six and a half by eight and a half inches. In the earliest ones the outlines were hand-colored the same way Currier and Ives prints were. These books are usually cut apart and the prints sold separately for 50¢ to $1. Nowadays a complete book should be worth a dollar a page to a collector.

415 Early poster advertising an excursion train. Neatly framed in black, $16.

416 There are so many prints left over from the nineteenth century that there are many books about them. But a homely, homey scene like this, a black and white lithograph that has been badly hand-colored, will start you out at the bottom of the heap for $6 framed. From here on everything gets better and costs more, and you should buy a guidebook devoted exclusively to prints.

---

417 French paintings in the Academy style are a fairly standard item in ornate gilded frames at around $85 to $125. This frame is twenty inches high.

418 Ancestor paintings, as they are called in the trade, go for around $85 if the artist is not especially well-known. You can even have them painted on an old canvas dating from 1830 or so to have a family resemblance for $125 in New York City. Just ask around at the dealers on the upper East Side.

417

418

419 Oil paintings can vary greatly in value, but many of the ones from the mid-1800s—when whaling was a big industry—were done by sailors home from the sea and they have a fairly standard value. A sixteen-by-twenty-inch on canvas or wood should run around $85, unless it is especially fine or interesting; thirty inches wide, $125. Weird or strange details, such as men being eaten by whales, will push up these prices.